Y0-BLS-696

Ideology of Adventure
Volume 2

Theory and History of Literature
Edited by Wlad Godzich and Jochen Schulte-Sasse

Volume 43.	Michael Nerlich *Ideology of Adventure, Volume 2*
Volume 42.	Michael Nerlich *Ideology of Adventure, Volume 1*
Volume 41.	Denis Hollier *The College of Sociology*
Volume 40.	Peter Sloterdijk *Critique of Cynical Reason*
Volume 39.	Géza von Molnár *Romantic Vision, Ethical Context: Novalis and Artistic Autonomy*
Volume 38.	Algirdas Julien Greimas *On Meaning: Selected Writings in Semiotic Theory*
Volume 37.	Nicolas Abraham and Maria Torok *The Wolf Man's Magic Word: A Cryptonymy*
Volume 36.	Alice Yaeger Kaplan *Reproductions of Banality: Fascism, Literature, and French Intellectual Life*
Volume 35.	Denis Hollier *The Politics of Prose*
Volume 34.	Geoffrey Hartman *The Unremarkable Wordsworth*
Volume 33.	Paul de Man *The Resistance to Theory*
Volume 32.	Djelal Kadir *Questing Fictions: Latin America's Family Romance*
Volume 31.	Samuel Weber *Institution and Interpretation*
Volume 30.	Gilles Deleuze and Félix Guattari *Kafka: Toward a Minor Literature*
Volume 29.	Peter Szondi *Theory of the Modern Drama*
Volume 28.	Edited by Jonathan Arac *Postmodernism and Politics*
Volume 27.	Stephen Melville *Philosophy Beside Itself: On Deconstruction and Modernism*
Volume 26.	Andrzej Warminski *Readings in Interpretation: Hölderlin, Hegel, Heidegger*
Volume 25.	José Antonio Maravall *Culture of the Baroque: Analysis of a Historical Structure*
Volume 24.	Hélène Cixous and Catherine Clément *The Newly Born Woman*
Volume 23.	Klaus Theweleit *Male Fantasies, 2. Male Bodies: Psychoanalyzing the White Terror*
Volume 22.	Klaus Theweleit *Male Fantasies, 1. Women, Floods, Bodies, History*
Volume 21.	Malek Alloula *The Colonial Harem*
Volume 20.	Jean-François Lyotard and Jean-Loup Thébaud *Just Gaming*
Volume 19.	Jay Caplan *Framed Narratives: Diderot's Genealogy of the Beholder*

For other books in the series, see pg. 443.

Ideology of Adventure
Studies in Modern Consciousness, 1100-1750
Volume 2

Michael Nerlich

Translation by Ruth Crowley

Theory and History of Literature, Volume 43

University of Minnesota Press, Minneapolis

G
522
.N4713
1987
v.2

Copyright © 1987 by the University of Minnesota

Originally published as *Kritik der Abenteuer-Ideologie: Beitrag zur Erforschung der bürgerlichen Bewußsteinsbildung, 1110-1750*, volume 2, copyright © 1977 by Akademie-Verlag, Berlin.

All rights reserved. No part of this publication may be reproduced, stored in a retrieval system, or transmitted, in any form or by any means, electronic, mechanical, photocopying, recording, or otherwise, without the prior written permission of the publisher.

Published by the University of Minnesota Press
2037 University Avenue Southeast, Minneapolis, MN 55414.
Published simultaneously in Canada
by Fitzhenry & Whiteside Limited, Markham.
Printed in the United States of America.

Library of Congress Cataloging-in-Publication Data

Nerlich, Michael.
  Ideology of adventure.

  (Theory and history of literaure; v. 42-43)
  Originally published as: Kritik der Abenteuer-Ideologie.
  Includes bibliographies and index.
    1. Adventure and adventures—Philosophy. 2. Adventure and adventurers in literature. I. Title. II. Series.
  G522.N4713   1987   904   86-19354
  ISBN 0-8166-1581-0 (set)
  ISBN 0-8166-1582-9 (pbk. : set)
  ISBN 0-8166-1540-3 (vol. 2)
  ISBN 0-8166-1541-1 (pbk: vol. 2)

The University of Minnesota
is an equal-opportunity
educator and employer.

Contents

9. Adventure in Bourgeois Order   249
10. The Metamorphosis of the *Chevalier*   284
11. The Foundations of Modern Ideology of Adventure in France   308
12. The Decay of the Alliance and the Department of the Nobility   343
13. The Decay of the Alliance and the Formation of the Antiabsolutist Opposition   359
14. The Decay of the Alliance and the Rise of the *Commerçant*   372
    Notes   407
    Index   433

Contents of Volume 1

Foreword: In-Quest of Modernity *Wlad Godzich*   vii
Preface   xvii
1. The Adventure of the *Chevalier*   3
2. The Adventure of the *Hidalgo*   20
3. The Counterrevolutionary Ideology of Knightly Adventure   31
4. The Adventurous Prince   45
5. The Business of the Adventurer   51
6. The Times That Bred Giants   76
7. The Merchant Adventurer Leaves the Ship   108
8. From the Glorification of Adventure to the Thesis of *Bellum Omnium contra Omnes*   183
   Notes   213

Ideology of Adventure
Volume 2

Chapter 9
Adventure in Bourgeois Order

Locke as Theorist of the Class Compromise

The scope of the present work does not permit us to explore the development of economic theory in the seventeenth century. Let us therefore mention a chapter in Jürgen Kuczynski's work, *Studien zu einer Geschichte der Gesellschaftswissenschaften*, "Wie eine Wissenschaft entsteht—dargestellt am Beispiel der Politischen Ökonomie"[1] (How a Discipline Arises: The Example of Political Economy). I am in full agreement with Kuczynski's statement that in England, especially after the revolution of 1640, "there was an unusually favorable climate for the development of scientific thinking in the area of political economy as a result of the harmonious relations between methodology and world view as well as because of the frequent appearance of thinker and profit-hunter in one person."[2] This is especially significant since the "profit-hunters" are representatives of the revolutionary avant-garde and of progressive science. In the phase of its revolutionary encounter with the absolutist reaction, the bourgeoisie is concerned with finding the most fundamental and radical explanation possible for the economic and political laws that move society; in this attempt it assumes that its own interests, which determine the direction of its theories, are the interests of all humanity, or it presents them as such, as Marx demonstrated in *The German Ideology*. What Bacon and Hobbes establish as universal laws of nature, theorists like Mun, Child, Davenant, and especially William Petty[3] confirm on the basis of their observation of the laws of economics:[4] they use political and economic categories to systematize the bourgeois claim to dominance in the guise of the universal *human being*.

The Glorious Revolution of 1688, specifically the Bill of Rights of 1689, had guaranteed in principle that Parliament would supervise the king; on the basis of the alliance of interest between noble landowners and capitalist bourgeoisie,[5] this implied control by the representatives of the "bloc formed by the new nobility and the urban bourgeoisie" (Kuczynski). The way was thus clear for the English bourgeoisie to move from the phase of its revolutionary rise, its revolutionary destruction of existing absolutist power relations, into the phase of guaranteeing, stabilizing, and justifying in theory and in practice the new power relations it dominated.[6] Kuczynski unfortunately does not discuss Locke's function in the next chapter, "Wie eine Wissenschaft verkommt—dargestellt am Beispiel der bürgerlichen Politischen Ökonomie" (How a Discipline Decays: The Example of Bourgeois Political Economy). But Locke was crucially important as an ideologue of the bourgeoisie in its transition from revolutionary to dominant class. "In both religion and politics," as Engels wrote to Conrad Schmidt in 1890, "Locke was the son of the class compromise of 1688."[7]

Locke's twofold function, in the development of the "subjective idealism" of Berkeley and Hume on the one hand and of the revolutionary materialism of the French Enlightenment on the other, was demonstrated by Marx in *The Holy Family* and by Lenin in "Materialism and Empirio-Criticism."[8] More recent examinations of the eighteenth century have also repeatedly treated this latter aspect, which is fundamental to epistemology and to the development of materialism and scientific socialism.[9] It seems to me that scholars have dedicated less time to the ambivalent nature of Locke's overall work, in both its economic and political aspects; these aspects, after all, caused Marx and Engels to respect Locke despite their revulsion at this "most uncompromising advocate of the flogging of vagabonds and paupers."[10] But it should be borne in mind that this (involuntary) founder of French revolutionary materialism, which "leads direct to *socialism*" (Marx, 1845),[11] at the same time in England

> championed the new bourgeoisie in every way—he took the side of the manufacturers against the working classes and the paupers, the merchants against the old-fashioned usurers, the financial aristocracy against governments that were in debt; he even demonstrated in a separate work that the bourgeois way of thinking is the normal human way of thinking.[12]

These statements not only reflect a development in Marx's judgment,[13] but also show an exact grasp of the ambivalence in Locke's writing, a result of the contradictions in their time of origin and the reflection of those contradictions in Locke's work. To vary a statement by Marx: not only were Locke's *Essay concerning Human Understanding* (1690) and the *Two Treatises of Government* welcomed with open arms by the revolutionary bourgeoisie across the Channel, that is, the French, but these works were incontestably welcomed by the English bourgeoisie, industrialists, men of commerce, aristocrats of finance, who were postrevolutionary or no longer revolutionary.

What at first glance seems paradoxical is quickly explained in view of the different stage of the class struggle in England and France. Briefly, we can state that Locke's *Treatises* attempt to explain bourgeois capitalist society as the result of human reason (or to speak with Marx, to prove "that the bourgeois way of thinking is the normal human way of thinking"). The revolutionary bourgeoisie in France found this broadly designed attempt at a bourgeois society based on reason just as opportune as it did the demystifying effect of Locke's materialist sensualism in the *Essay concerning Human Understanding*. Albert Soboul's summary of the overall development of the epoch shows why Locke's writings offered this ideological assistance: "Against the traditional social order, natural right was an effective weapon. It was a question of replacing the traditional order by one based on reason."[14] That was exactly what Locke accomplished, and his main achievement was to erase the disgrace that Hobbes was responsible for with his undisguised glorification of despotism as a force to contain the war of all against all. For Locke tries in his *Treatises* to give this anarchic principle, the law of free competition inherent in the capitalist mode of production, a rational, seemingly peaceful setting instead of the abhorrent despotism of an absolute monarch which Hobbes could not do without.[15] The English bourgeoisie, as the (co-)ruling class, desperately needed such a justification of their dominance, supported by reason and harmony; they too found the *Treatises* opportune, and Berkeley and Hume adapted Locke's epistemology to this need.

The political utility of Locke's economic theory for the ruling, postrevolutionary bourgeoisie interests us here: for both Hobbes and Locke (though with completely different premises), all human relationships are based on the principle of their utility in the struggle for individual survival.[16] In both thinkers, the instinct for self-preservation is the actual source of all human activity. But while in Hobbes, human beings are driven by fear to emerge from the state of the war of all against all into a relation of mutual utility, in Locke it is reason that from the outset, before a state of universal war can even arise, gives the impetus to such a relation of mutual social utility. Locke writes:

> The state of nature has a law of nature to govern it, which obliges every one; and reason, which is that law, teaches all mankind who will but consult it that, being all equal and independent, no one ought to harm another in his life, health, liberty, or possessions.[17]

This is the state governed by the law of reason on the basis of which the social contract is concluded. As Cornelius Meyer-Tasch summarizes it: "The state is formed by the free union of individuals. The decision for peace and welfare takes on social form in this *consensus.*"[18] Given this understanding of the state of nature, war, considered by Hobbes as the original state, must be seen as unnatural. As Locke puts it:

> The state of war is a state of enmity and destruction; and, therefore, declaring by word or action, not a passionate and hasty but a sedate, settled design upon another man's life, puts him in a state of war with him against whom he has declared such an intention, and so has exposed his life to the other's power to be taken away by him or anyone that joins with him in his defense and espouses his quarrel; it being reasonable and just I should have a right to destroy that which threatens me with destruction; for, by the fundamental law of nature, man being to be preserved as much as possible when all cannot be preserved, the safety of the innocent is to be preferred; and one may destroy a man who makes war upon him, or has discovered an enmity to his being, for the same reason that he may kill a wolf or a lion, because such men are not under the ties of the common law of reason, have no other rule but that of force and violence, and so may be treated as beasts of prey, those dangerous and noxious creatures that will be sure to destroy him whenever he falls into their power.[19]

It is of course important to ask about the criteria that decide when life is threatened, that is, when the right to preventive war or murder in self-defense takes effect. According to Locke, this right takes effect in the event of any attack on an individual's life, and since the individual needs property to survive or for self-preservation, then an attack on property also counts as a threat to the individual's existence, with all the appropriate consequences for the threatened individual:

> This makes it lawful for a man to kill a thief who has not in the least hurt him, nor declared any design upon his life any farther than, by the use of force so to get him in his power as to take away his money, or what he pleases, from him; because using force where he has no right to get me into his power, let his pretense be what it will, I have no reason to suppose that he who would take away my liberty would not, when he had me in his power, take away everything else. And therefore it is lawful for me to treat him as one who has put himself into a state of war with me, i.e., kill him if I can; for to that hazard does he justly expose himself whoever introduces a state of war and is aggressor in it.[20]

Without going so far as some of Locke's contemporaries and seeing behind the mask of the liberal representative of bourgeois reason "the naked features of a decided Hobbist, for whom the norms of the primitive law are nothing other than 'theorems promoting...survival,'"[21] we can state that Locke has cleared an unusually broad area for interpretation, which allows the bourgeoisie a representation of all their interests. Is not the competitor, especially the foreign competitor, to be considered an aggressor against property? Does competition not introduce a state of war, and must the (English) merchant not take preventive measures? What are the criteria for deciding whether an attack is taking place on someone else's property? And how can the boundaries of property (as set by natural law) be determined, beyond which one may not reach?

It is no coincidence that Locke's *Some Thoughts concerning Education* (1693) expressly recommends studying the most outspoken advocates of the thesis of self-preservation: Samuel Pufendorf, with his *De Officio Hominis et Civis* and *De Jure Naturalis et Gentium*, as well as Hugo Grotius, with *De Jure Belli et Pacis*. The apology for the natural-rational state of peace in society disguises that fact that it is bourgeois class domination that is being glorified. To be sure, in distinction to Hobbes, who believed thievery legitimized the claim to property, Locke calls *labor* the criterion for the rightful claim to property, the labor by which an individual appropriates the share of nature, which in principle belongs to all human beings, necessary for his subsistence and that of his family. But, as Marx determined in looking at Locke's views on interest,[22] Locke's thesis about individual appropriation according to "the limit of personal labor"[23] serves primarily to justify bourgeois property relations, the "inequality of individual property,"[24] and that means the exploitation of human beings by human beings (we will not set this out in detail, since Marx has done that so brilliantly). "Locke's view," Marx confirms, "is all the more important because it was the classical expression of bourgeois society's ideas of right as against feudal society, and moreover his philosophy served as the basis for all the ideas of the whole of subsequent English political economy."[25]

The Rotten Peace of "Useful Competition"

The criterion for justifying property, necessary for the sake of self-preservation, lies in Locke's concept of social utility, although it remains rather unclear what is actually meant by labor, since in Locke it includes precisely those activities proper to animals and picking and gathering wild fruits for nourishment.[26] With such a view of labor, simply taking and possessing something is just as rightful as owning *substantial* property, provided that no one else is hindered thereby in his right to self-preservation.[27] This very argument, which was easy to combine with the imputation that one felt threatened by the "savages," the natives of occupied countries and continents, was the favorite one for justifying the conquest of colonies and the extirpation or subjugation of their inhabitants (except for the Christian justification in terms of the obligation to carry out missionary work).

The amount of property is secondary for Locke's idea of the social utility of property, since it is not identical with the amount of social utility, for it is labor indeed that put the difference of value on everything; and let anyone consider what the difference is between an acre of land planted with tobacco or sugar, sown with wheat or barley, and an acre of the same land lying in common without any husbandry upon it, and he will find that the improvement of labor makes the far greater part of the value. I think it will be but a very modest computation to say that, of the products of the earth useful to the life of man, nine-tenths are the effects of labor; nay, if we will rightly estimate things as they come to our use and cast up the several expenses about them, what in them is purely owing to nature, and what to labor, we shall find that in most of them ninety-nine hundredths are wholly to be put on the account of labor.[28]

If we pursue this logic, then of course social utility cannot be measured by the inequality or the largeness or smallness of property, if so little utility arises from it and so much from labor; but as long as the property (for instance, a piece of land) is placed at the disposal (for instance of a tenant) to be worked, then property is not without (social) utility. The question of property relations is thus irrelevant, for these, according to Locke, are only symbolically reflected in gold, silver, or money (and even large landholdings are for him only symbolic property, for the owner can not exploit or consume them for himself alone):

> The greatest part of things really useful to the life of man...are generally things of short duration, such as, if they are not consumed by use, will decay and perish of themselves [like food—M. N.]; gold, silver, and diamonds are things that fancy or agreement has put the value on, more than real use and the necessary support of life.[29]

According to Locke, it is reprehensible only for one man to keep from another what he needs and what the other does not (does not consume):

> And indeed it was a foolish thing, as well as dishonest, to hoard up more than he could make use of. If he gave away a part to anybody else so that it perished not uselessly in his possession, these he also made use of. And if he also bartered away plums that would have rotted in a week for nuts that would last good for his eating a whole year, he did no injury; he wasted not the common stock, destroyed no part of the portion of the goods that belonged to others, so long as nothing perished uselessly in his hands. Again, if he would give his nuts for a piece of metal, pleased with its color, or exchange his sheep for shells...and keep those by him all his life, he invaded not the right of others; he might heap as much of these durable things as he pleased; the exceeding of the bounds of his just property not lying in the largeness of his possession, but the perishing of anything uselessly in it. And thus came in the use of money—some lasting thing that men might keep without spoiling, and that by mutual consent men would

take in exchange for the truly useful but perishable supports of life. And as different degrees of industry were apt to give men possessions in different proportions, so this invention of money gave them the opportunity to continue and enlarge them.[30]

Thus a justification was provided for the exploitation of human beings by other human beings in all "rational" harmony, supposedly in service of social utility, and the dominance of the bourgeoisie over the people or the proletariat was theoretically secured as "mutual exploitation" (in the exchange of what was appropriated through labor). "This theory came to the fore with Hobbes and Locke, at the same time as the first and second English revolutions," as we read in *The German Ideology*. "It is to be found even earlier, of course, among writers on political economy, as a tacit presupposition."[31] Marx and Engels continue by stating that for the bourgeois

> only *one* relation is valid on its own account—the relation of exploitation; all other relations have validity for him only insofar as he can include them under this one relation; and even where he encounters relations which cannot be directly subordinated to the relation of exploitation, he subordinates them to it at least in his imagination. The material expression of this use is money which represents the value of all things, people and social relations.... Liberation from the standpoint of the bourgeoisie, i.e., competition, was, of course, for the eighteenth century the only possible way of offering the individuals a new career for freer development. The theoretical proclamation of the consciousness corresponding to this bourgeois practice, of the consciousness of mutual exploitation as the universal mutual relation of all individuals, was also a bold and open step forward. It was a kind of *enlightenment* which interpreted the political, patriarchal, religious and sentimental embellishment of exploitation under feudalism in a secular way; the embellishment corresponded to the form of exploitation existing at that time and it had been systematised especially by the theoretical writers of the absolute monarchy.[32]

We must bear in mind the dialectical character of the "theory of utility or exploitation" as a "bold and open step forward" and as a justification of bourgeois class dominance. The development of this theory, which played a significant role especially in the French Enlightenment, is connected "with the various periods of development of the bourgeoisie," as Marx and Engels demonstrate:

> Hobbes and Locke had before their eyes not only the earlier development of the Dutch bourgeoisie (both of them had lived for some time in Holland) but also the first political actions by which the English bourgeoisie emerged from local and provincial limitations, as well as a comparatively highly developed stage of manufacture, overseas trade and colonisation. This particularly applies to Locke, who wrote during

the first period of the English economy, at the time of the rise of joint-stock companies, the Bank of England and England's mastery of the seas. In their case, and particularly in that of Locke, the theory of exploitation was still directly connected with the economic content.[33]

The bourgeoisie did not hesitate long in making the "theory of utility" specially developed by Locke the basis of their ideology of dominance:

> The economic content gradually turned the utility theory into a mere apologia for the existing state of affairs, an attempt to prove that under existing conditions the mutual relations of people today are the most advantageous and generally useful. It has this character among all modern economists.[34]

What Marx and Engels set out in an ironic, objective way in their 1845/46 critique of Max Stirner had moved Engels shortly before to passionate moral outrage. In his "Umrisse zu einer Kritik der Nationalökonomie" (Sketch for a Critique of Political Economy, 1843/44), Engels is still taking as a point of departure for his criticism the manifestations of (commercial) capitalism and of the use of bourgeois ideology in Malthus and Adam Smith, and in his "brilliant sketch" (Marx) he reaches fundamental insights not only into the annihilation of the other competitors, the way in which competition tends to eliminate itself,[35] but also into the consequences of competition for the society at large (its effect on the crime rate, for instance).[36] Engels is particularly outraged by the glorification of trade as a vehicle for humanitarianism and amity among peoples (an argument that is an integral part of the ideology of bourgeois theorists of the seventeenth and eighteenth centuries):

> Naturally, it is in the interest of the trader to be on good terms with the one from whom he buys cheap as well as with the other to whom he sells dear. A nation therefore acts very imprudently if it fosters feelings of animosity in its suppliers and customers. The more friendly, the more advantageous. Such is the humanity of trade. And this hypocritical way of misusing morality for immoral purposes is the pride of the free-trade system.... By dissolving nationalities, liberal economics had done its best to universalize enmity, to transform mankind into a horde of ravenous beasts (for what else are competitors?) who devour one another just *because* each has identical interests with all the others—after this preparatory work there remained but one step to take before the goal was reached, the dissolution of the family. To accomplish this, economy's own beautiful invention, the factory system, came to its aid.[37]

Perhaps it was because Engels in this work derived the particular dialectic between the social anarchy of production and the hierarchical subordination within the factory (within the material production), of the competitive battle, and of exploitation from the "system of free trade" that he later repeatedly placed such stress on the rules of that system as a consequence of the immanent laws of the capitalist mode of production. What riles him especially in this work is the "hypocrisy of the liberals"; they pretend to see the principle of peaceful coexistence among individuals and peoples in just this destructive competition. "This law with its constant adjustments, in which whatever is lost here is gained there, is regarded as something excellent by the economist,"[38] mocks Engels and determines that in truth there is no harmonious adjustment; instead there is a spasmodic adjustment that takes place between competitive "demand and supply" without the awareness or control of the process by the producer, in "trade crises":

> And each successive crisis is bound to become more universal and therefore worse than the preceding one; is bound to impoverish a larger body of small capitalists, and to augment in increasing proportion the numbers of the class who live by labour alone, thus considerably enlarging the mass of labour to be employed (the major problem of our economists) and finally causing a social revolution such as has never been dreamt of in the philosophy of the economists.[39]

The Armchair Adventurer

But at the beginning of the eighteenth century the English bourgeoisie and its ideologues (especially among the Whigs, the liberal bourgeois party) still believed in the harmonious development of the capitalist system and the peace-promoting principle of free trade, in part because of the beneficial influence of Locke's theories of reason. Only seldom did the shrill discordances of doubt disturb this ostensible harmony (especially in France, from Meslier, Mably, Morelly, Rousseau, and later even from the Marquis de Sade). In England there developed an atmosphere of comfortable social adjustment that was in fundamental contradiction to the increasing polarization within bourgeois class society, to the formation of the proletariat and of a petty bourgeoisie with a limited perspective on one side and to the policy of (colonial) exploitation and power politics on the other. The partisan battle between Whigs and Tories, between the originally anti-Catholic and hence progressive party of commercial and financial capital and the reactionary party of the established church together with the gentry and the squirarchy, distracted attention from the actual problems (which brought more sensitive spirits like Defoe or Swift to despair or cynicism). From the beginning, however, these two parties were not consistent in their differences, and they soon tended to slur them over and to dissolve into one another.[40]

The *Tatler*, a (Whig) periodical published from 1709 to 1710 by Sir Richard Steele (1672–1729), who under the name of Mister Bickerstaff gave his opinions on everything in life including trivial matters and thereby won a huge success with his public, reflects the satisfied, boastful mood of the age—a mood of "We've done it!" It is of interest to us how much philistine, deliberate irony is brought to bear in polemics against the gentry and squirarchy and their ideology of knightly adventure, which only shows the continued flogging of an already defeated opponent. This takes place on several levels.

First, it is beyond doubt that the criterion for social recognition is virtuous utility. Even and especially the tradesman is a gentleman, and he has at *least* as much right to this title as the courtier and the scholar.[41] This is, so to speak, the premise on which the whole *Tatler* is based. That is the background against which we must understand the settling of accounts with Fortuna as an employee, an image The *Tatler* uses again and again. The editor seems to find the joke particularly successful when he pretends to recognize Fortuna in the hired superviser of the women who spin the drum in a state lottery:

> This gentlewoman seemed an emblem of fortune; she commanded, as if unconcerned in their business; and though every thing was performed by her direction, she did not visibly interpose in particulars. She seemed in pain at our near approach to her, and most to approve us when we made her no advances.

It is surely to be taken as a good-natured joke that the irony with which Fortuna is treated here is also aimed at life as an employee: "She therefore appeared to be not only a picture of fortune, but of fortune as I liked her."[42]

A favorite target of Bickerstaff's mockery is the squire, who, according to the *Tatler*, is to be found everywhere and who is everywhere distinguished by his nullity. This nullity is ironically transferred to the origin of knighthood. At the beginning of world history the "great and heroic spirits" liked to complain about their hard fate, that the lady they loved wanted nothing to do with them:

> The hero in this distress was generally in armour, and in a readiness to fight any man he met with.... A lover of this kind had always about him a person of a second value, and subordinate to him, who could hear his afflictions, carry an enchantment for his wounds, hold his helmet when he was eating (if he ever did eat), or in his absence, when he was retired to his apartment in any king's palace, tell the prince himself, or perhaps his daughter, the birth, parentage, and adventures of his valiant master. This trusty companion was styled his Esquire.[43]

(This is also the context for the information that King Arthur is generally considered the first to eat roast beef and that the Knights of the Round Table always stuffed their bellies with roast beef before they began their debates.)[44] It is obvious that this critique of the knightly ideal, which becomes most politically explosive when it attacks dueling as a ridiculous continuation of the tradition of the knight-errant,[45] has no trace of Shakespearean greatness or of bourgeois-revolutionary force. It is oriented toward a Don Quijote reduced to a petty-bourgeois, English measure of reason. Just as Don Quijote went mad reading knightly romances, so a paperhanger, Mr. Bickerstaff's neighbor, becomes a fool after reading the sensational press of the time: the *Tatler* reports that he feels a calling to politics, which results in Mr. Bickerstaff's jovial scorn and the paperhanger's social ruin.[46]

However trivial the individual letters, commentaries, and essays of the *Tatler*, they still fit with the tendencies toward harmonizing the developing capitalist system and the peace-promoting principle of free trade (and they also filled a need as civilizing forces because a victorious class had to educate itself to competence as rulers).[47] Henry Fielding was the first to turn the broad genre sketches in the *Tatler* into finer irony, into the ironic critique of the bourgeoisie itself. From 1711 to 1712 Steele, together with Joseph Addison (1672-1719), continued the tradition of the *Tatler* with the *Spectator*. The *Spectator* appears as the gazette of a fictional club to which belong various members of the aristocracy, of commerce, and of the sciences. We will direct particular attention to Sir Andrew Freeport because he, or the way he is presented, illustrates especially well the moral attitude that called forth Engels's wrath. In the *Spectator* of 2 March 1711, the author makes it clear that English colonial policy is inhumane and that cannot be condoned. But the implicit criticism is presented in the joking tone of serious nonsense. Sir Andrew Freeport is an important London merchant,

> a person of indefatigable industry, strong reason, and great experience. His notions of trade are noble and generous, and (as every rich man has usually some sly way of jesting, which would make no great figure were he not a rich man) he calls the sea the British Common [a pun on "common property" and "prostitute"—M. N.]. He is acquainted with commerce in all its parts, and will tell you that it is a stupid and barbarous way to extend dominion by arms; for true power is to be got by arts and industry.[48]

The same Sir Andrew Freeport also declares on the appropriate occasion that merchants are to be thanked if poor people find work: the merchant pays the poor man for his labor, he lets others partake of his profits by preparing his freight and supplying his manufactures, he provides for more people than the aristocracy, who should be grateful to him, because without him they would not have the goods they desire—for all these reasons the merchant deserves the title of gentleman,[49] since his activities do not consist merely in calculations. Nevertheless,

> when I have my returns from abroad, I can tell to a shilling, by the help of numbers, the profit or loss by my adventure; but I ought also

to be able to shew that I had reason for making it, either from my own experience, or that of other people, or from a reasonable presumption that my returns will be sufficient to answer my expence and hazard; and this is never to be done without the skill of numbers.[50]

That is especially revealing for us: for the first time a merchant reports from his armchair on the adventures others undertake for him *ad majorem mercatoris gloriam,* "to the greater glory of the merchant." He is a gentleman.

Habakkuk Redivivus

In "The 18th Brumaire of Louis Napoleon" (1851/52), Marx analyzes the tendency of the French Revolution of 1789 to "[drape] itself alternately as the Roman Republic and the Roman Empire,"[51] a tendency that quickly disappeared after the establishment of "modern *bourgeois* society": "The new social formation once established, the antediluvian Colossi disappeared and with them resurrected Romanity—the Brutuses, Gracchi, Publicolas, the tribunes, the senators, and Caesar himself."[52] The "real commanders" of bourgeois society, writes Marx,

> sat behind the counter.... Wholly absorbed in the production of wealth and in peaceful competitive struggle, it [bourgeois society— R. C.] no longer comprehended that ghosts from the days of Rome had watched over its cradle. But unheroic as bourgeois society is, it nevertheless took heroism, sacrifice, terror, civil war and battles of peoples to bring it into being. And in the classically austere traditions of the Roman Republic its gladiators found the ideals and the art forms, the self-deceptions that they needed in order to conceal from themselves the bourgeois limitations of the content of their struggles and to maintain their passion on the high plane of great historical tragedy. Similarly, at another stage of development, a century earlier, Cromwell and the English people had borrowed speech, passions and illusions from the Old Testament for their bourgeois revolution. When the real aim had been achieved, when the bourgeois transformation of English society had been accomplished, Locke supplanted Habakkuk.[53]

But in 1719, Habakkuk once more burst into the polite society of Mr. Bickerstaff, Sir Roger de Coverley, Will Honeycome, and Sir Andrew Freeport—loud, bold, crude, greedy, and up to his neck in Biblical quotations. It happened in the following way: in (or around) 1660, Daniel Defoe was born, a Dissenter, a nonconforming Puritan, the next thing to a revolutionary. He rejected the clerical career which seemed to have been destined for him and tried his luck as a merchant. It was a matter of course that he, whose father was an artisan or small businessman, fought on the side of the progressive forces against the absolutist reaction, despite or precisely because of his commercial activity—considering the encouraging slogans of Bacon, Mun, and others about youth and trade. In 1685 Defoe took part in the failed rebellion of the Duke of Monmouth against James II, in 1688 he rode out to meet the Protestant liberator William of Orange when he landed in Dover, and in 1701 Defoe defended William against attacks by the reactionaries, who tried to denounce him as a foreigner, with the satire *The True-born Englishman*.[54]

Revolutionary élan carried the Whig Foe (later, somewhat more elegantly, Defoe) over his first disappointments as well: in 1692, after great initial successes, he went bankrupt for the first time. Despite enormous debts, in the amount of seventeen thousand pounds, he was undaunted, worked temporarily as a civil servant (one of his jobs was as chairman of the royal lottery), in 1697 founded a brickworks and wrote his first long piece on political economy, *An Essay upon Projects,* in which he made suggestions about founding a branch banking system, about road construction, naval policy, and protection from false bankruptcies.[55] Moreover, he continued to produce political treatises, circulars, and poems,[56] and his political activities brought him close to court and into favor with the king.

When the king died in 1702, Defoe's real time of troubles began, interrupted by short periods of success; with Queen Anne, the Tories came to power and the Dissenters were harassed. Defoe was moved to write another satire, *The Shortest Way with the Dissenters*. In 1703 he was arrested, sentenced to the loss of his fortune, to the pillory, and to indefinite imprisonment. Although the pillory was a public triumph for Defoe—the people cheered him and threw flowers at him—his political courage was broken (though not his conviction). While maintaining the appearance of belonging to the opposition, he entered the government or Tory service (which was not so dramatic a step as it might appear, in view of the diminishing differences between Tories and Whigs). In Tory pay, he published an opposition periodical, *The Review,* starting in 1704. In many respects this was the forerunner of *The Tatler* and *The Spectator*.[57] It appeared until 1713; it was written largely by Defoe alone and appeared at first weekly, then three times a week.

We will not discuss Defoe's activities in greater detail here: his activity as a political agent alternated with his work as a historian or as author of political, moral-practical, economic pamphlets and treatises. And in 1719, a surprise to everyone, the fifty-nine-year-old Defoe's first novel was published, *The Life and Strange Surprizing Adventures of Robinson Crusoe*. But despite the immense public success of this novel, the bourgeois intellectuals of the time were indifferent or even hostile to it. "That is closely connected with Defoe's...hostility to literature," as Norbert Miller, scholar of comparative literature in West Berlin, writes, "and with his no less striking ignorance in all questions of aesthetic and literary judgment."[58]

Doubtless: but that cannot be the whole explanation. For what explains how Defoe writes, if not what he writes? In order to answer this question, let us look at Robinson Crusoe. "From an economic point of view, Crusoe's actions represent an ethically advanced economic type," Robert Weimann states, "that is contrasted with the conservative view of the older generation, which was not oriented toward expansion."[59] Starting with the material we have presented here, we can say that this view is quite simply false (which only partly impairs Weimann's interpretations, some of which are excellent). Daniel Defoe undertakes such an exact positioning of his protagonist that it is unclear why Weimann did not start by determining whether that positioning was adequate with respect to the social reality of the time, the first great bourgeois revolution. Robinson sets out on his adventures in 1651: that is the year of Cromwell's Navigation Act, which, like the whole revolutionary movement that ended with the king's beheading in 1649, is naturally the result of a decades-long development. From the time of John Cabot on, England's great merchants were adventurers who had a view of trade that was "oriented toward expansion." The only important question is whether this type was still current in 1719, the year in which *Robinson Crusoe* appeared.

Robinson Crusoe's father, a small trader, remonstrates with Robinson (who has not studied anything and *consequently*, according to Defoe, has rambling thoughts and wants to go to sea). He urges Robinson not to try his luck:

> He ask'd me what reasons, more than a mere wandering inclination I had for leaving my father's house and my native country, where I might be well introduced, and had a prospect of raising my fortune by application and industry, with a life of ease and pleasure. He told me, it was men of desperate fortunes on one hand, or of aspiring superior fortunes on the other, and who went abroad upon adventures, to rise by enterprise, and make themselves famous in undertakings of a nature out of the common road; that these things were all either too far above me, or too far below me; that mine was the middle state, or what might be called the upper station of *low life,* which he had found by long experience was the best state in the world, the most suited to human happiness, not exposed to the miseries and hardships, the labour and sufferings of the mechanick part of mankind, and not embarrassed with the pride, luxury, ambition, and envy of the upper part of mankind. He told me, I might judge of the happiness of this state, by this one thing: viz. That this was the state of life which all other people envied; that kings have frequently lamented the miserable consequences of being born to great things, and wished they had been placed in the middle of the two extremes, between the mean and the great; that the wise man gave his testimony to this, as the just standard of true felicity, when he prayed to have neither poverty nor riches.[60]

The division of classes in the father's speech is extraordinarily precise. There are the upper classes, kings or the aristocracy, and "those who went abroad upon adventures, to rise by enterprise," that is, adventurers, great merchants; there are differentiated middle (to which the father himself belongs) and lower classes, the "mechanick part of mankind," which carry out material production, either as artisans or as wage laborers who are "sold to a life of slavery for daily bread."[61] The middle class (especially the upper part of it), equally distant from the social extremes, is, in contrast to the upper and lower classes, largely spared the blows of fate, is prospering, ought to risk nothing, and certainly ought not to go on adventures. This agrees, by the way, with the advice Defoe gives the small tradesman in *The Complete English Tradesman*, 1726. When he has a family, the tradesman should not engage in longer excursions than from the shop to the second floor, "and no further; when he is there, a bell, or a call, brings him down; and while he is in his parlour, his shop or his warehouse never misses him, his customers never go away unserved."[62]

In *Robinson Crusoe*, Defoe pointedly and precisely presents the ideology of moderation, the glorification of staying home, of diligent enterprise without risk, as the ideology of the middle class. He logically contrasts this with *something else* in the glorification of adventure, or he means to contrast it with something else. Is the "something else" the worldview of "an ethically advanced economic type"? Hardly. Weimann can arrive at this conclusion only by following a false intellectual-historical genealogy: Robinson as the descendant of the (Spanish) *pícaro* and as rising burgher. Weimann writes:

> With Robinson and Moll Flanders, for the first time a bourgeois hero is at the center of the novel, a hero who not only comes from a plebian milieu, like Gil Blas and Simplicissimus, but whose thinking and actions are already guided by bourgeois, mercantile impulses. This new hero is still surrounded by adventurous-picaresque circumstances: he is—at least in part—still the vagabond, the *pícaro* tossed about by the forces of nature and society. He is an adventurer, but already an adventurer with bourgeois coloring, an involuntary aventurier who makes his bourgeois attitude and morality prevail *despite* the adventurousness of his experiences. In the process of this encounter, his individuality distinguishes itself from the Spanish scoundrel's lack of a standpoint. The adventure is now no longer the irresponsible trick of a scoundrel, no longer an anarchic means of negating society, but is placed in the service of a socially constructive idea.[63]

Apart from the fact that the "lack of a standpoint" in many *pícaros* merely expresses the anarchy of the decaying feudal monarchy in Spain, that many *pícaros* (like their original, Lazarillo)[64] embody the desire for order (not all *pícaros* are the same), that Robinson is a completely voluntary "adventurer" (in contrast to nearly all *pícaros*!) and runs away from home against his father's will, we do not dispute the fact that Defoe used the literary means of the *novelas picarescas* and their English variations.[65] Many authors did the same, without, however, writing picaresque novels.[66] But in England, the bourgeois as adventurer has a three-hundred-year-long, respectable (and revolutionary) tradition, so that for England it is almost a tautology to talk about the "adventurer becoming bourgeois" (the novelty that begins with Defoe is that the bourgeois no longer wants to be considered an adventurer). It seems to me central for an understanding of the novel that Defoe is trying consciously and desperately to continue this centuries-old, respectable (and revolutionary) tradition. He knows its history quite well, not least from Hakluyt's *Principal Navigations*.[67] But Defoe would not have had to study Hakluyt; the Merchant Adventurers of London were still in existence, and the greatest political economists of the seventeenth century, whom Defoe, as an expert, would of course have studied, were members or opponents of the adventurers and disputed with them; the founder of the London Exchange, Sir Thomas Gresham, was an adventurer; Frobisher, Hawkins, Cabot, Drake, Raleigh—they were all adventurers. The whole heroic time of the revolutionary bourgeoisie stood under the banner of the adventurer, and *this*, the *past, heroic* time, is what Robinson and Defoe have in mind, not "an ethically advanced economic type."[68] Only a few months after *Robinson Crusoe*, Defoe published *The King of Pirates, being an Account of the Famous Enterprises of Captain Avery* and *An Historical Account of the Voyages and Adventures of Sir Walter Raleigh*, the idol of the revolutionary bourgeoisie of the seventeenth century.

It may be that Defoe felt himself transported back to heroic times by the infamous South Sea Bubble affair (a large-scale, failed overseas venture contemporary with John Law's experiment in France); Defoe scholars have suspected as much[69] (he did, after all, write a history of contemporary pirates in 1724 and did not hide his admiration: the material seems to have fascinated him). In any case, Defoe made several attempts to imitate the heroes of the past, politically and economically, and failed again and again. Was his optimism, his belief in natural right, in unlimited economic opportunity, the omnipotence of reason and diligence (which Locke had after all confirmed for him), mistaken from the beginning?

Daniel Defoe, who had given instructions for success in so many treatises and projects, wants to prove to himself and the world that the old revolutionary image of the world still holds, and to do this he takes a case that is much worse than his own, which he supplies with seemingly insurmountable difficulties: he writes *Robinson Crusoe*. He reconstructs the time of heroic bourgeois world conquest, but his "conscientiousness in detail" (N. Miller) causes him to project into this heroic construction the stagnation of the social relations of his time for the middle class or for the people. That works well in the first part of the novel, which deals with the artisan Robinson and his isolated island, but it leads to logical contradictions in the second, which treats Robinson as a large-scale merchant traveling throughout the world. Here Defoe goes beyond his (middle-class) relations—he loses his credibility. The second part is also an artistic failure (in comparison with the first part, with *Moll Flanders*, *Roxana*, and *Captain Singleton*). And how could this be otherwise at the time of the East India Company, of which Marx said: "The East India Company excluded the common people [Robinson, for instance] from the commerce with India, at the same time that the House of Commons excluded them from Parliamentary representation [1702]."[70] But it is at precisely this time that Robinson's individual adventures occur in Asia, which make him even richer than he was before, fabulously wealthy.

In truth, individual adventurers of the type of Drake, Frobisher, Hawkins, or Raleigh had become nearly impossible (at least for the private citizen: with the support of the monarch, a privateer like George Anson could still make fortunes in time of war). In *Robinson Crusoe*, Defoe contrasts the middle-class ideology of security expounded by Robinson's father with another, new variant of middle-class ideology: the glorification of the unrealizable individual adventure, which will become the favorite dream of the petty bourgeoisie. Just as it is unsurprising that Rousseau responded strongly to Defoe, it is to be expected that Defoe found little response among contemporary intellectuals: Robinson's thoroughly egocentric individual adventure is of no use to the French Enlightenment, which is concerned with proving the *social* utility of free trade, and in England no bourgeois intellectual can take such an individual adventure seriously any longer. On the contrary, the incorruptible critics like Swift mock and condemn what Defoe so desperately and honestly wants to prove (and who can doubt his sincerity, given the story of his life?): the possibility and utility of adventure.

An Adventurer, Undemanding by Nature

The bourgeois ideologues of the epoch must have had a hard time digesting Defoe's *Robinson Crusoe*, the apologists for the existing circumstances as well as their critics. The apologists were choking on Defoe's realism—the indirect revelation of the impossibility for the people to make (individual) fortunes within existing relations of dominance (which was tantamount to a revelation of the new class relations). The critics must have found the reconstruction of the past or the literary attempt to transport the heroic, revolutionary past of the bourgeoisie fictionally into an exactly observed present retrograde, naïve, even shady. This Habakkuk was useless for bourgeois ideologues of any stripe.

But not for the common people. As J. R. Moore says, *Robinson Crusoe* not only created a new literature, it also created a new reading public.[71] Its popularity among the lowest classes of readers was a source of jealousy,[72] and this, together with the already mentioned political reasons, explains the sometimes devastating judgments of his contemporaries (think of Swift, who would certainly not have written his *Gulliver* without *Robinson Crusoe*, but who claimed that he couldn't remember Defoe's name!). It also explains the immediate falsification of *Robinson Crusoe*, either through misleading translations and sentimental imitations or through the straightforward falsification by abridgement or transformation into a children's book.[73] The misuse of *Robinson Crusoe* by bourgeois (especially anti-Marxist) political economists, who, as Marx says, love "Robinson Crusoe stories,"[74] was and remains still more trenchant. In concrete terms, these political economists love to set up speculations about the Natural Individual, the hunter, the gatherer, understood as an individual:[75]

> The more deeply we go back into history, the more does the individual, and hence also the producing individual, appear as dependent, as belonging to a greater whole.... Only in the eighteenth century, in "civil society," do the various forms of social connectedness confront the individual as a mere means towards his private purposes, as external necessity. But the epoch which produces this standpoint, that of the isolated individual, is also precisely that of the hitherto most developed social...relations. Production by an isolated individual outside society...is as much of an absurdity as is the development of language without individuals living *together* and talking to each other.... The point could go entirely unmentioned if this twaddle, which had sense and reason for the eighteenth-century characters, had not been earnestly pulled back into the centre of the most modern economics by Bastiat, Carey, Proudhon etc. Of course it is a convenience for Proudhon et al. to be able to give a historico-philosophic account of the source of an economic relation, of whose historic origins he is ignorant, by inventing the myth that Adam or Prometheus stumbled on the idea ready-made, and then it was adopted, etc. Nothing is more dry and boring than the fantasies of a *locus communis* [a commonplace mind].[76]

Marx deliberately excludes the authors of the eighteenth century, including Daniel Defoe, from the reproaches he makes to modern economists. They were not concerned with constructing a fictional Natural Individual (of whatever sort),[77] but instead they made the liberated individual in a society of free competition the object of their reflection:

> In this society of free competition, the individual appears detached from the natural bonds etc. which in earlier historical periods make him the accessory of a definite and limited human conglomerate. Smith and Ricardo still stand with both feet on the shoulders of the eighteenth-century prophets, in whose imaginations this eighteenth-

century individual—the product on one side of the dissolution of the feudal forms of society, on the other side of the new forces of production developed since the sixteenth century—appears as an ideal, whose existence they project into the past. Not as a historic result but as history's point of departure.[78]

Robinson Crusoe demonstrates how right Marx is. As Robert Weimann correctly states: "The shipwrecked Robinson is not the natural individual celebrated by Rousseau... but an individual who acts in very particular ways in quite specific natural circumstances."[79] His way of acting was characterized by Marx in *Capital*:

> Undemanding though he is by nature, he still has needs to satisfy, and must therefore perform useful labours of various kinds: he must make tools, knock together furniture, tame llamas, fish, hunt and so on. Of his prayers and the like, we take no account here, since our friend takes pleasure in them and sees them as recreation.[80]

Marx's text offers, I believe, an impulse for an interpretation of *Robinson Crusoe* that makes the reception of this novel comprehensible, its success with a mass public and its relative failure with the bourgeois élite: "Undemanding though he is by nature, he still has needs." That is what is new and exciting for Defoe's petty-bourgeois, plebian public: that one of their own, from the hard-working middle class, realizes his own claim to happiness at a time some of the public experienced, at a time (up to 1705) in which the common people are trying to make a revolutionary claim to happiness and which at first only brings the bourgeoisie to power. In this time, a member of the common people, one of their own, advances his claim to fortune and realizes it (at least experimentally, in the novel) despite all difficulties. A plebian member of the middle class sets out to preserve and to continue the revolutionary inheritance of the bourgeoisie in practice, and as we will see, in theory as well. When blows of fate cast him up on a lonely island, he fights on for the fulfillment of his claim to happiness: then he finds this fulfillment in materially productive labor and finally also in the adventure trade—the claim to happiness is redeemed; one of their own has made it, Robinson, a plebian member of the middle class, their idol.

Claim to Happiness, Not Promise of Happiness

To avoid misunderstandings, let us be clear about this: Defoe has no intention of carrying out a plebian, middle-class "revolution." What he, or his Robinson (but also other characters from his novels), wants is success in the existing bourgeois society, using the methods of the (formerly) revolutionary bourgeoisie. The explosive power of his claim to happiness lies in the fact that he bluntly presents members of the plebian middle class and uses them as examples to demonstrate the claim to happiness; that is, he believes he can demonstrate (fictionally) the possibility that that claim can be redeemed. Defoe is still unbroken, despite all the defeats he has suffered: his glorification of adventure is a mixture of enthusiasm for the past, plebian protest, economic experience, political-moral challenge—Defoe/Robinson is a threatening, anarchic element in bourgeois society as it is consolidating itself. In Robinson's claim to happiness, in his setting out for distant parts, there is a historical perspective that must make the bourgeoisie shudder, and it is therefore quick to transform, to falsify, Robinson's claim to happiness into an illusionary promise of happiness. For even though Defoe's perspective is that of the plebian middle class, that is not to be understood in the modern sense: it is not that of the petty bourgeoisie, assimilated, dependent, vacillating between the classes. Robinson, with his claim to happiness, hurries on in advance of the proletariat, even though once his fortune is made he behaves like a capitalist, a slaveholder, a plantation owner.[81] (How could he behave otherwise? What other possibilities could he have seen for redeeming his claim to happiness?) He even believes that this *is* happiness, and the bourgeoisie, which at first drew back in horror from this anarchic, berserk man who was so unruly in wanting to force his way into their privileged class happiness, will see their opportunity in his error. It will deceive the member of the plebian middle class on his way to being an assimilated or vacillating petty bourgeois with the hope that adventure is a real possibility for solving his problems. Today the bourgeoisie attempts to convince the proletariat of that as well. The reason: the bourgeoisie had found, as Defoe ascertained indirectly (in constructing the fairy-tale ending for *Robinson*) or directly (in *Moll Flanders*), that the claim to happiness could not be redeemed in reality—in adventure. From that point on, the bourgeoisie permitted adventure. What Defoe had erroneously promoted, they now affably promoted. What Defoe had meant to be an entry into social reality, the bourgeoisie and its ideologues turned into a palliative, a dream, a substitute for the unachievable reality. The petty-bourgeois literature or ideology of adventure, which might well be one of the most significant means of psychological mass control, is the falsification of the plebian-middle-class claim to happiness of the type Defoe/Robinson/Captain Singleton into its opposite, into a renunciation of real (bourgeois) happiness and later, with respect to the proletariat, into a renunciation of the real happiness that could be achieved by the elimination of the class society in favor of an illusion—of indeterminate adventure beyond the real world.

"Naked from the Waist Upwards"

Of course, Defoe helped pave the way for this development: he tried to rise in the real world and did not succeed, suffered the shipwreck of his adventures on the French coast, went bankrupt, was on the run from his creditors and the forces of political reaction. Robinson, dominion over an island, wealth from individual overseas trade—all that had long ceased to exist in the age of the East India Company (at least as a historical law against which to judge the truth or fabulous nature of a story). Did Defoe not know that? It seems as though he did not want to take cognizance of it. He writes in *The Complete English Tradesman*:

> A tradesman sets up, falls, and sinks under misfortunes, and is undone. If he is a man of no spirit, indolent, deadhearted, and desponding, he is indeed utterly undone.... But the vigorous restless man of diligence never lies still there; he struggles, he strives with creditors, to get free; if that will not do, he gets abroad, turns himself round in the world; nay, I may say, turns the world round with his application...he never gives out.... Trade is like a rolling sea, that sometimes one wave washes a man overboard, the next returning surge washes him on board again.[82]

What has misled various interpreters who have studied this treatise (like Jan Kott) is its internal contradictions, which characterize the entire work of Defoe. To be sure, Defoe declares at the beginning that by tradesman he means small merchant, but he himself slips into talking in large dimensions again and again, or he brings these into the narrow space of the shop, glorifies small trade with the heroic perspective of world trade, and in the midst of prescriptions for the assortment of wares, bookkeeping, and domestic frugality (the tradesman does not go out, does not gamble, does not drink) opens a view on the breadth of the oceans dominated by British trade. And why not? "Trade may [itself— M. N.] truly be called an ocean; and those that sail in it, however experienced, have always need of directions."[83] Defoe (the bankrupt) gives these sailors directions with his instructions for shops from the perspectives of British trade policy, English commercial capitalism, that are as necessary as they are earthshaking: *sub specie negotii britannici*, "from the perspective of the British trader."

We can complete our picture by mentioning that the bankrupt, the member of the plebian middle class proudly points out over and over how many English traders come from the aristocracy or how many have risen into the aristocracy (an argument that was used frequently in the heroic epoch of the English bourgeoisie). Incidentally, this very argument is extremely important in the confrontation between the French bourgeoisie and aristocracy in the eighteenth century. As Defoe says, "trade is a very different thing in England than it is in many other countries, and is carried on by persons who, both in their education and descent, are far from being the dregs of the people."[84] This praise, too, from the mouth of a failed member of the plebian middle class, must have embarrassed not only the arriviste British bourgeoisie like Mr. Bickerstaff, but the capitalist landowning aristocracy as well. Someone wanted to join them, someone whose origins, whose thought (the involuntary caricature of their former revolutionary worldviews, long since repressed), whose behavior, whose boasting were *still* unpleasant to them. Later they would recognize how useful the inversion of such arguments was for inciting the masses in support of their imperialist policy.

The reasons that trade is so honored in England, according to Defoe, are:

> 1. That we are the greatest trading country in the world.... 2. That our climate is the best and most agreeable to live in, because a man can be more out of doors in England than in other countries. 3. That our men are the stoutest and best, because, strip them naked from the waist upwards, and give them no weapons at all but their hands and heels, and turn them into a room or stage, and lock them in with the like number of other men of any nation, man for man, and they shall beat the best men you shall find in the world.[85]

That this passage is full of stylistic howlers will not concern us here. But the structure of the argument is important. That England is the most important (trading) country is already as good as national doctrine; that trade is a noble occupation is beyond doubt for *The Tatler* and *The Spectator* and for gentlemen and does not require such rowdy propaganda. It is somewhat shocking, however, that the basis for all of this is the fact that the Englishman (think for instance of Sir Andrew Freeport) can beat up the best men in the world. (The extent to which such ideas are later adopted in Rudyard Kipling's apologetics of adventure is another question.)

In a positive application, that means that the plebian is still present in Defoe's disguise as trader, commercial theorist, and literary man; patriotic, proud of the aristocracy, and concerned with keeping a distance from "the dregs of the people." In the same way, in the successful adventurer merchant Crusoe there is still and always the indefatigable, diligent, puritanically narrow-minded island artisan Robinson, and in that Robinson there is the member of the plebian middle class, Robinson Kreutznaer. Even in Defoe's late economic treatises, the substance is unmistakably plebian, and it breaks through the external appearance again and again, as when he writes: "The French are eminent for making a fine outside, when perhaps within they want necessaries; and indeed a gay shop, and a mean stock, is something like one of those people, with his laced ruffles without a shirt."[86]

The Elan of Adventure in the Underworld

Defoe's affirmation of substantial, manly activity, of the rational dare, of adventure, which in his writings always has the *dual* aspect of business and adventure,[87] is ambiguous or can be read two ways from a dialectical point of view. In his polemical distancing from the "dregs of the people"[88] (by which Defoe means the criminal underworld) with the simultaneous glorification of the plebian qualities of the people (as for instance in the talk of their ability to beat up others), Defoe is *also* polemicizing against the ruling classes, against the aristocracy and the bourgeoisie, or their alliance. In *Augusta Triumphans, or, The Way to Make London the Most Flourishing City in the Universe* (1728), he takes a position on crime in the streets:

> Where is the courage of the English nation, that a gentleman, with six or seven servants, shall be robbed by one single highwayman? Yet we have lately had instances of this; and for this we may thank our effeminacy, our toupee wigs, and powdered pates, our tea, and other scandalous fopperies; and, above all, the disuse of noble and manly sports, so necessary to a brave people, once in vogue, but now totally lost among us.[89]

Defoe is, however, obviously an advocate of the manly element: we are once again referred back to the plebian element which he so admires that he traces it into the criminal strata of the London populace and more or less openly admires it there (after all, the complaint from *Augusta Triumphans* can be reversed; then the robber would be the representative of the "courage of the English nation" that was believed lost, for he defeated a gentleman along with six or seven servants). This state of affairs (and the personal rancor that Defoe despite everything must have felt for "fine" society that treated him so unfinely time and again) must be one of the reasons Defoe viewed famous/infamous figures of the underworld, like Jonathan Wilde[90] and especially John Sheppard,[91] with obvious admiration. His admiration, however, applied only to their joy in enterprise, their courage, and the goal of their actions (earning money), but not to their (criminal) rejection of society. Defoe rejects social rebels like the French robber Cartouche[92] as well as the amused glorification of crime he must have thought to see in the figure of Mackheath/John Sheppard and of Peachum/Jonathan Wilde in John Gay's *Beggar's Opera*, which appeared shortly before *Augusta Triumphans*.[93] His admiration is sustained by the conviction that such capable human beings could have done much if they had not been led astray:[94] "Sheppard and his master had now parted," we learn from Defoe about Sheppard's interrupted apprenticeship, "a woeful parting to the former."[95] And he tells us about Jonathan Wilde: "It must be allowed to Jonathan's fame, that as he steered among rocks and dangerous shoals, so he was a bold pilot; he ventured in and always got out in a manner equally surprising."[96]

The belief in the plebian's power to rise up runs through all Defoe's novels, especially *The History and Remarkable Life of the Truly Honourable Col. Jacque, commonly called Colonel Jack, who was born a gentleman, put prentice to a pick-pocket, was six-and-twenty-years a thief, and then kidnapped to Virginia: came back a merchant* (1722) and the famous story of the prostitute *Moll Flanders* (also 1722), in the foreword to which Defoe gives a programmatic summary of his belief in the rise of the plebian:

> Her application to a sober life and industrious management at last in Virginia, with her transported spouse, is a story fruitful of instruction to all the unfortunate creatures who are obliged to seek their reestablishment abroad, whether by the misery of transportation or other disaster; letting them know that diligence and application have their due encouragement, even in the remotest parts of the world, and that no case can be so low, so despicable, or so empty of prospect, but that an unwearied industry will go a great way to deliver us from it, will in time raise the meanest creature to appear again in the world, and give him a new cast for his life.[97]

Adventure Born of the Distemper of Wandering

> That evil influence which carried me first away from my father's house, that hurried me into the wild and indigested notion of raising my fortune...the same influence, whatever it was, presented the most unfortunate of all enterprises to my view; and I went on board a vessel bound to the coast of *Africa*.[98]

What distinguishes Robinson from other figures of Defoe's is precisely this: while fate has normally buffeted them into an unusual, socially disadvantaged position from which they try to free themselves by any means, especially through hazardous ventures or through the adventure trade, *Robinson Crusoe* (for a short time) presents a different perspective. Robinson is doing well. As things stand, he can expect sufficient income to live on: his self-preservation is, to use Locke's ideas, guaranteed; no one is threatening him, declaring war on him; he need not to fight for his place in society. Like his father, he belongs to the upper middle class that, if we accept the father's thoughts, should be satisfied with its position. But Robinson is not satisfied. Defoe must therefore find a cause to explain why Robinson leaves his security, runs risks, undertakes adventures, and Defoe shifts this cause to Robinson's inner life. Robinson explains to his mother "that my thoughts were so entirely bent upon seeing the world, that I should never settle to any thing with resolution enough to go through with it."[99]

Thus a new basis is created for the glorification of adventure: the individual does not set out on adventures for the sake of material gain; he is not driven by need but by curiosity. At least that is what Robinson claims, and Defoe has him repeat that claim again with emphasis. After Robinson has returned from his lonely island and has settled down as a rich merchant, he is seized—like Fortunatus before him—by restlessness again. After everything that happened to him in "35 years' affliction," one would assume

> that the native propensity to rambling, which I gave an account of in my first setting out into the world to have been so predominant in my thoughts, should be worn out, the volative part be fully evacuated, or at least condensed, and I might at sixty-one years of age have been a little inclined to stay at home, and have done venturing life and fortune any more. Nay further, the common motive of foreign adventures was taken away in me; for I had no fortune to make, I had nothing to seek: if I had gained ten thousand pounds, I had been no richer.[100]

Still, the "strong inclination I had to go abroad again, which hung about me like a chronical distemper," is stronger: Robinson wants to go off on adventures again, and only his wife's worry keeps him from putting "myself upon adventures, fit only for youth and poverty to run into."[101] Going off on adventures, the activity of adventuring, as the privilege of youth or as a necessity dictated by poverty—that is the "classic" justification, found in similar form from the time of Bacon and Mun on; moreover, it is always connected (as in Defoe himself) with the declared goal of becoming rich, of making a profit: "With these thoughts, I considered my new engagement; that I had a wife, one child born, and my wife then great with child of another; that I had all the world could give me, and had no need to seek hazards for gain."[102]

This chapter in *Robinson Crusoe* is an essential step toward the formation of the modern bourgeois or petty-bourgeois ideology of adventure in the nineteenth and twentieth centuries. Robinson's decision to travel practically hangs by a thread. To be sure, Robinson (Defoe) names all the actual economic or social reasons for adventuring, and Robinson behaves on his adventures exactly as these reasons suggest; that is, he acquires plantations, makes deals—every single adventure conforms to these goals. But Robinson begins to treat these material reasons as secondary. In contrast, say, to Captain Singleton or to Colonel Jack or Moll Flanders, he purports to engage in adventure for the sake of adventure because of the lure of distant places, of his "distemper of wandering,"[103] of "one blow from unforeseen Providence."[104] When his wife dies, he sets out again for overseas at the age of over sixty, and in 1693 he and his nephew (representing some businessmen) undertake "a voyage...to the East Indies and China, as private traders."[105] Robinson takes this opportunity to return to his own colonial realm, in order to travel from there on a large trading enterprise to Asia and then via Russia back to England, where he arrives in 1705. Of course, as Defoe himself declared, Robinson's story is partly a reflection of his own life. Doubtless Defoe was looking for a justification vis-à-vis himself and his family, but it is more significant that this berserk member of the plebian middle class engineered his optimism out of despair, ideologized his activities out of social necessity. In terms of world history, as we have shown, the time of the individual adventure, the time of the adventurers, was long since over. Certainly it was still possible to rise with élan, diligence, luck, and courage (and especially with a sufficiently large starting capital) and to fall again. But this was not the rule and became less and less so (put differently, the number of those who could no longer rise in this way became greater and greater). The conflict between the willingness to adventure and the factual impossibility of carrying it out that Defoe encountered throughout his life could therefore be resolved only by resignation or internalization. Defoe chose the second: the *adventurer*, who seems to him the image of an ideal human being, is the merchant whose portrait he draws in his periodical *The Review*.

> He knows foreign languages without books of instruction, geography without maps, his business books and the route of his trade voyages span the world; his foreign exchange, protested bills, and vouchers for goods speak all languages; and while he sits in his office, he has commerce with all nations and keeps up a universal correspondence with the most excellent and worldly part of human society.[106]

The Adventurer as Employee of the Yahoos

We must assume that Defoe cannot have been completely unaware of the fairy-tale character of his novels. In *The Complete English Tradesman,* he lets us see for whom he is really writing, for the employees:

> When merchants send adventurers to our British colonies, it is usual with them to make up to each factor, what they call a sortable cargo; that is to say, they want something of everything that may furnish the tradesman there with parcels fit to fill their shops, and invite their customers.[107]

The times were too prosaic in England and too revolutionary in France for the bourgeoisie to make anything of Defoe/Robinson's drive toward adventure. The French Enlightenment could make relatively little of a glorification of adventure for adventure's sake (who would be interested in that, against the background of the confrontation between feudal nobility and bourgeoisie?), and in England people were interested in other things (like building up colonial trade and building up manufacturing in the transition to industrial capitalism). This glorification of adventure was meaningless also to the growing army of manufacturing or industrial workers, or to those among them who could read or had time to[108] (Defoe's Friday in part represents the workers' opposition to adventure, their forced exploitation, as Engels demonstrates in his critique of Dühring.[109] What remained was the middle-class public, which devoured *Robinson Crusoe* avidly.

To the intellectuals, who had regarded the development of bourgeois (capitalist) society from an ironic distance or with disapproval, Defoe must have seemed almost like a confidence man, a swindler, a charlatan. If we disregard Smollett's work,[110] whose *Adventures of Roderick Random* (1748) uses the stylistic means of the picaresque in order to reflect the change from formerly voluntary, Robinson-like adventures to the exploitative situation of endured adventures, we come across criticism of the glorification of adventure quite early. While Fielding, in *Joseph Andrews* (1742) and *Tom Jones* (1749), tends humorously to reduce adventure in English bourgeois society to the appropriate dimensions of family gossip and luck in love, with *Gulliver's Travels* (1726), Jonathan Swift (1667–1745) carries out an attack on the glorification of adventure—directed probably not least against Defoe himself—that is as cynical as it is radical. The ship on which Gulliver sets out in 1726 into a satire on English conditions is called *Adventure*. What were still actual social and philosophical problems for Defoe, on which he discoursed as a student of Hobbes and Locke and as a follower of Drake and Raleigh in his fictional experiment,[111] are now categorically condemned from an intellectually purist point of view (which, compared to Defoe's, is quite unworldly): trade, colonial policy, and— especially—slavery. At the same time, Swift satirizes Defoe's ideological positions on adventure in *Robinson Crusoe*; these satiric passages in Swift read like a direct parody of Robinson's remarks on his inner drive toward adventure. Gulliver has returned from his first involuntary voyage to Lilliput, earns much money in London, but cannot stay in one place for long:

> I stayed but two Months with my Wife and Family; for my insatiable Desire of seeing foreign Countries would suffer me to continue no longer. I left fifteen Hundred Pounds with my Wife, and fixed her in a good House at *Redriff*. My remaining Stock I carried with me, Part in Money, and Part in Goods, in Hopes to improve my Fortunes....
> I took Leave of my Wife, and Boy and Girl, with Tears on both Sides; and went to board the *Adventure*, a Merchant-Ship of three Hundred Tons, bound for *Surat*.[112]

And at the beginning of Gulliver's third voyage to Laputa, we also find remarks that seem to be a persiflage of Defoe: "the Thirst I had of seeing the World, notwithstanding my past Misfortunes, continuing as violent as ever. The only Difficulty that remained, was to persuade my Wife, whose Consent however I at last obtained, by the Prospect of Advantage she proposed to her Children."[113] Let us note in passing that neither Defoe nor Swift, in his parody, believe that family, wife and children, domestic cares or idylls can be united with adventure. At any rate, Gulliver begins his fourth voyage to the land of the Houyhnhnms, the noble horses, as captain of the *Adventure*. This voyage begins in 1710.

Swift is hostile to bourgeois society in general, and particularly so to adventure or the glorification of adventure, but not from any plebian or (historically impossible) proletarian impulse. Swift is a conservative critic whose moral integrity, which would doubtless also have made him a rigorous critic of feudal absolutism,[114] leads him to scourge the exploitation of the common people, especially the Irish,[115] and all colonial exploitation with all its attendant phenomena. To be sure, he has a correct view of the horrifying manifestations of the transitional time from primitive accumulation to industrial capitalism, but he does not recognize (and unlike Defoe, does not even suspect) that only the forces that are creating this misery can liberate the forces that can overcome it. The fourth part of Gulliver's travels is the report on his stay in the land of the Houyhnhnms, the rational horses, and of the Yahoos, bestial humans. The bestial, inhuman character of the humans is denounced through a comparison of human beings with Yahoos. Gulliver tells his master, Dapple-Grey, about humans in Europe (England), and the dapple-grey finds his report credible because it exactly corresponds to the behavior of the bestial humans, the Yahoos, in his country. That is especially the case with the drive for possession and the resultant aggressiveness (competition) among humans/Yahoos—let us note by the way that Swift uses this opportunity to polemicize against trade and especially against the import of luxury goods.[116] The dapple-grey tells Gulliver he believes his story; after all, it confirms what he and his fellow horses had observed in the Yahoos, and it even explains what they had previously misunderstood. They had attributed the aggression that the Yahoos demonstrated toward each other to their ugliness, "which all could see in the rest, but not in themselves."[117] In reality this Yahoo wildness was the result of the same causes Gulliver gave for human wildness. The dapple-grey says to Gulliver: "For, if (he said) you throw among five *Yahoos* as much Food as would be sufficient for fifty, they will, instead of eating peaceably, fall together by the Ears, each single one impatient to *have all to it self.*"[118] This drive is especially noticeable in the Yahoo efforts to collect, bury, hide, and protect against others "certain *shining Stones* of several Colours" that are found in some fields of the country. The dapple-grey, Gulliver's master, says he had never been able to tell "how these *Stones* could be of any Use to a *Yahoo*, but now he believed it might proceed from the same Principle of *Avarice*, which [Gulliver] had ascribed to mankind."[119]

Swift combines this Hobbesian, biologistic construct (which is sharply distinguished from Locke's explanation of the interest in money as an interest due to aesthetic pleasure, for instance in shells), with Locke's concept of the reasonable, equal claim of all humans to a share of the "productions of the Earth," a view the dapple-grey represents. The horse does not understand the Hobbesian (Yahoo) principle of *bellum omnium contra omnes*, "the war of all against all": "For he went upon a Supposition that all Animals had a Title to their Share in the productions of the Earth."[120] For that reason he (or Swift) considers money to be merely a whim for the sake of which wars are waged, people subjugated, and humans exploited. Gulliver, reporting on his conversation with the dapple-grey, says the horse told him

> that when a *Yahoo* had got a great Store of this precious Substance, he was able to purchase whatever he had a mind to; the finest Clothing, the noblest Houses, great Tracts of Land, the most costly Meats and Drinks; and have his Choice of the most beautiful Females. Therefore since *Money* alone, was able to perform all these Feats, our *Yahoos* [i.e., humans—M. N.] thought, they could never have enough of it to spend or to save, as they found themselves inclined from their natural Bent either to profusion or Avarice. That, the rich Man enjoyed the Fruit of the poor Man's Labour, and the latter were a Thousand to One in Proportion to the former. That the Bulk of our People was forced to live miserably, by labouring every Day for small Wages to make a few live plentifully.[121]

This oppression, the misery in which exploited people live, also explains for Swift why merchants succeed over and over in finding people for dangerous sea voyages or to settle colonies. He has Gulliver say that

> they were Fellows of desperate Fortunes, forced to fly from the Places of their Birth, on Account of their Poverty or their Crimes. Some were undone by Law-Suits, others spent all they had in Drinking, Whoring and Gaming; others fled for Treason, many for Murder, Theft, Poysoning, Robbery, Perjury, Forgery, Coining false Money; for committing Rapes or Sodomy; for flying from their Colours, or deserting to the Enemy; and most of them had broken Prison. None of these durst return to their native Countries for fear of being hanged, or of starving in a Jail; and therefore were under a Necessity of seeking a Livelihood in other Places.[122]

Swift is showing the other side of the mythology of émigrés or colonists under the sign of adventure: if people could earn a living at home, if they were not starving there, they would not undertake the risks of these adventures, or forced into crime by their misery, people are compelled by the government to emigrate, to undertake an adventure. Swift's dismantling of the myth of adventure is perfect. The adventurer is the slave of a despot or the employee of a merchant who had earlier called himself an adventurer, but who is actually nothing other than a despot, a dirty Yahoo.

Adventure in the Intellectual World

But even the slave, even the person living in poverty, in exploitation, for whom Swift has so much sympathy, is a Yahoo. And here we see the lack of perspective, the lack of a standpoint, in his radical criticism of everything (in which Swift manifests his kinship with another radical-conservative critic, Molière's Misanthrope). Swift's condemnation of colonialism, for instance, is brilliant. He shows how bandits, pirates (the colonialists) seize possession of land and extirpate or enslave the populace:

> And this execrable Crew of Butchers employed in so pious an Expedition, is a *modern Colony* sent to convert and civilize an idolatrous and barbarous People. But this Description, I confess, doth by no means affect the *British* Nation, who may be an Example to the whole World for their Wisdom, Care, and Justice in planting Colonies.[123]

Of course, this description exactly fits English colonial policy. The contemporary reader understood that immediately and—laughed at Swift's ingenious trick, the only disadvantage of which was that it showed no alternative: Swift's strength, the satirical form, reveals itself on close observation to be the formal expression of his actual weakness, the lack of orientation. He does not like the bourgeoisie; he annihilates it. But the aristocracy is no better; he scorns it, whether prince or monarch. Does he like the people? But the people consist of Yahoos, and the boundaries he draws between the poor and the criminal elements are fluid. What remains? "The noble savage"? the unspoiled natural peoples? Not even that. What remains is a realm of rational horses because even the "noble savage" is a Yahoo in the last analysis.

Let us disregard the fact that Swift's lack of a standpoint also had a positive aspect; the criticism of the aristocracy or of feudal despotism did permit *Gulliver* to be received by the revolutionary French bourgeoisie (in contrast to Defoe's *Robinson Crusoe*) and to serve as a literary weapon for the Enlightenment (in Voltaire's *Candide*). Of course, Swift's satire is exactly aimed at the barbaric conditions in the colonies and in Ireland and the exploitation of the masses, and what he dismantles with this satiric form is the glorification of exploitation and colonialism under the banner and in the name of adventure. And here Swift has the clairvoyance of a genius. For the ideologues of public morality, anyone who sets off for overseas is not a captain in the pay of a trading company or the leader of a genocidal band, not a mercantile employee or a salesman, no impressed sailor or deported criminal. He is—and here we see the utility of *Robinson Crusoe* as well—a human being whose desire for adventure in exotic lands and outside the bourgeois order forces him to travel. In the birth hour of this myth of adventure, Swift is already using the scalpel of his satire to reveal the true motives, is unmasking its two-faced morality, its hypocrisy and lies.

The triumphal march of the myth of adventure in bourgeois society as it is becoming consolidated in fact makes increasingly impossible what its ideologues glorify and proclaim as a kind of "opiate of the people": adventure itself. Still, the myth cannot be contained, especially since it also tries to assimilate the positive sides of real adventure and since the glorification of adventure calls on the valuable qualities and potentialities of the individual such as élan in enterprise and curiosity. In fact, in the bourgeois worldview of the eighteenth century the adventurer comes into an inheritance that will later decay completely. But this inheritance had to do with the best potentialities awakened and liberated by the original adventure trade: the glorification of human thought, of experimental science, seen as equivalent to the discovery of distant lands, new worlds, as we already discovered in Francis Bacon's work. Bernhard Fabian has pursued this metaphorical way of thinking and seeing. He writes about the analogy between naval exploration and literature:

> As early as the seventeenth century these metaphors were applied to literature, in a secondary transfer. A new nature had opened itself, noble secrets of optics, medicine, anatomy, and astronomy were discovered; consequently, similar successes must be possible in literature, given similar efforts. So literature was discovered in the same way that American or the law of gravity was discovered.... A self-evident correlate to this conception was a naïve belief in progress. According to the contemporary conception, the natural scientist of the seventeenth century penetrated ever farther into ever broader realms, and as if conquering lands he strode from finding to finding.[124]

Fabian shows how in the Restoration era, when bourgeois heroism had come to an end internally and externally, the idea of the natural scientist as explorer was joined with that of the bold man, the hero: "The heroic ideal ... did not perish, but instead underwent a metamorphosis from which it emerged, 'spiritualized' through its application to the natural scientist."[125]

As evidence of this process, Fabian quotes from Thomas Sprat's *History of the Royal Society* (1667): "*Invention* is an *Heroic* thing, and plac'd above the reach of a low, and vulgar *Genius*. It requires an *active*, a bold, a nimble, a restless *mind*: a thousand difficulties must be contemn'd, with which a mean heart would be broken."[126] The qualities of the scientific "spirit" no longer distinguish it from the "spirit" of the adventurer or vice versa. Just one hundred years later, Edward Young in his *Conjectures on Original Composition*, 1759, "associated" with this "spirit" "the metaphor of the voyage around the intellectual world and the advance into unknown regions."[127]

The First Systematization of the Adventurer

It is impossible to give even a rough survey of the literature that appeared like a spring flood in England (but also in France and Germany, in Holland and elsewhere) toward the end of the seventeenth and in the first half of the eighteenth century under the key-word "adventure" or *aventure*, and that included the knightly-courtly, the picaresque, and the English beggar and criminal literary traditions[128] as well as the novels of colonization and exploration and travel literature in general. Fictional or factual memoirs also belong to that flood (especially the memoirs of infamous people). In short, there was almost no realm of social reality that was not furnished with the label "adventure" and marketed under it, thanks in large part to the changed social position of the writer or to the revolution in book production (both results of the general revolution of the relations of production in the direction of industrial capitalism). Books became mass goods, a development that liberated writers from the constraints of the feudal patronage system although the new system produced new constraints, namely the (partial) subordination of production to the interests of capital or the transformation of the author into a literary wage laborer.[129] In Arnold Hauser's somewhat one-sided characterization of this development, for which he mistakenly makes only the public, and not the producers, responsible (this kind of one-sidedness was the basis for the later construct of a "need" for "adventure literature" on the part of the "masses"),

> the sudden growth of the reading public leads to a sharp decline in the general standard [of literature—M. N.]. The demand is much greater than there are good writers to meet it, and as the reproduction of novels is an extremely paying concern, they are turned out in wild and indiscriminate profusion. The needs of the lending libraries dictate the pace and determine the quality of the output. Apart from the thriller, the subjects most in demand are the scandals of the day, famous "cases," fictitious and semi-fictitious biographies, travel descriptions and secret memoirs, in a word, the usual types of sensational literature.[130]

Laurence Sterne is wittier than Hauser in expressing his discomfort at the flood of sensational literature in the first volume of *The Life and Opinions of Tristam Shandy, Gentleman* (1760). He challenges a (fictional) female reader to read the previous chapter again, because she missed something (which is actually not there at all):

> I have imposed this penance upon the lady, neither out of wantonness or cruelty, but from the best of motives.... 'Tis to rebuke a vicious taste which has crept into thousands besides herself,—of reading straight forwards, more in quest of the adventures, than of

the deep erudition and knowledge which a book of this cast, if read over as it should be, would infallibly impart with them.[131]

The other side of the coin is (at first) the improvement of the social position of the writer, which is also reflected in an increase in his self-confidence. Even though we must distinguish between known and unknown authors and even though publishing practices were always directed at profits and hence at low royalties,[132] still the writer's social position had improved overall. As Hauser puts it:

> Now for the first time the writer as such enjoys the regard due to the representative of a higher sphere of life.... Now for the first time the ideal of the creative personality arises, of the artistic genius with his originality and subjectivism, as already characterized by Edward Young.[133]

Although, as we have seen, the ideal of the creative personality probably arose earlier, it is true that around the middle of the eighteenth century this view of the writer, the ideal of the creative personality, reaches a high point, which is expressed in the development of the ideology of adventure as well. On 7 November 1752, the first number of *The Adventurer* appeared, a periodical published by John Jawkesworth.[134] Here we find a treatise on the adventurer that we can regard as the first systematic presentation of the modern idealistic ideology of adventure. Life, we read, has generally been considered as warfare, and in it every man must struggle with difficulties and is exposed to dangers. For that reason, courage is the most necessary of all virtues. But it quickly proved that courage contributes little to the common weal without the "exercise of courage," something that is possible only if "immediate pleasure is rejected [!] and life itself set at hazard."

But since it is difficult to move human beings to renounce their pleasures without exchanging them for other pleasures, people began to glorify courage: "The pleasures of the imagination are substituted for those of the senses, and the hope of future enjoyments for the possession of the present.... Courage has been dignified with the name of heroick virtue; and heroick virtue has deified the hero" and compelled his veneration. But we must distinguish between kinds of courage. The essential element of true courage in the face of danger is "that this danger should be voluntary: for a courageous resistance of dangers to which we are necessarily exposed by our station [which can in any case not be avoided—M. N.], is considered merely as the discharge of our duty, and brings only a negative reward, exemption from infamy."

A soldier who is obliged by a command or through chance to carry out a dangerous act would not be admired for his courage. Only the man who voluntarily provokes risk can lay claim to being praised as a hero:

It is the man who provokes danger in it's [*sic*] recess [who seeks it out—M. N.], who quits a peaceful retreat, where he might have slumbered in ease and safety, for peril and labour, to drive before a tempest or to watch in a camp; the man who descends from a precipice by a rope at midnight, to fire a city that is besieged; or who ventures forward into regions of perpetual cold and darkness, to discover new paths of navigation, and disclose new secrets of the deep; it is the ADVENTURER alone on whom every eye is fixed with admiration, and whose praise is repeated by every voice.

This admiration can only be won if the voluntary risks the adventurer takes are not taken for the sake of greed or desire for power. The adventurer's risk must be not only voluntary, but also only for the sake of adventure itself and not to earn anything else; otherwise it does not deserve the name of adventure:

> If new worlds are sought merely to gratify avarice or ambition, for the treasures that ripen in the distant mine, or the homage of nations whom new arts of destruction may subdue; or if the precipice is descended merely for a pecuniary consideration; the Adventurer is, in the estimation of reason, as worthless and contemptible as the robber who defies a gibbet for the lure of a strumpet, or the fool who lays out his whole property on a lottery-ticket.

The true hero, who coincides here with the adventurer, is the man who freely takes risks and sets his life at hazard for others without wanting anything more in return than fame.

Unfortunately, the time is long past when the knights-errant could unite "the shout of the multitude, and the eulogy of the philosopher" in themselves in this way. Their deeds are described in *The Adventurer* in the style of *The Tatler*, and in obvious imitation of the same: encounters with dragons, sorcerers, and the like as well as emphasis on the renunciation of material reward and the undertaking of adventures for the sake of adventure. The knight-errant, *The Adventurer* determines, must now be replaced by the adventurer, who will earn this general praise, this universal fame—"and who is more truly a candidate for publick praise than an author?" The author runs risks for the sake of his honor alone (like the knight-errant); like the knight-errant, he "confides in the temper of his weapon, and the justice of his cause." He can even work magic himself because

> he also has the power of enchantment, which he will exercise in his turn; he will sometimes crowd the scene with ideal beings, sometimes recall the past, and sometimes anticipate the future; sometimes he will transport those who put themselves under his influence to regions which no traveller has yet visited, and will sometimes confine them

with invisible bands till the charm is dissolved by a word, which will be placed the last in a paper which he shall give them.

None of this is boastful; this is appropriate praise, for the dangers the author runs are great, and "danger is the measure of honour."

With *The Adventurer*, the original meaning of the concept of adventure in bourgeois thought has been transformed into its opposite: from adventure = goods, trade undertaking, and profit, it has come to mean a practical or intellectual deed abstracted from any kind of drive for gain. If the adventurer of the past took risks as a matter of course in order to make profits, struggling at the same time against risk or trying to keep risk as low as possible, we now hear that the adventurer is characterized by seeking out risks. If the goal of the adventurer of the past was to use his adventure, with as little risk as possible, to create the material base for a better, richer, finally also freer life, that carries no weight in the scale of the modern theorist: death would be preferable as a goal. But in any case, the goal is no longer the fulfillment of happiness, but the promise of happiness: the adventurer renounces his individual happiness in favor of a hope, the promise of future happiness—what Defoe by no means wanted, but what he involuntarily helped to prepare, has come about. Adventure will be used in the future to explain why the human being is forced to live so shabbily; the promise of future happiness and the contempt for the present will be used to distract attention from the misery of the present. The meaning of the life of a *true man* (women are cast in another role in capitalist society) is *adventure for the sake of adventure.*

Chapter 10
The Metamorphosis of the *Chevalier*

Primitive Accumulation in France

There can be no doubt that the material and intellectual bases for the modern bourgeois ideology of adventure were created by the English bourgeoisie's "naïve" revolutionary assault ("adequate" to Bacon's philosophy in the sense of the Marxist formulation) up to the crucial years 1649 and 1688 (to 1688 on the basis of political experience and without that revolutionary recklessness); in this process sea trade with all its described manifestations played a decisive role. The old courtly ideal of knightly adventure was in ruins and had been laid to rest, at the latest in *The Tatler* and *The Spectator*, even though the bourgeoisie was to preserve certain qualities of this idea of humanity, which were apparent especially in the ideal of the gentleman. If we disregard the sixteenth-century representatives of the English bourgeois, who had taken on a courtly coloration (but only in part), we can say that the English bourgeois, the bourgeois revolutionary, had acted (and traded) first and only then taken on manners; he was aided in this by the circumstance that the behavior of the English aristocracy (often even at court) tended to be rude and careless and that large portions of the English feudal nobility (to say nothing of the gentlemen adventurers) had quickly adopted the bourgeois methods of competition.

That is explained in part by the fact that the English feudal nobility had set the course for wool production and hence for the "agricultural revolution" with its enclosure policy as early as the end of the fifteenth and the beginning of the sixteenth centuries. This process was promoted by textile production and by the wool or textile trade (of the merchant adventurers) as much as textile production was promoted by the "agricultural revolution":

> Since the end of the century, this *inner* impetus had been supported by wealth streaming in from *outside*, thanks to maritime and colonial expansion. The circumnavigation of Africa, the discovery of the sea route to the Indies by Vasco da Gama, of America by Columbus... raised the scientific niveau and expanded the European idea of the world. But at the same time (that was the true goal of the "explorers") large-scale trade with exotic products, with slaves and metals, was inaugurated again and immensely expanded. A new era opened up for *commercial capital*... because... a world market was established, because its impulse concerned the *entire European system of production* and because large *states* (and not simply cities) profited from it to constitute themselves.[1]

What Vilar here expressly presents as a summary of the "primitive accumulation" analyzed by Marx is true in an exemplary way in England; however, it is true in principle in all large European states, even if there are local and regional differences and restrictions. In France, for instance, the revolutionary change in agriculture did not take place. The feudal structure of agriculture remained in place (albeit with some improvements over the Middle Ages),[2] and that means that the most important economic structure, the decisive mode of production, the basis for the entire economy (up to the French Revolution of 1789),[3] remained fundamentally unchanged: up to the French Revolution, the feudal landowners were thus the dominant class in France (even though they had others manage their lands and had themselves taken on some sort of duties at the court at Versailles). That also explains why every bourgeois who became wealthy tried to buy himself into the magistracy in order to enjoy the exemption from taxes granted to the nobility or to acquire feudal land holdings (or to do both).[4] Success proved such a bourgeois right: only someone with land holdings and a place in the nobility of magistrates could acquire permanent property in this society based above all on feudal agriculture.[5]

The Nobility of Magistrates as a Revolutionary Element

In France, too, the formation of the nation-state was accomplished according to the laws of class struggle exposed by Marx and Engels: the monarchy allied itself with certain elements of the bourgeoisie against the feudal nobility. But the stimulus for the bourgeoisie to enter an alliance with the monarchy in this essentially feudal-agrarian society was the rise into the class of noble landowners or into the *noblesse de robe*, the "nobility of magistrates" (and not, as in England, the permission to carry on overseas trade with certain privileges guaranteed by the monarch, which by the way did not exclude elevation into the aristocracy). Thus the purchase of noble titles played a considerable role. Most titles purchased belonged to fiscal or legal office:

> The development of the practice of purchasing offices had decided fiscal causes, because the sale of civil service positions became a considerable source of supplementary income for the king. Once this profitable custom had developed, it produced a stimulus to create more and more new civil service positions in order to continue to fill the state coffers. Francis I exploited such opportunities especially well. The consequence was a bloating of the civil service system, which became a more and more oppressive burden to the population and increasingly developed a parasitic character.[6]

As fitting as this description doubtless is for the time when the absolutist monarchy was prevalent, it cannot be seen as generally valid for the time of its rise. To be sure, the system of the nobility of magistrates was often oppressive, but the whole process has a social and political dialectic that prevents us from seeing it from a negative or primarily negative point of view, as so often happens.[7] We cannot make statements about what was or was not progressive (or revolutionary) in past times if we abstract from the objectively verifiable relations of production and from the forms and categories of thinking and acting of that age. One specific characteristic of the French manifestation of the class struggle that was analyzed by Engels and Marx is that when the French monarch was struggling for the absolute monarchy, he allowed masses of the bourgeoisie allied with him to rise into the aristocracy. We must not see this simply as an impediment to the development of capitalism in France as it has often been considered in the relevant literature because quite different limits were set on the development of capitalism in France than for instance in England. One important limit is that the "agricultural revolution" did not take place in France. The domestic market could not become functional before the country was politically unified, and in this phase overseas trade was as good as impossible without support by the national government because the merchant was able to establish a permanent foothold overseas only under the protection of a national government. During this time, the rise of the bourgeois into the nobility (of magistrates) or into the class of noble landowners is not simply an impediment, even in the direction of revolutionary change. On the contrary, the fragmented state of the country made this very establishment of an autonomous, relatively mobile system of civil servants an instrument to help the power of the monarchy prevail. Moreover, the king thereby bound powerful moneyowners to himself and converted them into royalist aristocrats, whom he used against the oppositional feudal nobility. Norbert Elias writes:

> Partly beside and partly within the new nobility a new noble hierarchy

was formed within which status depended far more on the title bestowed by the king and the pension going with it than on tradition. The effects on the structure of the nobility were very soon seen. As early as the second half of the sixteenth century almost all the names of the aristocracy are new names.[8]

The bourgeoisie, through its rise to the function of the civil service nobility, thus made a considerable contribution to creating the bases for establishing the absolute monarchy and hence also for developing the capitalist mode of production, a process that began during the formation of the absolute monarchy. The rise of the successful bourgeois into the nobility created space and stimulus for others to follow, for it was not the entire bourgeoisie that rose into the nobility (of magistrates), but always only the representatives who were most important economically and politically. Thus from the time it had become usual to purchase offices, under François I (1515-47) at the latest, there was something like competition among the bourgeoisie for the rise into the nobility, and of course powers were liberated to achieve that goal. But overall it can be determined that those who rose into the nobility, as paradoxical as this sounds today, were the specific French avant-garde of those "revolutionary elements" which, as Engels demonstrates, allied themselves with the "progressive element" of the epoch, the monarchy, in order to help the nation-state, the absolute monarchy, prevail against the oppositional feudal princes.

This is not the place to investigate in detail the development of the *noblesse de robe* in the epoch of the formation and prevalence of the absolute monarchy.[9] But as a general tendency we can state that, however mutable the various alliances between the monarchy and the Catholic or Protestant nobility and bourgeoisie were, the fundamental goal of the alliance of the "progressive elements" of the bourgeoisie and monarchy was the economic and political unification of the country under the absolute monarchy and not the prevalence of certain worldviews, as the designation "wars of religion" for the confrontations between feudal nobility and monarchy could lead one to believe. The idea of religious tolerance then joins with the idea of the absolute monarchy in this age too, as in the *Six Books of the Republic* by Jean Bodin, 1576. When Henri IV (of Navarre) entered Paris in 1594, after his conversion to Catholicism, six Parisian citizens from different professions published a song of praise to the victory of reason in the state, long hoped for and now achieved: the *Satire Ménippée*. This work tallies up for the bourgeoisie of Paris not only what they have lost through their conspiracies against the king, but also what they will win:

> We shall have a king [in Henri IV—M. N.] who will reestablish order and compel all petty [feudal] tyrants to obedience and duty, who will punish the licentious and rebellious, will extirpate thieves and bandits, will clip the wings of those with delusions of grandeur, will force those

who swipe or embezzle public moneys to cough them up, will force everyone to be content in his office, and will protect all the world in peace and quiet.[10]

Le Roi absolu à la quête de l'aventure

The process of forming this basic alliance between monarchy and bourgeoisie, with the peculiarly French feature of the rise of the "upper bourgeoisie" into the *noblesse de robe*, necessarily affected the movement of thinking and the development of new ideals of humanity. As early as the time of transition from the medieval feudal state to the absolute monarchy, at the time of the reign of François I, who can already be considered an absolute king (he was able to make the unified nation-state prevail, although not yet the absolute monarchy), the ideologues were beginning to create an artistic, theoretical basis for the absolute monarchy toward which they were working, and hence they were also beginning to create the foundation for the first unified national culture on French soil. This courtly-absolutist national culture, the production of which is inseparably linked with the names of the theorists and poets of the Pléiade—Du Bellay, Pelletier du Mans, Ronsard, Baïf, Pontus de Tyard, Jodelle—necessarily liquidated the culture of the urban bourgeoisie, which had until then been predominant. One reason for this liquidation was that the French bourgeoisie, unlike the English, did not have an autonomous economic-political and artistic-theoretical perspective, but rather saw its life goal in the rise into the *noblesse de robe* and applauded the artistic glorification of that group in the courtly-absolutist national culture; another was that the burgher (of the medieval city) or the small feudal lord or knight could no longer stand at the center of this culture: that place was occupied by the absolute monarch.

But especially in the epoch of transition to the absolute monarchy, contradictions are obvious and probably unavoidable. They are particularly obvious in the first attempt at a theoretical foundation for the necessary new national literature, Joachim de Bellay's *Deffence et illustration de la langue françoyse*. This work appeared in 1549, two years after the death of François I, and reflects Du Bellay's experience with the absolute monarch François I in the phase of national unification. This work, besides emphatically rejecting the literature of the medieval urban bourgeoisie, those "Rondeaux, Ballades, Virelaiz, Chantz Royaux, Chansons" and "similar spices that are ruining the taste for our language,"[11] calls for the erection of the sole fitting monument to the French nation (and of course that means to the absolute monarchy): the creation of "le long Poëme Françoys," the great epic poem. "Such a work would . . . bring [the poets—M. N.] immortal fame, would bring France honor, and would contribute to the glorification of our language."[12] For this "long French poem," which, according to Du Bellay, must be written in "vers Heroïques," the models should be not only the epics of Homer and Virgil, but also the *Orlando furioso* of Ariosto (1516-32), whom Du Bellay considers almost the equal of Homer and Virgil. Du Bellay addresses his poet-reader: "As far as I am concerned, choose," like Ariosto, "who saw fit to borrow from our language the names and the history [the legend of Roland—M. N.], one of those lovely old novels, for instance Lancelot or Tristan, or another, and shape that again into an admirable *Iliad*, an *Aeneid*, full of suffering and troubles."[13]

Du Bellay's poetics in general and his suggestions for the creation of an epic in particular have been subject to much criticism, which has usually emphasized his insufficiency in comparison with the normative neo-Aristotelian poetics of the Italian Renaissance and of French "classicism." Even René Bray, in his standard work, *La formation de la doctrine classique en France*, writes: "Du Bellay dreamed of a French epic. But what he imagined was bad."[14] What Bray means is that Du Bellay's idea of the epic was inadequately formulated and by no means corresponded to the model ideas that had been drafted by the so-called neo-Aristotelian literary theorists in connection with the first Latin translations of Aristotle's poetics in 1498 and with the first edition of the Greek text in 1503. Just as the discovery of the trade routes to the East Indies and America resulted from economic necessity, the "discovery" of Aristotelian poetics arose from literary-political necessity: this poetics—at least as interpreted by contemporary theorists—provided the framework for drafting a literature of the absolute monarchy. The literary genres it included, defined, and suggested for production were organized in a strictly hierarchical way and corresponded in a rough way to the class structure of society under feudal absolutism; if one disregards the smaller genres, neo-Aristotelian poetics is divided into three large genres: epic, tragedy, and comedy. According to prescription, comedy was the precinct of the "people": the nobility was not to appear in comedy. Tragedy, on the other hand, was reserved for the nobility. The heroic poem, the epic, which held first place, was previously unknown in this form and function; it was a new creation of the epoch of the transition to absolute monarchy and was considered the only fit genre to give literary shape to the ideal of the (absolutist) ruler and general.

Du Bellay's ideas of the "long Poëme Françoys" no doubt failed to correspond to the often minutely detailed (test-tube) ideas of the neo-Aristotelian theorists; they recommended Virgil's *Aeneid* as the model for epic production, which was supposed to correspond to the laws of verisimilitude.[15] Du Bellay offended just these theorists with his suggestion of taking material from the Grail legends, the *matière de Bretagne*: from this material one could create only material that was historically improbable. But Du Bellay's suggestion is more realistic in a certain way than an attempt at an epic based on nothing but theoretical prescription. Put differently, his suggestion reflects the contradictions in the real figure of the ruler at the time of transition to the absolute monarchy, for instance the contradictions in the role of François I, which Du Bellay was himself in a position to observe. As Norbert Elias correctly states, François I "represented a transition between the chivalrous and courtly types of king with perhaps an inclination toward the former rather than the latter."[16] To be sure, François I fundamentally unified the country and forced the feudal nobility into subordination;[17] he began the policy of representing the absolute monarchy in the courtly ritual and in artistic and literary glorification; and he fostered the sciences and the fine arts. Nevertheless, he personally led his armies, against Italy for instance, supported by "large portions of the nobility," which were "only too glad" to undertake these "adventurous campaigns" (in the hopes of booty);[18] and he personally participated in knightly tournaments. In these actions he embodied the *roi chevalier*,[19] who rode out on adventures as absolute monarch and thus kept himself from being fixed in a central administrative site or kept the country from administrative centralization. As Elias puts it:

> It is also characteristic for the situation of the court in the transitional period that the people who gather here, while living in more direct and constant dependence on the king than earlier, are still basically knights and warriors and not, as later, courtiers who occasionally go to war. The period is full of wars, military expeditions and their vicissitudes. We should think only of Francis I's imprisonment. So the court always had something of the army camp about it.[20]

From *Chevalier* to Mythic Hero

Another contradiction is that while the court of François I resembled an army camp, the style of living there still corresponded in many ways to the ideal that Castiglione had drafted in the *Cortegiano*. At the same time, a process began in France that would culminate under Louis XIV: the absorption of the petty and greater feudal nobility into the court and its being given offices in the ritual. Elias writes:

> How far the nobility is growing into the king's household in this process can be seen above all from the fact that under Francis I it becomes customary for the king and princes of the blood to be served by nobles even as regards lower functions such as that of valet. Nevertheless, all relations are in a state of flux in this period. The hierarchy of court people is more unstable, and the inheritance of offices is diminishing. Thus the mobility of the court and its military mode of life do not leave much scope for the formation of an inescapable etiquette.[21]

How is this king and his court to be portrayed and glorified? Symptomatically: François I had both the *Iliad* and *Amadís* translated. Du Bellay's ideas thus proved to be not so deviant after all: the external form was to be taken from antiquity and to provide the heroic framework that the king obviously did not yet fill, and the material was to be taken from the knightly romances, whose *chevaliers*, to be sure, did not have the stature of François I. Nothing was certain except that only the epic would do to glorify the absolute monarch or the absolute monarchy. This was the set of political-theoretical problems that had to be solved, problems both of the correct conception of the hero and of the genre that had yet to be developed. The great epic poem, the *chanson de geste* of the type of the *Song of Roland*, had long since become irrelevant, even nonexistent, for the society of the late Middle Ages and the early Renaissance. Its time had already run out with the counterdesign to the archaic hero of the early Middle Ages, with the courtly knight of *aventüre* and the transposition of the epic materials into the form of the courtly romance. Even the courtly-knightly romance was replaced by new literary forms in the course of the fourteenth and fifteenth centuries, forms that were appropriate to the developing needs of society, especially those of the rising urban bourgeoisie. The time before, during, and after the Hundred Years' War had no more need for heroic poetry.

When the development we have sketched allowed this need to arise, there was no possibility of connecting with an existing, contemporary, heroic epic poetry produced and received in France. Only in Italy had such poetry found a continuation, in a much altered, ironic-romantic form (which corresponded to the special social needs of Italian princely courts or of the patrician urban bourgeoisie) that often included elements from popular ballads (as for instance in Luigi Pulci's *Morgante*, 1482). In this form the *matière de Bretagne*, the legendary material of the courtly romances, combined with the popularized *gestes* (the *Reali di Francia*), survived and was able to produce significant works in the epics of Boiardo and Ariosto. However, because of their similarity to fairy tales, their irony, and their orientation toward an Italian Renaissance audience with their emphasis on love and exotic adventures, these epics were as little suited for use as propaganda literature as the modern courtly-knightly romances of the *Amadís* type.

Nonetheless, authors had to work with this material at first, especially since the necessary internal contradictions of the time of transition to the absolute monarchy might well have blinded the contemporaries to certain "impossibilities." Du Bellay's suggestions were therefore by no means as deviant as they appear to his later critics. Still, could figures like Tristan or Lancelot, the perfect ideal types of the individualist courtly knight of *aventure*, be protagonists of the heroic poem yet to be created, embodiments of the absolute monarch and hence also of the absolute monarchy, which was diametrically opposed to knightly autonomy and thus to individual *aventüre* or which had subsumed individual *aventüre* in negating it? Du Bellay must have had a few misgivings himself; he saw, after all, what had become of the *matière de Bretagne* in modern adaptation in the *Amadís* family of novels. At least with respect to these works he had to draw limits, although they did not and could not eliminate the fundamental contradiction, for the protagonists of these very modern adaptations of the *matière de Bretagne* were to be the protagonists of the absolutist epic as well. He writes:

> I want to make a remark by the way about those who occupy themselves with decorating and expanding our novels and who make books out of them that are, to be sure, written in beautiful, fluent language but that are actually much more suited to entertaining maidens than to teaching correct writing. I would like to advise them to use their great writing talent to collect the fragments from old French chronicles, as Titus Livius did with his *Annals*, or from other old Roman chronicles, in order to glean from them the whole material for a beautiful story.[22]

Du Bellay's friend Pierre de Ronsard (1525?-85) pursued this suggestion: in 1572 his epic *La Franciade* was published, dedicated to Charles IX (1560-74). As the title expresses, this work was to serve the glorification of the French monarchy: "I had an immense desire to honor the French royal house," Ronsard explains to his readers, "especially King Charles IX, my prince."[23] But the difficulties set in early: how can the poet glorify his king without offending the king with the glorification? For if the poet orients himself toward historical reality, he must necessarily injure the interests of parties or of persons whom the king defeated or whom he will still perhaps have to defeat. But it was by no means certain that the king had not already made allies of the defeated parties or persons, sometimes immediately after the confrontation with them, in the interest of a *realpolitik* compromise or for reasons of power politics. One can even say that this was the rule, which was expressly confirmed in 1572. After the Edict of Saint-Germain-en-Laye, which granted the Huguenots religious freedom with some restrictions, Charles IX allied himself first with the Huguenot leader, Admiral Gaspard de Coligny, and then the urging of his mother, Catherine de Medicis, had him killed during the infamous St. Bartholomew's night in 1572. The use of contemporary materials to prepare an epic poem glorifying the absolute monarchy was in fact a political impossibility.

Writings on literary theory also prohibited the use of contemporary materials; that prohibition might well derive from the historical form of that impossibility (of course we must also take into consideration the increasing autonomy of aesthetic norms, especially in later times). But if the poet withdraws into the past, if he for instance takes the story of some king of earlier times and makes a poetic example of it to glorify the absolute monarchy, historiography intervenes and relegates any fiction that deviates from historical truth to the realm of stupidity (without even having to call on Plato's view that poetry in general is a lie). Ronsard therefore dares to claim, he says, "that the poet who tells things as they are has less merit than the one who makes them up, but not for the purpose of creating a fantastic work like that of Ariosto, whose individual parts are anything but beautiful."[24] This is first of all a denial of De Bellay's assertion that the French heroic epic could continue the romantic-ironic poetry of Ariosto.

What remains is to reach back to the models of antiquity. But there are difficulties in this connection too, which result from the political task of neo-Aristotelian, absolutist poetics. Homer and Virgil had taken their material from mythology and legend, and their protagonists were gods, demigods, and archaic warriors. But the new epic poem has a historical task to perform, the glorification of the political idea of the absolute monarchy and of the figure of the absolute monarch. The poet's hands are tied in this attempt, however, because of the historical nature of his material and the political orientation that determines his selection. As Ronsard says, he bears "the burden of sixty-three kings" of French history "in his arms," and even the selection of one of these kings, who would have to represent his latest successor or the idea of the absolute monarchy, which he never embodied in actual history, will necessarily bring complications. Ronsard capitulates in the face of this task and excuses the choice of his hero—who finally turns out to be fictional—by alleging that King Charles IX did not want to see any of "his ancestors" receive favored treatment. For that reason he has oriented his epic toward the *naïve facilité*, the "naïve, carefree quality," of Homer instead of toward the *curieuse diligence* of Virgil, his "exactitude born of a desire to know" (a point scored against the neo-Aristotelian dogmaticists).

Du Bellay had still advised looking for the one great epic hero among the Lancelots or Tristans or changing a courtly knight into a representative of absolutism. Ronsard, aware that it was impossible either to follow this path or to choose a historical figure or an archaic hero from the world of Greek legend, tried a compromise. He chose a mythological hero, Francus, supposedly the son of Hector, whom he made courtly to resemble the knight of *aventüre* and integrated into French prehistory by naming him the ancestor of the French royal house, "because," as Ronsard boldly states, "the French people take it as an established fact" that this Francus traveled as far as Hungary after the fall of Troy:

> I had him come to Franconia, to which he gave his name, then to Gaul, in order to found Paris.... For it is probable [that is, in neo-Aristotelian logic, which Ronsard is here following: it is not improbable, the public can consider it possible—M. N.], that Francus made such a journey, the more so because he could have made it, and on this basis of verisimilitude I gave his name to my Franciade.[25]

Years later Ronsard returned once more to this problem and again excused his choice of hero with the statement that even Homer and Virgil took their epics "from old stories, just as we [create] stories of Lancelot, of Gawain, and of Arthur:"

> In emulating the two stars of poetry, I wrote my Franciade based on old sources, without worrying about whether they are true or not, whether our kings are Trojans or Germans, Scythians or Arabs, whether Francus reached France. For he could have come here, and so I used the possibility and not the [historical—M. N.] truth.[26]

Concentration at the Court

Ronsard's sentences reflect contemporary criticism of what he was defending, because a public that was not unfamiliar with the rational justification of the absolute monarchy by Bodin, for instance, that had to observe and suffer through the prosaic power struggles of its time, power struggles that were actually only conducted to see who would carry this absolute monarchy, and not in order to question the institution— such a public cannot have been pleased at Ronsard's painstakingly constructed apologies for the absolute monarchy that was uncontested and fundamentally accepted. In any case, giving up Lancelot in favor of a fictional, mythic-courtly epic hero did not solve the problem; in the last analysis it was insoluble. Ronsard's withdrawal into the fictional past, into ancient mythology in courtly guise, merely revealed that the glorification of the absolute monarch (or of the absolute monarchy) in the epic was accompanied by such great difficulties that it even had to disappear from the epic, as in the case of the *Franciade*.

The objective reasons for this, apart from those already mentioned, lie in the increasing factual de-heroization of the real individual king. In 1559 Henri II, son of François I, was so badly wounded in a tournament that he died. A year later, tournaments were prohibited. "With them," as Voltaire writes in the *Essai sur les moeurs et l'esprit des nations* (1756-69), "the old spirit of knighthood died; it scarcely appeared again, except in the romances."[27] By 1560 at the latest, and despite the later civil wars, a decisive change took place in the essence of the monarchy: the king lost his last active knightly link to the Middle Ages. After a short time of transition, in which he still took part in battles as a general (like Henri IV and even the young Louis XIV), he took up his fixed position at court as the center of the national government and—perhaps still more crucial—as representative of the absolute monarchy and hence at the same time of himself; in this function he was immobile.

> Francis I was still a knightly king, *le roi chevalier*. He was fond of tournaments and hunting; war for him was a splendid knightly game in which he put his life at stake.... The case was still similar with Henry IV who, when a Huguenot leader and a great vassal of the

kings of France, on receiving the news that their opponents were preparing for war, offered to settle the matter by personal combat with the enemy leader, the Duc de Guise.... After attaining power he embodied the transition between the late-chivalrous type of king and the court-aristocratic type that was to find its first perfect representative in Louis XIV, who no longer, like Henry IV, rode into battle at the head of his nobles. He had his wars fought more and more by generals with paid troops.[28]

This system seems to come out of joint again during the parliamentary and feudal-princely *Fronde* movement (1648-52), but in truth even this movement did not question the principle of the absolute monarchy. The absolute monarchy was able to structure itself internally and externally. This was factually expressed in the king's decision in 1661 to control state business himself, instead of leaving it as before to a prime minister like Richelieu or Mazarin; it was symbolically expressed in the centralization of the government apparatus at the huge court of Versailles, which was introduced in 1661 and realized in 1677. The personal participation of the young monarch in the campaigns against the Netherlands, for instance, had a rather representative character,[29] but was obviously already so obsolete for the function of an absolute monarch that Boileau was able to dedicate to him the letter "Contre les conquêts" (Against Wars of Conquest). This work expresses the (certainly not unjustified) view that there are a series of domestic political problems (especially of an economic sort) that must be solved before wars of conquest should be undertaken. In connection with this, it also celebrates a new type of hero or suggests to Louis XIV the *nonmartial hero* (the immobile absolute monarch) as an ideal, in hopes that he might end the costly martial ventures:

> Ce n'est pas que mon coeur du travail ennemi,
> Approuve un Faineant sur le thrône endormi.
> Mais quelques vains lauriers que promette la guerre,
> On peut estre Heros sans ravager la terre,
> Il es plus d'une gloire. Envain aux Conquerans
> L'erreur parmi les Rois donne les premiers rangs.
> Entre les grands Heros ce sont les plus vulgairs.
> . . . .
> un Roi vraiment Roi, qui sage en ses projets,
> Sçache en un calme heureux maintenir ses Sujets,
> Qui du bonheur public ayt cimenté sa gloire,
> Il faut, pour le trouver, courir toute l'histoire.
> La Terre conte peu de ces Rois bien-faisans.
> Le Ciel à les former se prépare long-temps.[30]

It is not that my heart hates work and wishes to see a slothful idler on the throne. But whatever vain laurels war might promise, one can be a hero without ravaging the earth. There is more than one glory. It is an error that one so often ascribes the first rank to the conquerors among the kings. These are among the least of the great heroes...a king who is truly king and who (moderate in his undertakings) knows how to preserve his subjects in a happy peace, who builds his glory on the public happiness—to find such a king, one must search through all of history. The earth knows very few of these beneficent kings, and heaven takes a long time to shape them.

To be sure, Boileau's warning hardly moved Louis XIV to change his aggressive foreign policy, but the king became more and more the center of an apparatus for pomp and administration that from the outside appeared almost immobile. One must, of course, be careful not to rush to conclusions about the dynamism or sclerosis of this organization: the impulses for a lively domestic and foreign policy were still emanating from this court, even if the king himself was leading a life that had nothing more in common with the knightly-kingly existence of a François I, and the former knightly campaigns had become national wars of conquest carried out by specialists in warfare. With this reservation one can agree with Norbert Elias that "in this way, therefore, the court mechanism revolved in perpetual motion, fed by the need for prestige and the tensions which, once they were there, it endlessly renewed by its competitive process."[31] This "perpetual motion," however, was both the luxurious apparatus of king and court with the potentate at the center and the motor of large-scale, absolutist power politics, including the wars that the potentate had others conduct without himself leaving the court.

In 1675, Bernhard le Bovier de Fontenelle (1657-1757), in his poem "La gloire des armes et des belles lettres sous Louis XIV," captured in verse this perpetual motion. He writes about the military successes of the young king in the campaigns against the Netherlands, then describes his building activity in Paris and Versailles, reports how Louis XIV put the feudal nobles in chains with his measures, and tries with startling clairvoyance to express the dialectics of rest and movement in rest. In so doing he emphasizes the novelty of the type of hero represented by Louis XIV, the absolute monarch, as opposed to the mobile feudal ruler of past times:

> Illustres conquérans, dont le dieu des combats
> De triomphe en triomphe accompagnait les pas:
> Et vous, qui par les soins qu'un doux loisir inspire,
> Eleviez avec vous les Muses à l'empire;
> Rois, qui fûtes toujours, par vos faits inouis,
> Le modèle des rois jusqu'au temps de LOUIS;

Si jadis entre vous l'ordre des destinées
Partagea les vertus des têtes couronnées,
Voyez et la nature et le ciel aujourd'hui,
Prodigues pour LOUIS, les réunir en lui.
Il en est parmi vous, dont les seules victoires
En faveur de leurs noms parlent dans les histoires.
Il en est qui, contens d'un august repos,
Ont trouvé dans la paix l'art de vivre en héros.
Mais que sans se fixer dans ces diverses routes,
Pour courir à la gloire, un roi des prenne toutes,
Qu'il aspire à la fois à ce double laurier,
De héros pacifique et de héros guerrier,
Qu'il accorde en lui seul des titres si contraires,
C'est ce que n'ont point vu les siècles de nos pères;
C'est de quoi nos destins, plus heureux et plus doux;
Ne donneront jamais le spectacle qu'à nous.[32]

Illustrious conquerors, whose steps the God of War has followed from triumph to triumph, and you who with the art that a sweet leisure inspires have helped the muses to dominance, kings, you who because of your amazing deeds have been the model of all kings up to the time of Louis: if in the past the will of fate has distributed the virtues among crowned heads, so you see today nature and heaven lavishly uniting these virtues in Louis. Among you there are some whose victories alone already speak in their favor in history. There are others who, content with august repose, have found in peacetime the art of living like heroes. But that one king should follow all these paths to gain fame without fixing on any one, that he should reach at the same time for the double laurel of the peaceful and the martial hero, that he unites in himself alone such contradictory titles—that is what the age of our fathers did not see, that is a spectacle our fate, happier and more temperate, has granted us alone.

Epic without *Aventure*

The wish for increasing centralization of function and representation in *one* place, the court at Versailles—which in fact already heralds the later development toward sclerotic immobility, the increasing (physical) immobility of the absolute monarch—is expressed in the ideas that Boileau developed about epic poetry in his *Art poétique*, published in 1674. Boileau saw perfectly well that the traditional neo-Aristotelian doctrine of the epic poem did not suffice for the production of authentically great modern epic poetry, and he was unhappy about neither this nor that contemporary epic poetry was as bad as he stated it was.

The agreement that theorists assumed or intended between the hierarchy of genres and the articulation of society in feudal castes necessarily had fatal consequences for the epic composed in accordance with neo-Aristotelian rules: the more exactly an epic followed the rules in its composition, the less useful and more irrelevant it must turn out to be. According to doctrine, the epic was to show a heroic undertaking, a military campaign (if possible, one ending in the establishment of a nation). Its ending, for reasons of propaganda, had to be happy. The protagonist had to be the aristocratic hero (the king) with his equally aristocratic retinue. Its element was the passage of arms, the battle. Non-nobles, burghers, the people in general were rigorously excluded as subjects sustaining the action and making history.

But that means logically that the more this theoretical concept was adhered to in writing an epic poem, the further the epic was removed from reality. The real world, the classes that moved and changed this world, were barred from the epic. If the ideal of the knight of *aventure* still expressed the aspirations of a class in its rise and decline, the epic hero of the neo-Aristotelian, absolutist epic, the absolutist hero, could express only himself: the ideal of the absolute monarch, abstracted from all actual involvement in the real world of class confrontations, the idea of the absolute monarchy. But the epic poem thus lost both its connection with social reality and its epic substance because just as the absolute monarch became physically immobile in his function as administrator and representative, the process of barring real history rendered obsolete, useless, and irrelevant the essential element of the Homeric and Virgilian type of epic poetry, the essential element of the epic in general: the warriorlike movement of the human being through time and space, and hence any form of *aventure*.

The standstill of warriorlike movement appealed to Boileau, and in his *Art poétique* he reinforced this tendency under the mask of faith in the neo-Aristotelian theory, putting the stress on the use of mythological *machina*, banning the idea of Christian poetry (to transform the revealed Christian truth into fiction would be heresy, he says):

> D'un air plus grand encor la Poësie Epique,
> Dans le vaste récit d'une longue action,
> Se soûtient par la Fable et vit de fiction.
> Là pour nous enchanter tout est mis en usage.
> Tout prend un corps, une ame, un esprit, un visage.
> Chaque Vertu devient une Divinité.
> Minerve est la Prudence, et Vénus la Beauté.
> Ce n'est plus la vapeur qui produit le tonnerre;
> C'est Jupiter armé pour effrayer la Terre;
> ....

> Ainsi dans cet amas de nobles fictions,
> Le Poëte s'égaye en mille inventions.
> Orne, éleve, embellit, agrandit toutes choses,
> Et trouve sous sa main des Fleurs toûjours écloses.
> Qu'Enée et ses vaisseaux par le vent écartez
> Soient aux bords Africains d'un orage emportez;
> Ce n'est qu'une *aventure* ordinaire et commune,
> Qu'une coup peu surprenant des traits de la Fortune.
> Mais que Junon constante en son aversion.
> Poursuive sur les flots les restes d'Ilion:
> . . . .
> Que Neptune en courroux s'élevant sur la mer,
> D'un mot calme les flots, mette la paix dans l'air,
> Délivre les vaisseaux, des Syrtes les arrache;
> C'est-là qui surprend, frappe, saisit, attache.[33]

Epic poetry, still more elevated, draws from the stuff of old myths and lives from free invention in the broad recitation of an extended action. To enchant us, every possibility is called into play. Everything takes on a body, a soul, a spirit, a face. Each virtue becomes a divinity: Minerva is prudence, and Venus is beauty. It is no longer the air that brings forth thunder; it is Jupiter, armed to affright the earth. . . . Thus in this mass of noble fictions, the poet diverts himself with a thousand inventions; he ornaments, elevates, embellishes, enlarges all things, and finds under his hand flowers perpetually in bloom. That Aeneas and his ships were driven by the wind and blown by a storm onto the coast of Africa is merely an ordinary, common *adventure*, a hardly surprising blow of the shafts of fortune. But when Juno, unswerving in her hatred, pursues the remainder of the noble Trojans on the sea, . . . when Neptune in wrath rises up out of the sea and calms the waves with a single word, stills the winds, saves the ships, snatches them from the Syrtis, that is surprising, striking, grabs and holds the attention.

The fictional immobilization of the king in the mythological apparatus corresponds perfectly to Jean-Baptiste Colbert's (1619-83) attempt at transforming Versailles into a huge mythological perpetual motion machine, into a decorative play whose rules are no longer determined by knightly ethics and warrior impulses but by ballets, operas, card playing, and so on. Because what Colbert (and the active bourgeoisie) needed was peace. Evidently this ran counter to the interests of the reactionary feudal aristocracy and that part of the absolutist nobility that espoused aggressive military politics (represented by Colbert's antagonist, minister of war Michel Le Tellier, Marquis de Louvois). Their most fanatic literary propagandist was Jean Desmarest de Saint-Sorlin, author of (bad) Christian epic poetry glorifying war. He attacks Boileau's ideas on epic poetry expressed in the *Art poétique* that Desmarest had read in manuscript form four years prior to its publication (*Comparaison de la langue et de la poésie françoise, avec la greque et la latine, et des poètes grecs, latins, et françois*, 1670 [Comparison of the French, Greek, and Latin Languages, Poetry, and Poets]). Desmarest understands perfectly well Boileau's intentions and denounces them unambiguously: Boileau's alleged respect for the Christian religion is hypocritical, he says. What Boileau intends, Desmarest states, is the destruction of the warrior epic, and he accuses him of—high treason.[34]

Desmarest de Saint-Sorlin died some few years after, and Boileau was promoted to the position of official royal historiographer and was, to some extent, neutralized by this promotion. In the *Querelle des Anciens et des Modernes* (Quarrel of the Ancients and Moderns), which "officially" began in 1687 with Charles Perrault's reading of and lecture about his poem "Le siècle de Louis le Grand," the discussion about the political function of epic poetry does not seem to have a primary importance. But this political function reveals its lasting importance in Fénelon's *Les aventures de Télémaque*, written as a prince's mirror for the son of the ruler. To be sure, there are travel adventures and martial events in the story of the protagonist Télémaque, son of Odysseus; but they are displaced into a mythological unreality and serve as a glorification of adventurous mobility, whether knightly or bourgeois in orientation. Praise of the absolute monarchy is beyond question, even if the monarchy described by Fénelon contradicts that of his king in many respects: display and luxury are damned as criminal (apart from other allusions to events at the court of Versailles).[35] It is no coincidence that this epic was written not in heroic verse but in prose.[36] When it appeared in 1699, against the will of its author, it earned him the disfavor of the king, who could no more overlook the numerous complaints about his practice of ruling than could other contemporaries. But such complaints run completely counter to the political task of the "long poëme Françoys" as Du Bellay imagined it and as neo-Aristotelian literary theory understood and required it.[37]

The *Chevalier* in the Salon

The development of the epic (from theory to failure) reflects fundamental problems of social development in the age of the absolute monarchy. We have considered only the problem of presenting the absolute monarch in the neo-Aristotelian epic and have seen that it contributed significantly to destroying the knightly ideal of adventure. No impulse for the development of a modern ideology of adventure could emanate from the transposition of this ideal into epic poetry, originally attempted by Du Bellay for the purpose of glorifying the absolute monarch. On the contrary, every sort of ideology of adventure had to be eliminated from the ideal of the absolute monarchy. De Bellay merely led the courtly-knightly ideology of adventure toward its exit. The knightly adventurer no longer had any important state function, due to the essence of the absolute monarchy.

That does not mean that the knightly adventurer no longer played a role in the epoch we are treating. Apart from the fact that elements of the knightly ideology of adventure furnish the first beginnings of a military glorification of the soldier's life (as in the *Bible du soldat* by Blaise de Monluc) during the time of transition to the absolute monarchy, the knightly ideology of adventure had an important political function (even on the side of the monarchy) as long as the confrontation between the monarch and the oppositional feudal nobility was not finally decided—that is, until the defeat of the *Fronde* in 1652. The translations of *Amadís* and the romances based on the *matière de Bretagne* were the most popular reading matter in the time from Henri II to Henri IV; the story was even spread that Henri IV himself was a great fan of the knightly romances: *Amadís*, it was claimed, was "the Bible of kings."[38]

Nonetheless it is evident that the advocates of the absolute monarchy could favor the glorification of the knight and hence of the feudal splintering of earlier times only to the extent that elements of the knightly ideology of adventure could be integrated and "refunctioned" to become elements of the glorification of the absolute monarch, a process that was dependent on the power relations of the classes and strata and that presented difficult problems for ideologues and artists, as Du Bellay illustrated. It is, for instance, obvious that the treatise *Le Prince* by Jean Louis Guez de Balzac (1597-1654), in which the ideal of a *roi chevalier* is presented, had to be rejected by the representatives of absolutism (in concrete terms, Richelieu) because when it was published (1631), the strategy of simple, explicit assimilation of the knightly ideal into that of the absolute monarch was already superfluous for the monarch and had become harmful. In his confrontations with the feudal nobility, the king was forced again and again to make political, economic, and ideological concessions, just as he was forced at the same time by the class-antagonistic alliance of parts of the bourgeoisie with the throne to distance himself ideologically from his ally the bourgeoisie.

This is the terrain on which—as a sort of ideological-artistic compromise—"heroic preciosity"[39] arose. The king tolerated it on the one hand, even used it himself (especially—although with less impact— during the time of increasing division between bourgeoisie and absolutist nobility after 1670); on the other hand it opened up a social-ideological field of activity for the oppositional feudal nobility. The most important sources for this "heroic preciosity" were doubtless the old and new knightly romances, the Italian and Spanish pastoral romances (especially Iacopo Sannazzaro's *Arcadia* of 1502 and Jorge de Montemayor's *Diana* of 1559), Tasso's epics, and Plato, mediated by the Italians. In fact, for both the absolutist nobles assembled at court and the feudal aristocracy conspiring in the salons (like that of Madame de Rambouillet) and their retinues, the knight (of romance literature), educated according to the laws of the *Cortegiano* and similar treatises[40] and purified by the (novelistic) pastoral spirit, is still the ideal of humanity at the beginning of the seventeenth century, an ideal memorialized by Honoré d'Urfé in the many volumes of his *Astrée* (1607-27).[41] *Astrée* influenced the production of novels throughout the seventeenth century and of other literary genres as well (and not just those with a feudal, reactionary orientation, as Norbert Elias believes).[42]

To be sure, "heroic preciosity" reached its first high point in the circle of the feudal-noble *Frondeurs*, especially at Condé's court, in the work of Gautier de Costes, Sieur de La Calprenède (1610-53), among whose writings are the massive heroic-historical novels *Cassandre* (10 volumes, 1642) and *Cléopâtre* (12 volumes, 1647). In these works historical events, knightly *aventüres* (often of a very anachronistic sort),[43] and descriptions of battles, duels, and love stories are blended into a pasty, often indigestible mix. Inspired by these novels, Georges de Scudéry (1601-67) and his sister Madeleine (1607-1701), who in 1641 had already published the novel *Ibrahim ou l'illustre Bassa*, began to produce their heroic-galant novels, *Grand Cyrus* (1649) and *Clélie* (1654), which contains the famous Carte de Tendre, the psychological-allegorical presentation and classification of love. In fact, Madeleine de Scudéry's interest shifted increasingly from narration, the report of adventures, to psychological analysis and the art of portraiture, to which we owe the minute, often long-winded, character presentations of current "société galante."[44] After the defeat of the *Fronde* in 1652, Madeleine de Scudéry's works helped lead "heroic preciosity" to inwardness, thus creating a new, politically explosive quality in the metamorphosis of the knightly ideology of adventure, a quality that became effective especially in the time after the dissolution of the alliance between the absolutist monarchy and the bourgeoisie.

Aventure and the Rules of Tragedy

The determined advocates of the progressive aspects of the alliance between absolutist monarchy and active bourgeoisie found the nostalgic glorification of knightly adventure in the guise of "heroic preciosity" highly retrograde (and dangerous). Molière's *Précieuses ridicules* of 1659 and especially Boileau's pitiless satiric dialogue "Les Héros de roman" of 1664-65 both bear witness to this. Their engagement can be explained only if we bear in mind the politically explosive nature of the *précieux* ideology. Paul Bénichou has correctly pointed out that the novels of knightly adventure and precious literature in general had a retardant effect on the developing absolutist ideology and the corresponding literature in the second half of the century. Bénichou discusses this especially with respect to Pierre Corneille (1605-84):

> The stern Corneille . . . seems far removed from the Carte du Tendre and the romantic artificialities with which one identifies precious literature today. But despite their artificialities, precious novels are full of heroic and generous emotions and actions, and Corneille's greatness of spirit is always linked with feelings of love, as corresponds to the tradition of knightly literature.[45]

Bénichou cites many authors who valued the knightly romances or Corneille (in connection with these knightly romances) or who condemned them (like Voltaire), but we will not pursue his argument further, since he does not raise the important question of the social and political motivation of the various recipients. But one detail will serve to show how Corneille's adherence to the knightly ideology, correctly identified by Bénichou, created very serious problems for Corneille: what becomes of *aventure*, the essential element of knightly romance in drama, in the tragedy of absolutist society? Corneille's extensive and subtle reflections on the rules of neo-Aristotelian poetics for tragedy must be considered from the point of view of this central question as well because that point of view reveals the political significance of the seemingly pedantic discussion about the "three unities" in tragedy. According to the rules, the unities of time, place, and action must be strictly observed, and the discussion about the length of time (twelve or twenty-four hours) and the size of the place (a room, a square, a city) often seemed to be in the foreground.[46] The context of the argument was always determined by the principle of neo-Aristotelian verisimilitude. Is it probable for the viewer that what is being played on stage takes place in a time of, say, several years, although the viewer watches for only a few hours, or in different cities or countries, although the actors do not leave the space of the stage? The answer was categorically negative: the action must be so designed that it can take place in a single place in a probable, short time.

One can imagine what that meant for the knight of *aventure*; he was banned from tragedy on principle. More precisely, the mobility of the petty nobles, knights, and feudal princes—the medieval aristocracy—could no longer express itself in tragedy, as opposed to the knightly romance. Instead, tragedy made clear that the power struggle between feudal princes and the absolute monarchy had been decided in favor of the latter: "The limitation of tragedy compared to the novel is the touchstone on which to test the relation of necessary and probable [stage] actions," as Corneille writes in 1660.

> We in the theater are hindered by the place, the time, the [technical— M. N.] difficulties of the presentation, which for example keep us from showing many persons at once, for it must always be feared that

one of them is not carrying out any action or is in the way of the others. The novel knows none of these constraints . . . it places the characters it has speaking, acting, or dreaming, in a room, in a wood, in a public square, whatever their special action demands. To do this, [the novel—M. N.] makes use of a palace, a whole city, a whole kingdom, the whole world.[47]

In other words, the protagonists of knightly romances, to the extent that they were still regarded at all and not given up along with the knightly romances themselves (which Corneille in fact did not do—think of *Clitandre*, 1632, or the *Cid*, 1636), were forced from the unlimited breadth of the world into the narrow limits of tragedy. Corneille tried to transpose the qualities correctly diagnosed by Bénichou, the heroic virtues of the knight of *aventure*, into qualities of the new tragic hero, but precisely the quality of *aventure* falls victim to the political rules of verisimilitude: the breadth of the world is blocked off; even the size of a kingdom is taboo. But where can action still take place, action that is adequate to the greatness of the tragic hero as he must be conceived in absolutism? What place can seem probable as the scene of such action for a public in absolutist society? Corneille mourns that not even the "public square," where all the ancient authors had their kings speak, can now be used because the absolute monarch no longer speaks there:

> We no longer even take the liberty of bringing the kings and princes from their chambers, and because the differences and the opposition of interests of those who live in one and the same palace prevent them from speaking openly and revealing their secrets in the same room, we must find a different [dramaturgical—M. N.] way to establish the unity of place if we want to keep it in our writings.[48]

The reflection of the change in political power and place in the formation of the absolute monarchy cannot be overlooked in Corneille's musings on the unity of time, place, and action. In the world of knightly adventure, movement into a distance that was theoretically unlimited was a characteristic of existence in the knightly romance, of the existence of the knight of *aventure* and of the noble in general, in the ceaselessly changing medieval feudal state. This movement is no longer possible, as Jean Racine also learned. In 1660 he wrote an "Epître au Roi" (Letter to the King), which precedes his *Alexandre le Grand*, first produced in 1665 by Molière. In this letter Racine describes the new quality of the absolute monarch Louis XIV, whom he compares at first with Alexander. To be sure, he writes, Louis XIV also has Alexander's warrior qualities, but, he continues, "Your Majesty took a newer and more difficult way to the peak of fame than Alexander." There have been many young conquerers, but "no one has yet seen a king who at Alexander's age already had the leadership qualities of an

Augustus, whose fame reached to the end of the world without his traveling far from the center of his kingdom."[49] In the tragedy *Alexandre le Grand*, Racine tried to subsume these contradictions between (absolutist) administrator-king and (knightly) warrior-king in a dramatic dialectics. He failed, and the laws of the neo-Aristotelian genre of tragedy played a decisive role in his failure; it is basically impossible to treat an absolute monarch as a tragic figure. For reasons of literary politics, he must be shown to conquer more or less unchallenged and this in near immobility, like the Alexander of the play. The movement of the absolutist hero in tragedy must be shifted to other dimensions, must take place in other dimensions: the movement shifts close to the hero and, in the last analysis, is portrayed as a mental conflict in the hero, a conclusion Racine drew but before which Corneille recoiled. Even in tragedy the movement of *aventure* was at an end, even if Corneille—struggling with himself, with the critics, and with his public—pleaded for one last compromise: let the place of action be—the city![50]

The *Honnête Homme*;
or, The Formation of Bourgeois-Aristocratic Opposition to Adventure

When Corneille talks of the city, in the seventeenth century he can only mean the unity of the court and the urban-courtly, bourgeois-aristocratic sphere of influence: *la cour et la ville*, "court and city," is an established concept.[51] As early as 1565, Ronsard writes:

> Because our France obeys only one single king, today we are compelled to speak his courtly language if we want to achieve any kind of honor. If this is not the case, then our work, however learned it may be, will be disparaged or (perhaps) treated with complete contempt. And because the advantages and evidences of favor come from such a place, we must often bow to the judgment of a noblewoman or a young courtier, even when they know very little about good and true poetry because they practice the craft of arms or other worthy professions.[52]

The place of which Ronsard speaks is the king's court, and the judgment on literary production has been shifted from the competence of the specialists to that of the courtly public, to which belong, besides the nobility of the sword, members of other "worthy professions," as corresponds to the formation of the alliance between monarchy and bourgeoisie. For if the inclusion of the bourgeois avant-garde in the nobility (of magistrates) takes on qualities of upholding the state, then this too must affect the general development of a worldview.

If we take as a point of departure the situation of the class struggle we have analyzed, we can state: first, the bourgeoisie sees its highest social goal in the rise into the nobility; second, the bourgeoisie tries to imitate the nobility in its way of living and thinking; third, the way of living and thinking is determined by the form of living and earning a living toward which the bourgeoisie is striving or which it has achieved, that is, living as a rentier or from real property; fourth, since despite the rise, a social difference remains between bourgeoisie and feudal nobility of blood (a difference that the feudal nobility uses against the *noblesse de robe*), the *noblesse de robe* introduces bourgeois ideas into its way of thinking, and those ideas tend particularly in the direction of an aristocratic-egalitarian valuation of the human being in general. Overall it is a question of shaping a worldview and a common language that is sustained by the affirmation of the court, of the absolute monarchy, by respect for the bourgeoisie or for the human being in general (as the neutral vanishing point of common interests), and by the efforts for equality with the nobility. For even though both nobles and members of the bourgeoisie are involved in shaping this worldview, which is centered around the concept of *honnêteté* (honesty, probity, integrity) and the *honnête homme* (the bearer of this ideal), still it is a development driven primarily by bourgeoisie ideologues, as Maurice Magendie has convincingly shown;[53] after the defeat of the *Fronde* this changes radically.

One of the poles of this new worldview (or, better, attitude toward the world) is formed by Castiglione's *Cortegiano* along with its (Spanish and) French successors; and the other pole, mainly by Michel de Montaigne (1533-92), whose *Essais* became a true catechism of the art of living and the attitude toward the world. Montaigne is the actual creator of the ideal of the *honnête homme*—the definition, instructions for education, and perfection of whom were propagated by dozens of handbooks in the seventeenth century. The most famous of these was doubtless Nicolas Faret's *L'honnête homme ou l'art de plaire à la cour* (1630).[54]

To schematize, we can state that the *honnête homme* is a detached, wise person who hates all excess and all impropriety, who prefers the philosophical golden mean (not to be confused with mediocrity), who is educated without becoming a pedantic specialist, who is courtly, who knows how to behave in society, especially in the society of ladies, who does not talk about certain things (for instance, personal troubles, money), and so on. As Auerbach writes, "Integrity [Honnêteté—M. N.] is not a class ideal ... for it is not in principle linked to birth or to the life style of a certain caste."[55]

That is correct, to be sure; but on the other hand we can say that without the specific form of the alliance between monarchy and bourgeoisie in France, the ideal of *honnêteté* could not have arisen: in its most essential substance it is the ideal of the feudal noble or magistrate living on the income from his land or on a royal pension—or of the bourgeois (poet, scientist) who frequents the court or its circle. In itself this ideal is not very significant, but as a norm for the daily praxis of living at the court and in its sphere of influence (*la cour et la ville*), it is extremely important at this time, "when national credit began to develop with income values bearing a set interest and the type of the rentier emerging for the first time."[56] The oppositional feudal nobility (especially theorists like Méré) contributed or propagandized a variant of this type, which made useful activity, earning money, a taboo and which elevated *oisiveté*, "worldly indolence," to the true content of life; this variant became a great obstacle for further social development in France. As an ideal for the noble, the *noblesse de robe*, or the bourgeois individual living at court and in its sphere of influence, it represents the logical complement to the apparent immobility of the absolute monarch.

Chapter 11
The Foundations of Modern Ideology of Adventure in France

La cour, la ville, et le monde infini

The massive rise of the bourgeoisie into the *noblesse de robe* lost its progressive function at the moment when the absolute monarchy was established and the monarch no longer needed the magistrates as a means to push through its goals. On the contrary, from that moment on the rise of the active bourgeois to tendentious stagnation in the *noblesse de robe* or to feudal landownership, along with the consequences those positions entailed for one's worldview, became an economic impediment, a political danger for the existence of the absolute monarchy. As paradoxical as that at first seems, in the last analysis even the total centralization of state power at the court ran counter to the real needs of the absolute monarchy. To be sure, centralization helped to force the refractory feudal nobles into subordination, but from economic, political, and ideological points of view its disadvantages are evident (from the orientation of the bourgeoisie toward a state pension and ground rent to the withdrawal of the feudal landowner to the court):

1.1 Under the absolute monarchy, there are no longer any economically independent regions. Larger resources are necessary to provide for and govern the land. The constantly growing army also demands larger expenses.

1.2 The bourgeoisie is buying aristocratic titles; no one wants to take over government posts in the provinces (especially not the nobles); the small feudal farmers who leave their land do not have enough money to buy military commissions, which are purchasable at this time.

2.1 The absolute monarchy has created the opportunity to build an efficient domestic market, which it desperately needs in order to exist: it needs commercial and manufacturing activity.
2.2 The bourgeoisie is buying property; the nobles are becoming courtisans in office.
3.1 The absolute monarchy needs overseas trade to become independent of the importation of raw materials via third countries or to be able to compete with these countries.
3.2 The bourgeoisie is crowding to the court or to the sphere of influence of *la cour et la ville*.
4.1 The absolute monarchy needs explorers and travelers in order to expand; it needs scientists, engineers, and builders in order to develop production technology in such things as manufacturing, shipbuilding, road construction, and canal building.
4.2 Bourgeois intellectuals are receiving offices at court; their work is subject to ideological censorship;[1] the *honnête homme* is the educated antiscientist par excellence (to say nothing of the *courtisan*).

After the absolute monarchy had prevailed, at the moment when it would have been necessary to mobilize all forces to fill the operative fields that had been created, to develop trade and manufacturing, all those forces were assembled at court, and the dominant ideal was the ideal of a person of private means. In this historical situation, with France's greatest national rivals conducting global politics, the ideologues of *honnêteté* were propagating the principle of *oisiveté*, "idleness," and were making the taboo on the idea of earning a living the highest value of their ethical system. At this moment when, thanks to Kepler, Copernicus, and Galileo, the vista on infinity had been opened, the French *honnête homme* was looking at his mirror image at court, or if he wasn't quite up to that, in a salon. At this moment, when Bacon was discovering the precondition for overcoming our lack of knowledge, for the natural sciences, in the practical alteration of the world, Descartes was decreeing the primacy of a priori dogmatism and the secondary importance of experiment. Descartes, who not only revolutionized the methodology of the natural sciences but also played a crucial role in shaping the ideal of *honnêteté*, is a perfect example of the fundamental contradiction in this social structure: while he was theoretically dealing with the infinite, *le monde infini*,[2] he writes in *Regulae ad directionem ingenii (Rules for the Direction of the Mind*, 1629): "If in the matters to be examined we come to a step in the series of which our understanding is not sufficiently well able to have an intuitive cognition, we must stop short there. We must make no attempt to examine what follows; thus we shall spare ourselves superfluous labour."[3]

The Unstoppable Movement

The contradiction, the tensions in this system can be overlooked as little as the inner contradictions in Descartes's work. Just as the following generations tried to overcome these inner contradictions in Descartes's work (so that D'Alembert in the *Encyclopédie* was able to claim that the "spirit of experimental physics" had been developed by Bacon and Descartes), from the very beginning the most varied forces were clamoring for a resolution of the tensions, the removal of the internal contradictions of the social system. In this phase there was, therefore, no immobilism of the sort Paul Hazard diagnosed in his otherwise brilliant introductory chapter to *The European Mind: The Critical Years (1680-1715)* (New Haven, 1953). In the transition from the medieval feudal system to the absolute monarchy, the manifestations of social movement changed, but even at court, at the motor of the entire system, the movement did not actually stand still. In its very origin the absolute monarchy was dependent on the forces which would eliminate it, and until its end in 1789 the dialectic of antagonistic, centrifugal and centripetal forces would not come to a halt. To be sure, the centripetal forces probably reached their climax in the era from 1660 to 1683, but their subsequent weakening reveals that the opposing forces must have been still greater. Just how great is shown by the fact that the representatives of the centripetal forces were at the same time the representatives of the centrifugal forces. Henri IV himself led the negotiations on trade treaties with other nations (of which Heinrich Mann gave an impressive portrait in *Henri Quatre*); trade, manufacturing, and crafts were promoted by privileges, and in this time we even see the first beginnings of a national colonial policy. In 1603 Henri IV sent Samuel de Champlain (1567-1635) to Canada (*La Nouvelle France*), where he founded Québec in 1608. In 1627 Champlain published his apologia for colonial politics: *Voyages et découvertes faites en la Nouvelle France depuis 1615-1618* (Voyages and Discoveries in New France between 1615 and 1618). After the first trading company he founded suffered reversals, he founded a new company in 1628 with Richelieu as the nominal head.

Two years before, Richelieu had become "Grand Master of Shipping and Trade." In 1635 he founded the *Compagnie des Iles d'Amérique*, with its main branch in Guadalupe; in 1642 he founded the *Compagnie d'Orient*, for trade with India. It seemed that the dream of Antoine de Montchrestien (1575-1621) was fulfilled with these two companies. In his *Traité de l'économie politique* (Treatise on Political Economy, 1615), Montchrestien had envisioned a France owning fleets and conducting a trade or colonial policy on a world scale; he believed the French had the spirit of enterprise to do this.[4] But in truth, the colonial successes of Richelieu were none too great, due primarily to the structure of the companies (which in turn was determined by the inner structure of the absolute monarchy in France). Apart from the fact that harbor cities like Saint-

Malo and La Rochelle did all they could to sabotage the companies out of fear of the trade privileges that the companies were granted, on the one hand, the interconnection of feudal-national government and private-capitalistic initiative stood in the way of a development like that in England, and on the other, despite Henri IV, Louis XIII, and Richelieu, internal conditions were so unstable that there were considerable impediments to a continuous foreign policy, which was especially true for the regency of Mazarin and the time of the Fronde. Nonetheless, it must be stated that precisely this national system of the absolute monarchy pushed for the development of productive forces (in overseas trade as well), although these forces were hostile to the absolute monarchy in the last analysis. In order to exist, the absolute monarchy promoted what would annihilate it and attempted, although in vain, to keep in check through supervision those forces that needed a free development. In the long run, as history proves, that was not possible; but the national system certainly inhibited the development that was being called for and promoted at the same time.

The First Disintegration of the Alliance between the Monarchy and the "Revolutionary Elements" of the Bourgeoisie

In this time, which was in need of activity and energy, the transformation of rich burghers into rentiers or officials began to be a political and economic hindrance. The rise into the *noblesse de robe* had in part fulfilled its historical purpose, to the extent that it helped to establish the principle of the absolute monarchy; the absolute monarchy had prevailed and instead of newly ennobled landowners or masses of magistrates, it now needed a bourgeoisie active in finance, trade, and manufacturing. The corresponding reorientation of the monarch's policy toward the nobility began, significantly, under Henri IV, who for the first time annulled titles of the *noblesse de robe* toward the end of the 1590s. Not much later, however, he was forced to recognize them again. Henri IV also decreed the first ban on dueling in 1602; both acts indicate how multifarious the monarch's strategy would be in relation to the whole nobility, the feudal nobility, and especially the purchased nobility. It was a question of weaning the feudal noble from his private, militaristic form of existence—by going so far as to forbid duels—and pointing him toward other tasks at court or outside the court; and of renewing that branch of the nobility which had purchased its titles, and to great extent become useless, with a new nobility recruited from the potent financial or commercial bourgeoisie. That also explains an apparent contradiction: while the king from this time on repeatedly annulled the noble titles he had previously distributed or sold, he also distributed new ones (although relatively fewer and fewer of them). At the same time, he tried to prod the nobility into activity as commercial capitalists. In 1627 a royal edict, probably inspired by Richelieu, stated that no one conducting large-scale trade would lose his privileges of nobility; in 1629 an *ordonnance royale* determined that the nobility was allowed to conduct overseas trade, in person or through a middleman, without losing its priviliges (especially tax exemption).[5] This (not very successful) measure was flanked by two bans on dueling, one from 1624, the other from 1626. And while Richelieu elevated active commercial burghers into the nobility (ennobling the head of the merchants' guild and of the lay assessors of Lyon in 1634, 1638, and 1643), in 1640 he annulled all noble titles purchased since 1610.

Blocking the uninterrupted access of the bourgeoisie to the nobility through the purchase of titles and at the same time declaring trade (and certain manufacturing activities)[6] as something not unworthy of the nobility had the obvious goal of removing the stigma of being not *honnête*, of being inappropriate, of being socially second-rate or contemptible from earning a living.[7] In this context also appeared the first reference to the commercial capitalist activity of the English nobility, which had become current in England as early as the sixteenth century. The English nobility, as an example, proved that trade was not only an occupation worthy of the nobility, but also a patriotic deed. At the same time a polemic was mounted against *oisiveté, fainéantise* (inactivity), *paresse* (laziness), and *utilité, activité*, and similar qualities were elevated to the fundamental values of true *honnêteté*. The transition to this new view of *honnêteté* is indicated by François de La Mothe le Vayer (1588-1672), who was elected to the Académie Française in 1636 and served as a tutor to the royal family from the fifties on. To be sure, he still believed that fruitful leisure was the most desirable condition for himself,[8] but it is obvious that by this he meant intellectual work.[9] But the second place in his scale of values is unconditionally occupied by the active life, which provides the precondition for *repos*, "leisure," "rest," in the last analysis a time of reproduction that is not to be confused with *oisiveté*, which La Mothe le Vayer equates with *fainéantise* and both of which he strictly condemns.[10] This unrestricted condemnation of *fainéantise/oisiveté* also explains La Mothe le Vayer's attitude toward the social activity of trade. He discusses the problems associated with this, using the relationship between commerce and *noblesse* as an example. Trade, he says, is degrading in its origin, but not in its goal, "for its basic goal is to lend aid where nature is not sufficient ... which makes trade not only legitimate, but even necessary and quite commendable."[11] La Mothe le Vayer is so radical in his pleading that he does not even distinguish between large-scale and small-scale trade: both are worthy, because quantity does not affect quality, the essence of the matter. With express reference to the authority of Jean Bodin in evaluating trade, La Mothe le Vayer closes his proof with the image of the "Gentils hommes d'Angleterre," the "Nobles of England," "who run most of the shops in London and in their other cities, without doing damage to their status thereby."

Because the historical situation in France was so different from the English situation, it is more than dubious that such considerations were able to comfort the feudal nobility, deprived of their power and partially impoverished, or the endangered nobility of "usurpation." Blame for this must be apportioned not least to Richelieu's financial policy and that of his successor Mazarin; both men allowed themselves to become more and more dependent on reactionary feudal-noble[12] finance capitalists or speculators. A clear policy cannot be determined, not even with respect to the sale of offices. The *traitants*, the "tax collectors," who worked on commission, aroused particular displeasure. Alain Niderst, whose summary I will use here, writes:

> An oppressive tax law, the reduction of pensions, which were often paid poorly or with great delay, the abuse of the sale of offices, the establishment of new offices that devalued the already existing ones and elicited the displeasure of their occupants—those were the measures by which all observers characterize the power of the traitants and that gave rise to such hostility that even the ministers were affected by it. Richelieu's centralist authoritarianism and his wretched financial policy were thus the two main causes for the Fronde. In this movement we can see a revolt of the old [feudal—M. N.] powers, of the noblesse de robe, and of the backward-looking bourgeoisie against the new classes promoted by the monarchy.[13]

Colbert's Plea for the Participation of the Absolute Monarchy in Primitive Accumulation

In 1654 the *Fronde* was defeated. In 1656 Mazarin (certainly not without the cooperation of Colbert) revoked all titles of nobility acquired since 1634 and thereby continued Richelieu's policy, which now served definitively to disempower the former *Frondeurs*. In 1661 Mazarin died; Louis XIV personally took over the leadership of his state affairs and called Jean-Baptise Colbert (1619-83) into his royal council.[14] In 1664 Colbert gave the king in council a remarkable lecture on the condition of world trade and of French trade as well as on the measures that had to be taken to bring French trade up to the world level. Colbert began by excusing himself for bothering the king with such mundane things as trade policy (a distant echo of the *honnêteté* taboos, which had now become linked with respect for the absolutist hero): the great states of the past, ancient and modern, with which the state of the French monarch could be compared, did not conduct trade, to be sure; but if we must now think about this sort of thing, it is because circumstances make it necessary.[15] Before the fourteenth century, Colbert continues, no trade was conducted on the ocean (especially the Atlantic Ocean). Only the Mediterranean enjoyed this advantage, and the oldest cities known to history became rich thereby. Before 1480 Venice and—at some remove—Marseille conducted all the large-scale trade with the valuable Indian goods, which were brought by caravan through Persia and India to Venice and sometimes also to Marseille and then distributed throughout Europe from there: this created Venice's power, which at that time was the goods depot of Europe.[16]

Through the discovery of the trade route to the East Indies around the Cape of Good Hope, the Portuguese then rose to become a colonial world power,[17] and after them the Spaniards, with the discovery of the West Indies and then America.[18] Finally, the Netherlands won their independence through overseas trade and became a world power, and the English in turn followed their example: the Netherlands and England ruined the two Catholic world powers by their trade policy, "and the two powers, which [today— M. N.] are so powerful, are heathen."[19]

After Colbert has presented this "large-scale trade, which is the only trade worthy of note," he mentions the smaller trading centers, from the Levantine trade to the Baltic trade, and then treats the question whether it makes sense for France to turn to overseas trade. He first enumerates all the reasons that speak against it: the most powerful states never conducted trade, so trade is an affair of weak states; France has such a superfluity of natural products that "industrie et parcimonie" would be harmed by trade, and so on. But in addition, Holland's trade would be ruined, which would be a disadvantage because Holland is dependent on France and was protected in the past, because Holland takes care of trade for France.[20]

On the other hand, the reasons for conducting overseas trade are the promotion of industry and frugality, which would be difficult in view of the mentioned superfluity of agricultural products, but it is after all especially glorious to overcome difficulties. If the king could add to the agricultural wealth of France the wealth produced by technology and diligence in trade ("l'art et l'industrie du commerce"), it would be easy to imagine how "the power and magnitude of the king would increase wonderfully."[21] Whatever had to be spent to build up the navy would soon be recouped through an appropriate policy of protective tariffs for the French ships, and Holland would not be ruined; at most there would be a slight decrease in Dutch trade.[22] The power of the king on land, moreover, is greater than that of any other European power, but at sea it is less: colonial trade is the only means to equalize this state of affairs.[23]

At this point the decision has actually already been made (it was never really open to question), but Colbert still analyzes the situation of the French economy at the beginning of Louis XIV's reign (1661), in order to know under what conditions the building up of trade would take place if it were undertaken. The cloth manufactures, the paper factories, production of iron, silk, linen, soap, and all other manufactures are almost ruined. Dutch imports have worked against their reconstruction. If France produced enough to be able to export, it could keep money at home[24] (with which Colbert strengthens the mercantilist credo).

The reasons for the poor condition of French domestic trade are first, the debts of the cities and communities, which have hindered the establishment of a system of communication, the basis for all trade "from province to province, from city to city;"[25] second, the legal disputes that have arisen from these debts; third, the profusion of duty payments everywhere on the highways and riverways, which ruin the public communications network; fourth, "the horrible huge number of offices for sale;"[26] fifth, the excessive taxes that weigh on all goods; sixth, the tax tariffs of the five great tax authorities ("des cinq grosses fermes");[27] seventh, piracy, which has caused great losses on innumerable ships[28] (and against which France could not protect itself because of the lack of a competent navy). The poor condition of French foreign trade was caused primarily by the lack of shipbuilding and the dependence on foreign imports.

The means Colbert suggests to reanimate trade and manufacturing will not be detailed here. They consist in part of an energetic program to increase the social and political esteem of the merchant class,[29] in subsidies to build up manufactures and to found trade enterprises, in subsidies and tax relief for anyone who buys or builds ships or wants to conduct overseas trade, in building up the road and river system while dismantling customs barriers, in making the rivers navigable, and in the energetic support of the West and East Indies trading companies.

The Renewal of the Alliance

All of Colbert's suggestions are—who could doubt it!—in the interest of the monarchy, but they are just as much and just as indubitably in the objective interest of the bourgeoisie. For while the absolute monarchy had indeed established itself politically, it was not fully formed. It was still expanding, rounding off its boundaries, founding colonies, providing the political and structural framework within which capitalist productive forces could develop. And that means that the alliance between the king and the "revolutionary elements" did not end with the *Fronde*, but renewed itself instead. As long as the possibilities for the development of the capitalist mode of production offered by the specific forms of the epoch were greater than the impediments the epoch erected, the fetters it laid on, this alliance would endure.

However, the renewal of the alliance depended on new forces in the bourgeoisie that were not oriented toward the ideal of the man of private means and *oisiveté* but rather toward commercial and manufacturing activities. With this, the seed of the later destruction of the alliance was already planted; Colbert himself placed the fetters on his new allies from the very beginning, those fetters that would then become too tight. His highest economic goal was, as we saw, to make the French economy independent; in keeping with his mercantilist convictions, he planned to achieve this by increasing exports and reducing imports (especially of luxury goods). For this reason, he saw one of his chief tasks in the establishment, promotion, and subsidization of manufactures, especially for textile production. As Robert Mandrou puts it:

> In this way fewer gold and silver coins were supposed to flow out of France, and the occupations necessary for the satisfaction of consumption were to develop in the land itself. To reach this ambitious goal, the controller general exhausted himself for twenty years in tireless work. His concern about producing cloth and weapons of the quality one was accustomed to from foreign imports is betrayed by a flood of regulations, in which the norms to be observed are determined to the smallest detail: for the warp and the weft, even for the dye substance to be used. The most important of these regulations was decreed in 1669. To judge by the explanations of the directors and master craftsmen, it represented a substantial handicap for the innovators.[30]

Despite the impediments he himself placed in the way, Colbert in the last analysis still gave a strong push to the development of manufacturing, thanks not only to his own unimaginable energy but also to that of his collaborators: the *noblesse de robe* and the active bourgeoisie on the one hand, the progressive nobles on the other—and the people groaned and succumbed beneath the huge exertions and burdens that were loaded on them,[31] while the old feudal nobility bored itself in Versailles with games, intrigues, and luxury. Colbert conjured up a navy and a trading fleet, and anyone who in his opinion showed too little pluck had to put up with hearing about it from him: "One must try to infuse everyone in our navy with 'esprit d'entreprise,' the spirit of enterprise."[32] Colbert had wharves built, canals dug, rivers straightened, and harbors laid out. Mandrou states:

> He called trading companies into being that had a trade monopoly in a certain region, in the north, that is in the Baltic, in the West Indies, the Levant, and the East Indies. The charter of these companies was worked out in Versailles, the original financing came partly from the royal treasury, partly through contributions by the large cities and especially the directly interested harbors. The administration of the companies was handled by members of the noblesse de robe who were chosen by the king, or knowledgeable merchants were recruited for this purpose in each of the regions traveled.[33]

That entrepreneurial élan was again hindered by state regimentation interests us less in this context than the fact that an energy was at work here that was appropriate to the magnitude of the monarchy.

The Active *Honnête Homme*

The situation was remarkable: the representative of the absolute monarchy (who, to be sure, must at the same time be considered as the representative of the progressive forces of the bourgeoisie) not only led the bourgeois trade and manufacturing capitalists, but also often had to push them forward. For this purpose, in fact, a large educational and propaganda machine was set in motion in which Colbert played a very special part. No one except Louis XIV himself had as much power in his hands as Colbert, made controller general of finances in 1665, minister of the marine in 1666, minister and director general of the fine arts, of manufactures, and of royal construction. He dominated not only the economic life of the time, but also the intellectual life: in 1663 he founded the Academy of Inscriptions, in 1666 the Academy of Sciences, in 1671 the Architectural Academy, and from 1667 to 1671 he had the observatory built. He distributed pensions and grants to French and foreign artists, poets, scientists, and he ordered all of social life just as he ordered and (over-)administered the country.

It is obvious that Colbert's measures were significant for all sectors of economic and intellectual life. Intellectual and social life were also often linked, especially in the work of educating the nobility and the bourgeoisie. At first Colbert continued the policy of his predecessors: in 1661 and 1664 decrees were issued or renewed against the usurpation of *noblesse*; from 1665 on all noble titles in each province had to be checked by commissions appointed for that purpose and all usurped titles were extinguished;[34] in 1666 another decree was issued against the usurpation of noble titles, and on 13 January 1667 still another decree stated that anyone who had assumed the title of *chevalier* or *écuyer* (squire) simply on the basis of a court order or a notarized document would be punished.[35] In 1679 dueling was definitively forbidden. A complement to these decrees were those issued in 1664 on the occasion of the refounding of the East and West Indies trading companies. These decrees clearly stated that nobles were and had always been permitted to conduct trade without forfeiting their titles, and decrees in 1669, besides reconfirming this right, strongly emphasized the significance of sea trade as quite worthy of being conducted by nobles.

The immediate success of these efforts was moderate, but throughout the whole eighteenth century the possibility was taken into consideration of moving the nobility to take an active part in trade so that wealth would circulate and the whole economy would benefit, and Colbert was always cited in discussions on this topic. He believed that the lever with which he could dislodge the *noblesse* from their *oisiveté* was sea trade, overseas shipping, the merchant marine.[36] The names of his ships and galleys reflect something of this strategy of attracting the nobles and the bourgeoisie through glorification of overseas shipping (they also demonstrate something of the modern ideology of adventure): *Le Glorieux,*

Le Furieux, La Tempeste, L'Invincible, Le Tigre, L'Hercule, La Fortune, L'Aventurier.

But whatever Colbert was announcing or having propagandists like François Charpentier[37] announce, an article of faith exists in all the statements: any idler is a useless parasite, a *fainéant*, a sloth, not worthy of the designation of *honnête homme*. Colbert was the *chef de file*, the leader of that part of the ideology of *honnêteté* at the center of which was work. From 1661 on, the false claims of interested researchers notwithstanding,[38] Colbert's ideology was the mainstream, borne by the alliance between monarchy and bourgeoisie; in the eighteenth century this ideology would develop further in opposition to the throne. Colbert wrote to his son, the Marquis de Seignelay, on 11 June 1670, that his *honnêteté*, like that of anyone else, rested on three things: first, on the duty of serving God, "for this first duty necessarily entails all others"; second, on fulfilling his duty to his father, and not because he is his biological father, but rather out of gratitude for the social position that his father's work has secured for him, and also "for the trouble and work" that his father has put into raising him; third, on *work*. Colbert continues in this letter, which he sent with his son on a journey to Rochefort:

> After these first two points, and to address now the details of what he [Colbert's son—R. C.] is to do during the journey, I should like him to begin by reading the naval code . . . and should like him to take along the treatises of Clairac and to study the one on marine terminology without delay, and to instruct himself about seafaring during the entire journey.[39]

In 1671, at age twenty, Seignelay traveled to Italy, and Colbert gave him the following instructions: "The two most important principles according to which this trip should be designed are diligence and caution."[40] Seignelay was to study, was to appropriate useful knowledge. For instance, in Genoa he was to pay heed to the "situation, the economic power, the size of the population," and "since all this knowledge can be gained in two or three days at the most, he is not to stay there longer, but rather to continue across the sea to Livorno or across the mountains to Parma."[41] "During the whole journey he is to see to it that he conducts himself in a mannerly, decent, and polite way toward everyone, while of course observing differences in station."[42]

Honnêteté without useful work, without industry was simply inconceivable for Colbert: his son, as he writes in another letter from the same year, when Seignelay was beginning his first official duties, was always to bear the king in mind, who demonstrated a "prodigieuse application," a "wonderful devotion" to work. That this attitude toward work, industry, and the fulfillment of duty was not just a whim applied to his family is shown throughout Colbert's official correspondence and in innumerable official decrees and edicts. And since all virtues derived from work—above which are only love of God and respect for one's father (unlimited respect for the king should be added to this list)—all vices derived from *fainéantise* or *oisiveté* (which he differentiated as little as the later *encyclopédistes* would). Colbert combated *fainéantise/oisiveté* with a regular passion, whether he was pushing his governors (even those from the upper nobility, even those from his own family) to work, nagging them about details in a sometimes insulting way,[43] or whether he was founding trading companies or manufactures "pour bannir l'oisiveté et la fainéantise parmy le peuple," "to drive idleness and laziness out of the people."[44]

Agnès; or, The Tidings of a Better World

As our discussion makes clear, it is false to claim what is often claimed, that the (bourgeois) intellectuals, the scientists, artists, and writers of the age who cooperated with the throne or worked at court sold themselves to the oppressor of their class, of their people, to the despotic power, for the sake of a pension. The reality is more complicated than such clichéd thinking can reveal: in judging the absolute monarchy in the epoch of interest to us, we must not start with the image of the absolute monarchy as it developed in France in the course of the eighteenth century (and still less as it developed in other places and at other times). Of course there was oppression and censorship,[45] but at the same time the most various progressive forces (in the intellectual realm as well) were set in motion by those same powers that practiced oppression and censorship. We can only decide whether the whole system was reactionary and misanthropic by weighing *all* the factors; it is, as we have demonstrated, a question of the dialectics of quantity and quality, and in the second half of the seventeenth century the judgment on the entire system of the absolute monarchy in France must be that, in the framework of the economic and political realities and possibilities, the overall tendency was *progressive*. The alliance that supported the state, an alliance composed of the different parties of the nobility and the bourgeoisie, was progressive in its overall tendency. This is expressed clearly in the actions of its most important representatives, Colbert and the (young) king. The promotion of trade and manufacturing was objectively in the interest of the bourgeoisie (although the specific form of this promotion became more and more burdensome as time went on), as was the propagation of an ethic based on *utilité* and *travail*; moreover, it was still clearly aimed against the reactionary forces of the false or feudal or purchased *noblesse*.

Numerous documents testify to the fact that Louis XIV, at least in the early phase of his reign, fully supported the struggle to establish this new ethics. In this context, the royal edict of 18 September 1664 is particularly interesting. In this edict, Louis XIV names the goal of the measures he and Colbert are taking:

> bannir le fainéantise et divertir, par les occupations honnestes, l'inclination si ordinaire de la plupart de nos sujets à une vie oisive et rampante sous le titre de divers offices sans fonctions ou sous de fausses apparences d'une médiocre attache aux bonnes lettres[46]

> to banish indolence and by means of honest work to drive out that tendency, common among so many of our subjects, to an idle and spiritless life carried on under the pretext of various offices with no function or under the false colors of a poor attachment to literature.

The edict is unmistakably addressed to those nobles who were filling no actual need in administration or who had usurped their titles, and to the ideologues and belletrists who represented reactionary forces, especially those of the conspiratorial feudal nobility of the former *Fronde*. This is the same cast of characters that Molière attacks in his comedies: from the *Précieuses ridicules* (*The Precious Damsels*), 1659, to the braggart poetaster of the *Misanthrope*, 1666, to the *maître de philosophie* in the *Bourgeois Gentilhomme* (*The Would-Be Gentleman*), 1670, whose ridiculous lectures on prose and poetry contribute to driving *le bon sens*, reasonable thinking oriented toward *activité, travail,* and *utilité,* out of the good bourgeois.

Molière is, in fact (not only in his critique of the *précieux*, that is, of the ideological representatives of feudal reaction), the most perfect artist-propagandist of Colbert's policies and hence of the alliance between the monarchy and the "revolutionary elements" of the bourgeoisie. This sometimes had quite unpleasant consequences, as the history of the production of Molière's plays shows: the various parties of society that he attacked often had enough political power to make his life difficult. The fact that in these confrontations, Molière could always rely as a last resort on the personal support of the king (though for political reasons it was sometimes given with reservations) demonstrates the significance of his artistic-propagandistic function. When Werner Krauss states that Molière "presented the *whole* world of the seventeenth century. Molière's comedy, like all genuine comedy, is a total interpretation of existence,"[47] we must place certain restrictions on his claim. It is true that in Molière's comedies nobles appear and are mocked, but not all of the nobility: the king, of course, is not an object of comedy, nor is the butt of Molière's mockery ever the *useful* nobility, that is, the nobility of the sword and of the court which supports absolutism. With other premises, the same is true of the bourgeoisie: in Molière's comedies the bourgeoisie is ridiculed, but (with *one* large exception, which we will treat later) only that faction that is allied with the reactionary nobility or that imitates it. Where the bourgeoisie does not fulfill its (revolutionary) tasks in the alliance with the absolute monarchy, Molière attacks it, exposes it for what it is: counterrevolutionary, retrograde, narrow-minded. In short, Molière mocks both the nobility and the bourgeoisie, but it is the reactionary factions of the nobility and the bourgeoisie that he makes fun of. The revolutionary factions of the nobility and of the bourgeoisie are spared Molière's criticism (for instance, the commercial and manufacturing capitalists as certainly the most important faction of the bourgeoisie, but even financial capitalists). Not only that, but they are the victors in the end, with fine regularity and revolutionary optimism. But when the reactionary forces are so strong that *le bon sens* of the progressive forces cannot triumph, then the king intervenes directly in their favor, for Molière's point of view is clearly situated in the alliance between the monarchy and the "revolutionary elements" of the bourgeoisie (which is not identical with *la cour et la ville*).

This state of affairs, which can easily be deduced from a reading of Molière's comedies, explains the fact that Molière does not *annihilate* the opponents he makes fun of (except for Tartuffe and Don Juan). That is quite in keeping with the policy of the court and of Colbert; it is in keeping with the objective interests of a victorious class or of a victorious alliance between two classes in the class struggle: to bring social relations into order and to establish the state of the absolute monarchy, all forces are needed, even the other parties of the victor's own class, which have just been defeated. Moreover, we must bear in mind that after the victory, the victor needs allies in both camps, and none of the warring parties would welcome it if an ally were to continue the struggle against members of its own class. These relations and forms of behavior had other designations, but we must not overlook the fact that objectively, class relations corresponded to this basic structure; that is the only explanation for the constant appeals to reason, the summons to active cooperation in the interest of the common good (and that means for Colbert always in the interest of the absolute monarchy as well).[48]

Molière's comedies again and again sound the appeal to support the society (of the victors) with *bon sens* and activity, to join the cause of the progressive forces, of *utilité*, of *honnêteté* founded on *utilité* and *industrie*, of *bon sens*. He mocks the counterrevolutionary or conservative forces, but in every case the mockery is followed (in a quite revolutionary way) by a conciliatory gesture and the invitation to cooperate in the new society,[49] for which he wrote plays that can with full right be called political didactic plays.[50]

A perfect example is *L'école des femmes* (*The School for Wives*), 1662, in which Arnolphe, a member of the bourgeoisie who pursues the wrong policy in Colbert's sense, is confronted with a faction of the bourgeoisie that is socially useful, active, and rational in Colbert's (but also in a historical) sense. The first act of the play reveals much. Arnolphe has usurped a noble title, calls himself Monsieur de la Souche, and leads an inauthentic life by using his wealth to lead a double life. He has a rich bourgeois house in which, as we can see from his speeches (1.1.143-44), he holds a salon. The salon puts him in contact with the sophisticated world, into which he bought his way with his title. This is the world of the *précieux*, the world of the ideology of *honnêteté* based on *oisiveté*; and this is the world in which the emancipation of women is discussed and propagated from the point of view of the precious novel à la Scudéry, a significant fact for the play. But Molière uses the figure of Arnolphe to show the reverse side of this sophisticated society of the *précieux* and the new nobility: Arnolphe has a second house that he has strictly isolated from *le monde* and where he keeps as a prisoner Agnès (1.1.145ff.), a young girl he bought when she was four. He allows her to grow up in ignorance because he wants to marry her and believes that this is the only way to ensure his domestic happiness.

Arnolphe's friend Chrysalde, who belongs to the party of the active bourgeoisie that does not want a noble title, makes fun both of Arnolphe's newly acquired title (1.1.165ff.) and of his anxiety and schizophrenia about women. When Arnolphe explains to him that he does not mind if a woman is stupid as long as she has *honnêteté*, Chrysalde asks him what kind of *honnêteté* is founded on stupidity (1.1.107-8). Arnolphe's rival Horace, who belongs to Chrysalde's party, argues in a similar way; he blames Arnolphe for Agnès's ignorance and finally triumphs (see 1.4.319ff., among others). Horace is the son of Oronte, a rich bourgeois who comes to Paris with a merchant named Enrique, who acquired a fortune through colonial trade in the West Indies after 1648. Oronte wants Horace to marry Enrique's daughter, whom Enrique had left behind in the protection of a peasant woman when he went to America. Of course, this daughter is none other than Agnès, whom Arnolphe bought when she was four years old: he loses her to Horace. Arnolphe's attempt to construct for himself a retrograde world outside reality and against the movement of his class thus collapses.

But who is Arnolphe and what kind of a world is it that he wanted to possess for himself alone, at the exclusion of real life? Molière's social analysis or his polemical propaganda is as brilliant as it is effective (the reaction to the play proves that; characteristically, the *précieux* salon nobility felt attacked, although it was not directly presented on stage: a representative of this retrograde nobility even assaulted Molière).[51] Arnolphe is not just some strange, eccentric individual; instead, he is a friend of all the other members of the bourgeoisie who appear in this play: Chrysalde, Oronte, and Enrique. They all belong to one and the same social group or the same class, the bourgeoisie, which had taken different courses of development from the time of the *Fronde*. Enrique followed the path of socially useful activity propagandized by Richelieu, Mazarin, and at the time the play was produced, by Colbert; he opens new horizons through overseas trade and acquires wealth. Arnolphe, on the other hand, tries to halt social development or to preserve the earlier state of the bourgeoisie and to lead the life of an *honnête homme* according to the model of *oisiveté*, the life of a man of private means. This form of existence reveals that the reverse side of reactionary preciosity is nothing other than dull bourgeois narrow-mindedness. Molière's criticism of Arnolphe's *vieux jeu*, "old-fashionedness," unmasks the misanthropy of the old feudal system that the reactionary feudal nobility mourned for, and it unmasks the prolongations of this system up into the present of the absolute monarchy. At the same time, *The School for Wives* finally documents the optimistic, philanthropic perspective of the development of the forces of production in the time around 1662 (it is no coincidence that it is the commercial bourgeoisie who—as in *The Merchant of Venice*—liberates the oppressed woman from the feudal prison that has kept her ignorant and imbecile). Chrysalde, Oronte, and Enrique want to share with their friend and fellow bourgeois Arnolphe the origin of a better world here—and Molière wants to share it with his public. Anyone who wants to be happy must not lock himself up, must not lock up other human beings, must not orient himself toward the wretched past, must be active, and must run risks, even in marriage.[52]

Portrait of a "Revolutionary Element"

But most of all, anyone who wants to be happy must be active in commerce and manufacturing. In 1675 Jacques Savary's *Parfait négociant* (The Perfect Merchant) appeared, dedicated to Colbert; this is a handbook for merchants and manufacturers which undertook a "measurement" of the active burgher, of the "revolutionary element," as the progressive contemporaries saw it. From an artistic point of view, the portrait of the *commerçant* or *négociant* painted by Jacques Savary (the two concepts are used synonymously, and until well into the eighteenth century they also mean the manufacturing capitalist) is not the equal of Molière's artistically perfect character sketches, nor is it comparable with them; but it has the advantage not only of presenting the useful (objectively revolutionary) commercial or manufacturing capitalist whom Colbert was promoting and whom Molière allows to triumph in his comedies, but also of presenting him in a systematic way.

It is all the more advisable for us to consider this portrait, because Savary's *Parfait négociant* functions as a key to a whole realm of political and economic reflection in France. Even in the eighteenth century it was reprinted often (the edition of 1715 is the most comprehensive and the best); it provided Savary's son, Jacques Savary de Bruslons, with a model for his *Dictionaire Universel de Commerce* (1723), and it still served as an authority even for Diderot's *Encyclopédie*. Moreover, another circumstance suggests the *Parfait négociant* to our attention: Sombart uses it as evidence in constructing his bourgeois type.

According to Sombart, the *Parfait négociant* is simply one of the numerous "text-books" or "treatises" preaching "middle-class virtues" which, he says, have shown no development since the Italian Renaissance: the *Parfait négociant*, like other books of a similar type, seems like a French translation of Leon Battista Alberti's *Della Famiglia*.[53] Quite apart from the fact that such an intellectual-historical understanding abstracts from the real context of the production and reception of texts (Seneca in the fifteenth century has a different function from Seneca in the seventeenth or twentieth century), a glance at these two works relegates Sombart's claim to the realm of pseudohistorical constructs (to give just one example: Savary of course did not design his book as a chronicle and glorification of his family, as Alberti did in a way almost typical of Italian merchants; Savary gives glimpses, for example, into the historical development of trade and of the forces of production).

But more important than the strategy of falsification is its goal: since Savary attempts to present the systematic nature of trade (and later of manufacturing as well), Sombart immediately takes the opportunity to demonstrate the antientrepreneurial and (of interest to us) the antiadventurous *bourgeois* spirit, oriented toward order, modesty, hierarchy. We have already seen that just the opposite is true, that bourgeois order stands in an indissoluble dialectical relation to the anarchic production of capitalism: Savary is one of the thinkers who prepared the ground on which the modern bourgeois ideology of adventure has grown, in France as well as elsewhere. What appears as order in his writings is—we must not forget this—a manifestation of the capitalist mode of production, a manifestation of the forces that will do away with the feudal system. In the seventeenth century, during the time of Racine, La Fontaine, Boileau, and Molière, Savary creates an ideal of humanity that represents a useful *honnête homme* who is radically different from the heroes of a Corneille, a Racine, from the image of the courtier (to say nothing of the figures from novels à la Scudéry). And this useful *honnête homme* has the reality of his existence on his side. He actually does appear "self-confidently," to quote Hazard; the *commerçant*, Savary determines, is an instrument of providence because he alone provides access to the products of nature (as commodities) that Providence has strewn all over the earth. In so doing he brings about peace and friendship among the human beings who enter into the exchange through him—and this is an important argument. There cannot be the slightest doubt of the utility of trade: on the one hand the "largest part of the kingdom" conducts this activity *honnêtement*, and many of the *commerçants* have made "fortunes considérables," which, as in Shakespeare, is seen exclusively as something positive. They thus created the opportunity for their children to acquire noble titles; here Savary admits how much the increase of commercial activity can be linked with the bait of the desired rise into the nobility. Moreover, through this activity the wealth of the kingdom or of the prince would increase proportionately to trade.[54]

Of greatest importance are the qualities which Savary believes youths who want to become *commerçants* (and hence the *commerçants* themselves) must have. First, as to the understanding, they must have a good imagination, for this is necessary for crafts, manufacturing, and trade. It consists in being able to invent new materials, in being pleasant in purchasing, selling, and trading, in being subtle and quick with plausible arguments [*argumens naturels*] when an answer is necessary, if one finds mistakes, in being able to write well, to know arithmetic and all other things necessary for the merchant's occupation.[55]

Second,

as to their physiques: they must be strong and robust and equal to all hardships encountered in travel on sea and on land, which... [the commerçants]... must undertake in the provinces of the kingdom, to the places where the manufactures are, where the fairs and markets are held, and into foreign lands in order to buy, to sell, and to distribute goods there; to make bales and to transport bales of great size without straining themselves.[56]

Third,

it would be desirable that all these good qualities were joined with good appearance, for this always benefits a merchant, because most people prefer to have to do with a good-looking man... than with another who does not have the same external advantages.[57]

Fourth, along with these last qualities, which make it clear that Savary is already thinking of the *employee*, the "commercial wage earner," the *commerçants* (or their successors) must also know "double-entry and simple bookkeeping" and "even [learn] the Italian, Spanish, and German languages, because these are very necessary for those who want to conduct trade with foreign lands."[58] Fifth, merchants (or aspiring merchants) should study even history books,

both of France and of foreign countries, and the books that report on travel and trade, for this kind of reading schools the judgment of young people in a wonderful way. They learn from them in theory what they must practice if they want to conduct trade with foreign countries, for they learn from them the customs and practices of the people with whom they will associate, as well as what goods they need for the manufacturing they want to do.[59]

Sixth, what is without utility must not be studied. It is not advisable to go to a *collège*, because one learns Latin there: "grammar, rhetoric, and philosophy."[60] In view of the school situation of the time, this advice is not without *bon sens* and can also easily be linked with the polemic of the *honnête homme* against pedantry.

Since the *Parfait négociant* was written not only for the independent *commerçant* but also for the employee, Savary gives advice on the direction and subordination of apprentices and employees in trade[61] and of wage laborers in the manufactures.[62] That is one side of a coin whose other side concerns us here: the whole world agrees, Savary writes, that large-scale trade is more honorable than commerce *en détail*, which remains "perched within the walls of the city" in which it is conducted.[63]

> It is quite another matter with large-scale trade, for those who conduct it have to do only with two sorts of people, namely with the manufacturers to whom they give commissions . . . and with small-scale traders, to whom they sell chests, bales, and whole consignments of goods. Large-scale trade is conducted in many kingdoms and states not only by non-nobles, but even by nobles . . . , but that is never true of small-scale trade, for that has something servile about it, while there is nothing in large-scale trade that is not honnête and noble.[64]

Moreover, the dangers inherent in the *grosse aventure* trade ennoble it.[65] There is nothing offensive about large-scale trade if as a noble one only invests money in a limited partnership (*société de commandite*), for in this case the noble gives money to a merchant who needs it and works with it. It is apparently a matter of secondary concern that the noble reaps profits thereby without dirtying his own hands.[66]

In any case, this is the *commerçant-honnête homme* whose portrait Savary paints and who is superior to the nobility in almost every respect. He does not need to furnish elaborate proofs of his *utilité*. He needs skills that are completely unknown to the courtier but which would relativize the courtier's self-importance if he had them. He has to have physical qualities that the courtly nobility, the courtiers (as opposed to the knightly nobility of the past) no longer need. He has to know foreign languages, while the courtly nobility understands only (its own) French. He has to move into the world—and this is perhaps the most important thing—open himself to the world and conquer it (Savary writes, full of pride and bitterness, "that it was the French who were the first to discover all the lands that the Spaniards, Portuguese, English, and Dutch today possess"),[67] and such conquest at this time was still a strenuous and sometimes dangerous undertaking. At the same time, except for *aventuriers* like Gramont and career diplomats, the nobility and the noble bourgeoisie (who were becoming fewer and fewer relative to their class, but soon in absolute numbers as well) strive to get to court, to Versailles or close to it, to Paris, in order to remain there (again in contrast to the knightly nobility) and to stiffen into ever greater immobility, along with the king.

In France Too, Usury Inhibits the Spirit of Enterprise

In Molière's *School for Wives*, the figure of the active bourgeois that Savary tried to describe in its essential qualities is called Oronte or Enrique. This figure embodies *le bon sens* and defeats the representative of that faction of the bourgeoisie oriented toward false or useless, unearned noble titles and the ideal of the man of private means who locks himself into a retrograde ghetto out of fear of movement, fear of bursting narrow horizons, fear of the emancipation of women. Molière juxtaposes these figures not only with the ridiculous or tragicomic figures of burghers led astray by this reactionary ideology (like Orgon in *Tartuffe*, 1664, Monsieur Jordain in *The Would-Be Gentleman* or Georges Dandin in the play *Georges Dandin*, 1668), but also with a representative of the medieval economic system, the feudal usurer. In 1668, *L'avare* appeared (*The Miser*—in the seventeenth century *l'avare* meant less a niggardly man than a rapacious, grasping one, hungry for profits),[68] a play that not only manifests striking affinities with Shakespeare's *Merchant of Venice* but also reveals in what detail Molière had dealt with the essential problems of the economic development and discussion of his age. In fact, the protagonist, Harpagon, is a usurer of the Shylock type: while he greedily accumulates money and property, he mortifies himself and his environment with inconceivable, inhuman greed (as Franz Mehring wrote in 1905 in his discussion of "Molières 'Geiziger,'" Harpagon is "both a miser and a usurer").[69] Out of miserliness, out of fear of diminishing his property, Harpagon oppresses his daughter Elise and his son Cléante as Shylock oppressed Jessica. Cléante cries out to his sister: "It is really past bearing. Could anything be more outrageous than the niggardly way he treats us, the absolute penury in which we have to live? What is the good of having money when we cannot use it until we are too old to enjoy it?"[70]

Cléante loves Marianne, a young woman who lives with her mother in straitened circumstances, and Elise loves Valère, who has smuggled himself into Harpagon's house as a servant. Harpagon, however, wants to marry Elise to a rich older man named Anselm and wants to marry Marianne himself; he does not know at first that his son also loves her. The inevitable happens: Elise gets her Valère, Cléante his Marianne, because the rich Anselm whom Harpagon wants to force on Elise is the father of Marianne and Valère (a shipwreck had separated the family). They are reunited in Harpagon's house, and a happy end is a certainty.

The political and artistic significance of this play is diametrically opposed to the banal plot, which of course appears more banal in such a short summary. With the help of this plot, Molière criticizes or glorifies important elements of the social development of the seventeenth century. Harpagon is very rich: he makes a living by lending money, by usury. Molière places him on stage as he has just received ten thousand ecus. Out of fear that the money could be stolen, he hides it in the garden of the house. Molière scholars have correctly pointed out that Plautus is a model; in his *Aululuria* a treasure is also buried. But in the age's discussion about usury, the burying (or hiding) of a treasure generally serves as an example for the fruitlessness of hoarding; sometimes (as in the case of Thomas Wilson, who quotes Jesus Sirach in his *Discourse upon Usury*) the Bible is also called upon. One thing is certain: hoarding for the sake of hoarding was generally considered to be sterile and criminal, and burying ten thousand ecus only strengthens the impression of Harpagon the monster that the audience must already have received from the exposition of Elise and Cléante.

Harpagon is, like Shylock, the type of the old feudal-medieval usurer who either removes his money from trade and manufacturing through hoarding or—when he lends it—creates a serious impediment to trade and manufacturing through his usurious interest.[71] "The exclusion of money from circulation would constitute precisely the opposite of its valorization as capital, and the accumulation of commodities in the sense of hoarding them would be sheer foolishness," as Marx writes,[72] but Harpagon commits just this double foolishness (although, as far as the burying goes, only temporarily): he buries his money in the garden, or he lends it as usurer's (consumer) credit, and he tries to foist off on his customers his goods accumulated "in the sense of hoarding," from his "four-post bedstead to a lizard's skin" (169-70). "He must have a big storeroom full of lumber somewhere," says Cléante's servant, La Flèche (173).

The necessity of bringing money into circulation was of course known to Molière's public. On 30 April 1672, Colbert wrote Louis XIV from Paris: "Since I have been here, I have been working with great success on reestablishing credit, which had suffered extraordinary disorder and decay. For this purpose I charged various merchants with putting their money back into trade, and several even volunteered to support M. Martel of Alliez, whose bankruptcy, if it were to occur, would cause various tax collectors and tax lessees a loss of more than eight hundred thousand pounds, which on the basis of the other bankruptcies that the one in Alliez would have caused, would indirectly have become a burden on Your Majesty."[73] Louis XIV answered laconically: "I am very glad about what you have written me about credit.... I am quite content that you have stopped the bankruptcy of the man from Alliez."

By *crédit*, Colbert understands the "ease with which one finds money without having to pay high interest."[74] Anyone who had to pay high interest, say of 20, 30, or 40 percent, like the king himself at the beginning of Colbert's term of office, had no *crédit*. On the other hand, anyone who had taken out an *emprunt*, a "loan," could go to court if the interest was usuriously high: The law unburdens him and condemns as guilty of usury and as a criminal the man who made him [the plaintiff—M. N.] the loan, and attaches his capital, which belongs to the king.[75] In fact, a decree of December 1665 had set interest at 5 percent, but the law was constantly broken in a more or less open way,[76] especially since it was difficult to prove usurious transactions and customers in need accepted the high interest rate of the usurers in desperation (like Cléante in *The Miser*), particularly if the deception was concealed with nasty tricks. Molière exposes such a credit deception (168-70). Harpagon offers a loan at 5½ percent interest, which almost corresponds to the decree. But the transaction entails numerous clauses for the borrower. First, the borrower is informed that the moneylender has to procure the money from a third party, to whom he of course has to pay high interest, 20 percent. The rate of interest for Harpagon's customer is thus raised to 25 percent. Second, however, Harpagon's customer is not permitted to receive the whole sum of fifteen thousand francs in cash, but has to buy the junk mentioned above for a deduction of three thousand francs. This yields an actual usurious rate of interest of 45 percent for Harpagon's customer, a rate of interest forbidden by law, but according to Colbert's own information not a rarity.

It is a special device of Molière's that Harpagon's customer is his own son, which neither the father nor the son know at first because they conduct the transaction through a go-between. Molière is showing again the varying (old-fashioned or modern) behavior of members of the same class, here in questions of finance, but also in questions of general way of living or of social activity. Cléante wants to take out a loan in order to free himself and his sister from their servitude to the medieval-feudal usurer. He tells his sister that he is determined to go abroad "and risk whatever future Fate may send us. I am already doing my best to borrow some money." If his sister agrees, she can go with him; they would leave their father and "no longer be the slaves of his unbearable avarice" (152).

For the public of the year 1668, there could hardly be any doubt that when someone talked about setting off for distant lands to make his fortune, that meant going to the East or West Indies. The public must also have been quite aware of the target of *The Miser's* polemic. On 28 May 1664 the West Indies Trading Company was reconstituted, in August 1664 the East Indies Trading Company was founded, and immediately before the production of *The Miser* in 1668 Colbert had mounted an advertising campaign for the Compagnie de Commerce du Nord. As quasi-public enterprises these companies desperately needed private capital as well: Colbert presented his projects to all potential donors, arranged real advertising and subscription campaigns, turned to all bankers and *commerçants*, all officials, the members of the state council and the parliament, and to the clergy, exhorting them to invest money. The king himself provided a good example: he invested a million (he later increased his investment)—all largely in vain. To be sure, Colbert did succeed in meeting the investment goals in Paris, where he could intervene directly. In the provinces, however, the advertising campaign and the threats and extortion applied in connection with it were by no means so successful. Investments were sparse, grudging, often accompanied by rebellious or inappropriate speeches. The owners of capital who were addressed were skeptical about the newfangled enterprise and remained sitting on their capital like Harpagon on his treasure or invested it in real property; that is, in a metaphorical sense they buried it like Harpagon instead of investing it in colonial trade.[77] Who at court could fail to see what Molière was being ironic about, whom he was attacking, when he mocked and ridiculed the narrow-minded hoarding of treasures?

The Problem of the "Common People" in Molière's Works

The Miser is of great importance for the solution of another problem that scholars up to the present have addressed repeatedly (and in view of their points of departure, their work has necessarily been fruitless or has yielded contradictory, irreconcilable results). While reactionary Molière scholars have tried to misuse Molière for their arguments or for the purpose of falsifying history, another branch of scholarship has gone to the trouble of refuting Molière's cooptation by the forces of reaction by using the (usually positive) presentation of maids and servants in Molière's plays as evidence of his "revolutionary" attitude.[78] I believe it is apparent from the discussion above that the attempts to claim Molière for the reactionary camp are diametrically opposed to historical truth. But the arguments in favor of a "revolutionary" Molière on the basis of his presentation of maids and servants has little to do with historical reality. They rest on a false understanding of what was revolutionary in the seventeenth century or on the assumption of a "revolutionary consciousness" that Molière could not have had and which, if he had had it, would have been objectively false (to borrow our contemporary terminology, it would have been "leftist-radical"). When did maids and servants ever make a revolution? Certainly not in the seventeenth century, and not later either: fundamentally it was in the interest of the common people, the employed masses of the age, to promote trade and manufacturing, even if the exploitation in the manufactures was pitiless and the wages were starvation wages.[79] From an objective, correct viewpoint, that means that at the time of Colbert, even with respect to the employed populace including the "maids and servants," the only people capable of acting in a revolutionary way and hence of representing the interests of the common people were those who represented the interests of the commercial and manufacturing bourgeoisie (which often coincided with the interests of the absolute monarchy) in an active and an ideological way. Molière was one of these; in his plays, with few exceptions, the maid or the servant conspires to help the party that triumphs in the end, the party of *bon sens*, the party of the active, socially useful bourgeoisie or of the court nobility and of the king, who are allied with this bourgeoisie. This context of interest and action is presented in *The Miser* in a particularly exemplary way: not only do Harpagon's children suffer from his avarice (the bourgeois next generation, condemned to inactivity by usury and by what does not appear in this play but otherwise is pilloried time and again, the desire for false *noblesse*), but the common people in general also suffer—the servants Jacques, Frosine, La Flèche. Therefore it is by no means a coincidence but rather a clear political statement when La Flèche digs up Harpagon's treasure and gives it to Cléante, for only Cléante can become active with the capital. The alliance between the young, progressive bourgeoisie willing to run risks and the common people is thus established, but it is intensified in the course of the play: Marianne and Valère are not children of the bourgeoisie but of the nobility. They marry into the young, active bourgeoisie—the political message is clear.

Alceste; or, Optimism

There is one instance in which Molière went beyond representing plebian interests through the bourgeoisie, beyond the alliance between (commercial or manufacturing) bourgeoisie and the common people (peasants, artisans, manufacturing workers), and thus aroused Boileau's pointed displeasure. Shortly before Molière's death, Boileau wrote in *L'art poétique*, 1664: "In this ridiculous sack in which Scapin hides / I no longer recognize the author of the Misanthrope."[80] Boileau's observation is quite correct, and the connection between the *Misanthrope*, 1666, and the *Fouberies de Scapin* (*Scapin the Scamp*, 1671) is no accident. For it is not Scapin who hides himself in a sack; rather, Géronte sticks him into a sack and thrashes him. And Géronte is—a merchant, who has undertaken a sea voyage with his business friend Argante "to look after some business in which they were both interested."[81]

In this late comedy, for the first and only time Molière shows two large-scale merchants as hardhearted individuals, greedy for profits and avaricious, stupid and narrow-minded. The normal alliance between the common people and the (commercial) bourgeoisie becomes for a short moment a class confrontation (Scapin deceives Argante and Géronte, whom he also thrashes) and gives us a glimpse of future confrontations, which must have shocked the convinced representative of the absolutist alliance between bourgeoisie and nobility, Boileau. Molière could perhaps have been the greatest writer of comedies, Boileau believes, but *Scapin*, which he particularly cites in his twisted formulation, prevents us from reaching this judgment, for in *Scapin* Molière showed himself to be too much the "ami du peuple," the "friend of the common people."

No wonder Boileau ranked the *Misanthrope* higher than *Scapin*, since this play coincided with the interests of his party. If one considers Molière's comedies from the point of view of the progressive alliance including the king, the absolutist upper nobility, and the ennobled or non-noble commercial, manufacturing, and financial bourgeoisie, one will find in them an unimpaired revolutionary optimism. The *bon sens* of the acting characters of this social group triumphs again and again (and it triumphs, as we have shown, in alliance with the rest of the Third Estate, the common people). Of course, all these victorious figures were *honnêtes gens*. But as a political thinker Molière could not fail to see that the price of progress, whose artistically perfect propandagist he was in the theater, was contradictions, dishonesties, even crimes. The ideology of *honnêteté* as the expression of the self-contained, well-balanced human being who was in harmony with the society of his age, that very ideal that the bourgeois apologists of later times called upon and call upon to justify the feudal injustice of the seventeenth century, became an internal problem for Molière in all its contradiction. It was not the counterattacks of the reactionary forces whom he had attacked that caused him problems, but the irrefutable criticism from the *conservative* forces, whom one could accuse neither of idleness nor of dishonesty, nor of being ridiculous.

When these morally upright conservative opponents point out the contradictions between the reality of class antagonisms and the harmonious, optimistic ideal of *honnêteté*, oriented toward utility and rationality and represented not only by Molière, then the apologists of the official (Colbertian) policy can easily be suspected of hypocrisy. Boileau, for instance, called for "égalité de l'âme," "spiritual balance,"[82] a quality that was supposed to distinguish the *honnête homme*, and condemned the *faux nobles*[83] who loved empty show or the true nobles who had bought their titles and who proved themselves to be unworthy of their forebears by their *oisiveté*; he damned merchants who thought only of profit (and not of the good of the absolute monarchy as well, of the state), who had no *honnêteté*. This and similar statements almost provoked counterpolemics. François de La Rochefoucauld's (1613-80) *Réflexions ou sentences et maximes morales* appeared in Holland in 1664: "The virtue of worldly people is nothing but a phantom called forth by our passions, to which one gives an honorable name [*nom honnête*] in order to do whatever one wants with impunity," we read in the second maxim, and in the third: "All human virtues are lost in *intérêt* [interest, profit, social position—M. N.], like the rivers lose themselves in the ocean." The fifth maxim contains a whole program: "Shame, laziness, and fear are often the sole causes of keeping us to our duty, while all honor for that is accorded to our virtue."[84]

On the face of it, La Rochefoucauld's maxims represent a systematic destruction of the ideal of *honnêteté* based on social utility, *bon sens*, and unimpeachable virtues; however, they also represent a fundamental destruction of the ideology of the *honnête homme* altogether. La Rochefoucauld performs a thorough investigation of that *honnêteté* based on *utilité* and *bon sens* and discovers behind its ideals *intérêt* and vices, though to be sure, he (like Mandeville after him in England) is willing to grant that vices (such as *intérêt* and pride) have socially useful effects.[85] The maxim "Our virtues are often nothing but disguised vices" corresponds to "There are people who are applauded in society and whose only merit is the vices that make social intercourse easier,"[86] or even to "Interest, which is blamed for all our crimes, often deserves to be praised for our good deeds."[87]

On the basis of his dialectical method of thinking, La Rochefoucauld even comes to insights like "Avarice is more opposed to economy than prodigality,"[88] which however was meant less as praise than as criticism of *liberalité*, prodigality. In any case, the material motives of human action are mercilessly exposed by La Rochefoucauld and the concept of *honnêteté* is called into question: "It is difficult to judge whether an upright and honnête action is the result of integrity or of slyness."[89] And anyone who still clings to this ideal after its demolition must put up with being called a hypocrite: "Hypocrisy is the respect of vice for virtue."[90]

This criticism must have struck Molière, who in his own way tried to expose hypocrisy and immorality, for he answered it with one of his best and most difficult plays, in which he dealt with it passionately, even desperately: *The Misanthrope*. At the very beginning of the play, the misanthrope Alceste terminates his friendship with Philinte, the representative of *bon sens*, of the affirmation of society and of activity within society despite all reservations, because this representative of *bon sens* is a hypocrite. Alceste is a rigorous, conservative judge of morals who tears the mask of *honnêteté* from the world around him by comparing deeds with speeches, with the ideals of *honnêteté* (and that this misanthrope is no insignificant opponent, not a *précieux*, for instance, Molière emphasizes unmistakably: Alceste tears apart a *précieux* poem and praises a folksong as an artistically perfect expression of the true emotions of the common people). In fact, if one applies the misanthrope's own strict measure, he is not wrong: hypocrisy is rampant around him, people bend the law, profiteer, chase after profits, denounce each other, enter into intrigues, lie, and cheat. But Molière does not make fun of this conservative critic (it has occasionally led Molière's interpreters astray that Alceste is not a comic type—no, he is an opponent to be taken seriously, whom one would want for a friend). Molière does not condemn him but confronts all Alceste's criticism with the figure of Philinte, Molière's response to Alceste. Molière confronts the flight from the world (which has Jansenist overtones) that must result from Alceste's total condemnation and denial of society with Célimène, who loves Alceste but who does not want to follow him into isolation from society and who leaves him for that reason, and with Philinte, who affirms the world, affirms the change for the better, even though it must be bought with injustice. And Philinte tries to win even his sharpest critic to the cause of progress: Molière's play ends with Philinte's declaration of intent to realize the goal he had proclaimed in the first act. When

Alceste forbids Philinte to follow him and to try to convince him of the necessity of a realistic attitude toward society, Philinte answers, "Say what you please. I shall stay right beside you."[91]

Janus-Headed Colbert

And still, contradictions were present, as in every society with class antagonisms, and what might seem to the reader of today like a harmless little joke represents a precise political position for the viewer of that time, for Boileau, for example. "It shall need more than a few years in the galleys to daunt a brave heart," as the rebellious Scapin declares in 1671 (336). The subject of discussion is the inhuman practice of using galley slaves, a practice that the king and Colbert not only knew about but expressly ordered. Galley sentences were pronounced for the most insignificant crimes (courts were officially charged with providing galley slaves because reinforcements were hard to come by). Police raids occurred from time to time; hundreds of innocent people were deported from regions where there were peasant revolts and sent to the galleys, where they were chained and treated worse than animals (when French reinforcements dried up, Russians, Turks, Negroes, and Indians suffered this fate: later, after the revocation of the Edict of Nantes in 1685, Protestants were the favored victims). And anyone who was once in the galleys—and this puts Scapin's boast in sharp relief—had every chance of staying there for the rest of his life, of dying there, still chained, even if his sentence had been served sometimes over thirty years ago: "An official report submitted on 5 July 1674...showed the practice of that time with respect to length of sentences. Of thirty-four individuals discussed in the report, eight had been sentenced between 1652 and 1660 for two, four, five, or six years, and they were still in the galleys in 1674."[92]

Did Colbert, the Christian *honnête homme*, know nothing of this? Of course he knew about it, but he thought he needed slaves for his galleys, for the navy that was so dear to him (although galleys did not have much military application). So he passionately conducted a policy of slavery and was bitterly unhappy when galley slaves died out from under him. "It is a great misfortune," Colbert wrote on 5 November 1652 to the Director de la Guette in Toulon, "that new galley slaves are dying every day. No matter what pains you have been taking, you must double them and not omit to do anything in your power to keep them [alive]."[93] A humane impulse? By no means—a question of economics. "A group of people who have a great deal of experience in the galley question," he wrote to De la Guette's successor Pierre Arnoul on 29 March 1669, "say that our galley crews cannot be good because you give the slaves too much freedom and nourish them too well. This is all the worse since nothing counteracts the value of a slave so much as fat and a belly."[94] Two years later he wrote to Arnoul by special order of the king, telling him to release twenty of the hundred slaves who had been chained *past their sentences*; those twenty should be the oldest and the sickest.

> In order to explain His Majesty's will exactly, . . . I must tell you that it is necessary for you to note each year on the sick lists that you send which sicknesses they have. His Majesty wishes that in selecting the ten who are to be released, you choose the oldest, provided that they have sicknesses that are also burdensome. But as to those who have a dangerous sickness like epilepsy, sickness should be considered before age. In buying slaves you must come to an understanding with the Marquis Centurion so that the two of you do not compete with each other.[95]

Colbert wrote this in the same year that the *Fourberies de Scapin* appeared. Two years later, in 1673, the Bishop of Marseille "anxiously" intervened for the first time in favor of the galley slaves who were held past their sentences.[96] Not much changed at first. The *honnête homme* of the seventeenth century was simply a slaveholder, among other things (although certainly not with a perfectly clear conscience). But he was not only a slaveholder, and that obviously makes the presentation of the *siècle classique* so difficult. From 1660 to 1690 there was a huge commercial and manufacturing revolution in France in which tendentious anarchic forces were liberated *within the feudal-absolutist system* without allowing the representative mask of the *roi soleil*, the "sun king," or of the courtiers, the *honnêtes courtisans*, to slip. The *honnête homme* was an artist of courtly ceremony and a slaveholder, a plunderer and a bandit in one. With the same lack of scruple with which Colbert shanghaied galley slaves, he sent young women, orphans or prostitutes, overseas by force to serve as women for the colonists and to populate the colonies for France, to produce children.[97] Any settler who wanted a woman got one; the woman had no choice in the matter. But sometimes the women did not survive the rigors of the sea journey or the work in the new climate. The women who were sent to Canada, as Colbert wrote in 1670 to the Archbishop of Rouen, "proved not robust enough to withstand the climate or the work on the land. It would be better to send peasant girls."[98] To this end, he continued, he was appealing to the archbishop, on whom he certainly could rely, since there was enough poverty in the area around Rouen.

Besides galley slaves and forcibly deported women, Colbert was concerned with a further human object, even more than with these first two since this last was a commercial ware: Negro slaves, whom he mentioned most frequently with the phrase, "commerce de nègres et bestiaux," "trade in Negroes and animals."[99] Colbert gave the French Negro traders free rein: not only were they to export Negroes from Guinea to the West Indies (for which the state paid a bounty per head), but they were allowed to sell Negroes freely to the Spaniards, who were otherwise seen as enemies, "because Negroes are a good that they never disdain."[100] On 10 November 1670 his correspondent de Baas, governor of the Antilles, wrote him about the Negro trade that Negroes were "the best and most valuable ware that can enter this country."[101]

The *Honnête Homme* as Privateer

All of this was of course known to people of the time; it was not hidden and people often made their living from it. Still, people observed the strategy of *honnêteté*, which repeatedly gave critics the opportunity to scourge *fausse honnêteté*, "hypocrisy." Boileau's satire "Sur l'homme" (On the Human Being) of 1667 shows just how prevalant hypocrisy was. Boileau describes the corruption of human beings, who are inferior to animals in every way, since in contrast to animals (unnatural impulses like) ambition, passion, acquisitiveness, and hatred move humans to deeds that cannot be made to harmonize with *égalité d'âme* and *sagesse*, "wisdom." In Boileau's system of vices (which he skillfully contrasts in a dialectical way with the human betrayal of reason), acquisitiveness has first place: all other vices derive from this:

> Le sommeil sur ses yeux commence à s'épancher.
> "Debout," dit l'Avarice, "il est temps de marcher."
> —"Hé laissez-moi."—"Debout."—"Un moment."—
> "Tu repliques?"
> —"A peine le Soleil fait ouvrir les boutiques."
> —"N'importe, leve-toi."—"Pourquoi faire aprés tout?"
> —"Pour courir l'ocean de l'un à l'autre bout,
> Chercher jusqu'au Japon la porcelaine et l'ambre,
> Rapporter de Goa le poivre et le gingembre."
> —"Mais j'ai des biens en foule, et je m'en puis passer."
> —"On ne peut trop avoir; et pour en amasser,
> Il ne faut épargner ni crime ni parjure."[102]

Hardly does sleep leave his eyes, when Avarice says, "Up, it's time to start." "Oh, leave me be." "Up!" "Just one moment." "You're talking back?" "The sun has hardly opened his shop." "That's no matter; get up." "What for?" "To sail the ocean from one end to the other, to look as far as Japan for porcelain and amber, to bring back from Goa pepper and ginger." "But I have plenty of goods, and I can do without more." "You can never have enough; and to amass them, you must fear neither crime nor perjury."

Did Boileau actually condemn the colonial trade that was so dear to Colbert?

No, his strategy was much more nimble than that. Overseas trade must be clothed in an *honnête* costume, or in order to attract the nobility, even a noble, heroic one. In short, here too one had to behave as one did in all other areas of politics and of (courtly) daily life: one had to use the *honnête-homme* strategy to distance oneself from what was practiced. People set up fictional "others" in order as men of honor to disapprove of what the fictional others did, although in reality it was they themselves who were constantly doing the criticized deeds. For that reason Boileau is able to polemicize with pathos and a moral aimed against the acquisitiveness of the merchant who charged his son of tender years to have nothing else in his head than the rate of interest and profit, which must necessarily lead to the development of a poor character. Become hardhearted, my son, the merchant cries to the next generation:

> become an Arab, a privateer,
> be unjust, brutal, deceitful, treacherous, false,
> do not be stupid enough to be generous.
> Bleed the unfortunate dry so you become fat, my son.
> And make your fortune with the atrocities with which you
>   circumvent Colbert's burdensome restraint.[103]

Boileau's last lines indeed show the height of hypocrisy. That Boileau reproaches the merchants of his time with behaving like privateers and committing atrocities to slip past Colbert's moderate policies is an almost cynical claim that can be understood only against the background of the initial quarrels between Colbert and Boileau[104] and the subsequent pointed advances of the poet to the controller general,[105] as well as against the background of the general *honnête-homme* strategy. For Colbert himself made use of piracy in the most varied forms on all levels, just as he allowed any kind of atrocity as long as it yielded a profit. And the most important representative of *honnêteté*, which was allegedly based on piety and actually based on utility, accedes to an argument that is almost Hobbesian to justify his means. In 1669 Colbert wrote a memoir for the king on the question "Which of the two alliances, that with France or that with Holland, can be more advantageous for England?" Colbert states his central idea, from which all else follows: "in war and in peace, trade causes a constant battle among the nations of Europe over who will make the greatest profit. The Dutch, English, and French are the protagonists of this battle."[106] Although Colbert, as an *honnête homme*, modifies his tone shortly afterward and speaks of trade as an "eternal and peaceful war of intelligence and industry among all nations,"[107] we must still conclude that he prepares and practices this (commercial) war in a most Machiavellian, militaristic way. Colbert says that there are twenty thousand ships in Europe, a number that would seem to be sufficient to supply the needs of the continent's population. Thus it is not to be expected that this number would change. But the proportions might: of the twenty thousand ships, the Netherlands has fifteen to sixteen thousand; England has three or four thousand; and France has five or six hundred. If France and England wanted to increase their trade or their merchant marine, this would logically occur at the expense of the Dutch. For that reason England would have an interest in an alliance with France against the Netherlands.

We will not discuss how realistic these views of Colbert's are; instead, we will consider the means he employed to reach the goals he set, which were far from those that Boileau praised as "prudence importune" in contrast to the piratical spirit of the merchants. Colbert saw privateering as an excellent means; he knew it brought much gain to England. Privateering means *faire la course*, and anyone pursuing this line of work was a *corsaire*; the man who financed this business was an *armateur* (the current term for shipowner). But a *corsaire* was a man of honor, and privateering was an honorable business. The *corsaire* was a private person (privateer) who received a so-called *lettre de marque*, a "letter of privilege," from the sovereign. The *lettre de marque* gave him the right to hold up (commercial) ships of the national enemy and to plunder them in time of war. If he was in possession of the *lettre de marque*, he was considered not as a criminal, in contrast to the pirate who operated without a *lettre de marque* but rather on his own; instead, when things went wrong for him he was treated as a prisoner of war.

But these rules were not observed too strictly.[108] The boundaries between piracy and legitimate privateering were fluid, and the legality of the matter depended on the whim of the prince; on the quiet even piracy was always tolerated when it was practiced against the ships of rival nations and when the profits were considerable, either indirectly (through damage to a national rival) or directly (through tribute from the pirate or privateer) (Ranke was still outraged about Mazarin, who split fifty-fifty with *corsaires*).[109] Despite legends to the contrary and despite his official policy toward privateers (especially the famed ordonnance of 1681 that made the *lettre de marque* obligatory and set forth the conditions under which one was permitted to privateer),[110] Colbert did little to contribute to differentiating between piracy and privateering. In 1666, for instance, he expressed his joy at the fact that there were enough *armateurs* along the coast of the English Channel ready to privateer "and disturb English trade."[111] To be sure, not much later he wanted to join with the English in privateering against the Dutch. On 27 March 1672 he wrote to the Lieutenants Généraux of Normandie and of Poitou:

> The decision the king has reached, to declare war against the Dutch on water and on land in a few days, compels His Majesty to bring all means into play in order to conduct the war as vigorously as possible; and he wishes his subjects in the maritime provinces, in addition to the

forces that they will provide on land and on water, to equip the greatest possible number of ships for privateering in order to eliminate [Dutch] merchant ships and to let them feel the anger of the king.[112]

A few years later the Countess of Soissons and Madame de Montespan, in the ship Le Hardy (The Bold One), engaged in privateering;[113] this was probably partly in hopes of the "grand profit" about which Colbert wrote confidently in discussing the war of privateering against Holland.[114]

Colbert's favorite recourse in building his navy was the Normandy privateers who were active in the English channel and whose most famous representative was doubtless Jean Bart. "In 1675 the *Gazette de France* mentions Captain Jean Bart, armateur from Dunkirk, for the first time," and Armel de Wismes continues, telling us that "accompanied by Captain Keyser, he captured twenty-six Dutch fishing boats and two frigates with twelve cannon each, which were accompanying them."[115] Just a year later Jean Bart received a golden chain as a gift of the king.[116] And eighteen years later, during which time Jean Bart had ample opportunity to score magnificent victories against the Dutch and English fleets, he was made a noble.

By the time Bart died in 1702, he had become legendary. But there is no contemporary French literary monument to his deeds. Christian Reuter gave him a small monument in Germany in 1697, with the introductory lines to the second part of *Schelmuffsky*:

> Let the pirate Bart make a show with his corsaires
> Of how he won much booty on the wild sea,
> He will never by far achieve the fame
> That Schelmuffsky won through his travels.[117]

The silence into which Jean Bart disappeared at his death and which is bemoaned by his biographer de Wismes is probably due to the rules of *bienséance* that were still in effect, seemliness within the framework of *honnêteté*, because as late as 1774 the *Nouveau dictionnaire historique-portatif* notes after a report of Bart's life:

> He could neither read nor write, for he had learned only to form his own name. He spoke little and poorly. He knew nothing of the bienséances and expressed himself and behaved like a sailor. When the Chevalier de Forbin brought him to court in 1691, the wags in Versailles said: Let's go look at the Chevalier de Forbin, he has brought a bear along.... [Jean Bart] was quite suited to executing bold deeds, but incapable of carrying out any larger plan.[118]

Even though there was a taboo against the *corsaire*, privateering was still practiced, and that was quite in keeping with the behavior of an *honnête homme*;

one had to watch his every move in order to judge him properly, despite his *honnêteté*. Well into the eighteenth century (it was not until the middle of the nineteenth century that privateering was internationally condemned: by that time it had become insignificant), in an interpretation of the ordonnance of 1681, the jurist René-Joseph Valin (1695-1765) wrote:

> As venerable and established as this manner of warfare is, there are actually so-called philosophers who disapprove of it. According to them, one cannot serve the state and the prince by this means, because the profit that results from it goes to individuals and is illegal or at least detrimental. But that is nothing but the language of bad citizens who are trying to bluff by hiding the actual reason for their indifference toward the weal and advantage of the state behind the impressive mask of a false wisdom and an artificially refined conscience. As much as these are to be censured, just as much should we praise those who generously invest their property and their lives in the dangers of privateering.[119]

To be sure, everything points to the fact that Valin means the philosophes of the Enlightenment, but who exactly he has in mind is hard to determine, because several of these philosophes were passionate partisans of privateering and even of piracy.

The *Aventurier* in the Service of the Absolute Monarchy

Three years before Boileau's satire "Sur l'homme," with its vain polemic against overseas trade, Colbert had founded the *Compagnie des Indes Occidentales*, the "West Indies Trading Company," successor to the *Compagnie des Isles d'Amérique*, furnished with trading patents by Richelieu in 1635. The *Compagnie des Indes Occidentales* was to conduct trade with the West Indies or with the French possessions of Martinique, Guadalupe, and Saint Christophe, which had been conquered by the so-called *aventuriers*. *Aventuriers, boucaniers* (buccaneers), *flibustiers* (freebooters): the concepts are hard to distinguish from each other. The important thing is that the French *aventurier/boucanier/flibustier* of the seventeenth century cannot be equated with the English merchant adventurer (for which reason even Diderot's *Encyclopédie* gives each of them a separate article). To be sure, adventurer and *aventurier* are united by the element in which they move, the sea and ship travel; to be sure, privateering, which can hardly be distinguished from common piracy, is one of the side occupations of the merchant adventurers or of the great trading companies in the sixteenth, seventeenth, and even eighteenth century;[120] still the adventurers (or their captains) remain essentially what they were from the beginning: commercial shippers.

The *aventuriers*, however, originated as pirates or freebooters; they did rise to the rank of legitimate privateers or were so closely related to these that a sharp conceptual division would contradict historical reality. At the beginning of the seventeenth century (they were often Huguenot refugees or emigrants), they appeared together with English freebooters around the islands of the West Indies, calling themselves *flibustiers* or *aventuriers*, and conquered several of the islands occupied by the Spanish, for instance Tortuga. The history of this conquest of colonies by French *aventuriers*, which was probably well known to contemporaries through Oexmelin's *Histoire des aventuriers, flibustiers et boucaniers* (1678-86),[121] is presented in the *Histoire philosophique et politique des établissements et du commerce des européens dans les deux Indes* (Philosophical and Political History of European Possessions and Trade in the Two Indies) by Abbé Guillaume Thomas Raynal, which appeared in three different editions between 1772 and 1781, with the collaboration of Pechmeja and Diderot.[122] After English and French pirates had taken possession of the islands, Raynal reports that they began pirating Spanish trading ships. Spain defended itself and drove the pirates out again, but they were not ready to give up their conquest. Still, they realized

> that they could avoid destruction only if they ceased living in anarchy. They immediately sacrificed individual freedom for a secure society and put Willis, an Englishman,...at their head. Under his leadership, toward the end of 1683, they again took possession of an island they had held for eight years; and in order not to be driven out again, they fortified it.[123]

The English soon tried to make the French totally dependent on them, which provoked "the partisanship of the national spirit"[124] in the French pirates. They therefore turned to the governor of the French king, De Poincy, who drove out the English and guaranteed the French pirates sole dominance over the island. "These enterprising people," as a chapter heading in Raynal reads, "are recognized by the court at Versailles when their position became firm, and they are given a governor."[125]

> In the meantime the progress of this adventure was slow and did not attract the attention of the mainland until 1665. It was not that not enough corsaires and pirates had been seen roaming about from one island to another; but the number of farmers, who were the real colonists, was very restricted. It was felt to be necessary to increase that number, and a nobleman by birth from Anjou, named Bertram Dogeron, was put in charge of this difficult matter.[126]

In plain language, when the court noticed that piracy was both lucrative and detrimental to national rivals, it turned its attention to the conquests of the pirates and placed itself de facto at their head. (Aristocratic) governors were appointed to supervise the pirates; they placed no restrictions on piracy itself, but were charged with conducting the actual policy of colonization, that is, settling French colonists and building up colonial production (plantations, especially for sugar cane).

> The execution of this plan was full of difficulties. It was a matter of establishing social order on the ruins of a wild anarchy; of bringing independent piracy under the hallowed and strict order of the laws; of reawakening human feelings in souls which had become hardened by vice; of replacing destructive murder weapons with the innocent tools of agriculture. Making barbarians, used to leisure and the companions of their craving for piracy, decide in favor of an industrious life; inspiring violent men with patience... to prefer the taste for peace to thirst for blood, to inspire with the fear of danger those who found pleasure in seeking it out, and with respect for life those who held it in contempt; finally to teach those who had respect for nothing and who were in a position to deal freely with all nations to respect the privileges of an exclusive society that was established in 1664 for all French colonies.[127]

Chapter 12
The Decay of the Alliance and the Departure of the Nobility

The Failed Integration of Primitive Accumulation

The insoluble dilemma in which the absolute monarchy found itself is illustrated more clearly than almost anything else by the monarch's, or Colbert's, attempt to exploit the wildest, or as Raynal says, most anarchic manifestation of primitive accumulation for the absolute monarchy, by trying to integrate it into the rigid system of administration and order. Raynal notes this attempt with great acuteness despite his tendency to moralize. The *aventuriers* had conquered the islands, had acquired wealth with their piracy against Spanish ships; now the monarchy wanted to pocket the profits it had had no part in generating. The *aventuriers* were not in agreement. Despite the "partisanship" of their "national spirit," they were by no means ready to share their profits with the king. But the governor Dogeron was an extremely skilled tactician, and, as Raynal writes with involuntary cynicism, "his views infused his upright spirit with only noble and just means."[1] One of the "noble and just means" was that he provided the *aventuriers* with "patents from Portugal in order to attack the Spaniards even after they had made peace with France. That was the only way to keep the national allegiance of men who would rather have become enemies of their country than give up piracy."[2]

This process has an exemplary character above and beyond its status as anecdote. Although we cannot say that the colonial undertakings of Richelieu, Colbert, and their successors were completely unsuccessful, they can by no means be compared with the English or Dutch undertakings. The reason is that within France, where the basis would have to have been established for French participation in primitive accumulation, this accumulation took place only in the tamed and restricted, government-directed enterprises of Colbert and his successors. Where manufactures should have become industrial plants, *manufacture dispersée*, "cottage industry," which Diderot's *Encyclopédie* still considers the best form of production,[3] remained the dominant form. And where trade should have allowed manufacturing or industrial mass production to circulate, it stagnated, except for the *traite*, the Negro trade in Bordeaux and Nantes; at most it had a false boom once in a while, as in John Law's brilliant but hopeless experiment of a bank to finance overseas trade between 1716 and 1720.[4] Even where it seemed possible to participate in certain forms of primitive accumulation, as for instance in the West Indies, the circumstances in France prevented these attempts from bearing fruit. Over and over, literature on the subject blames governmental overdirection for the failure of Colbert's attempts and those of his successors. It is doubtless true that this contributed to the failure, but it was not the main cause. This becomes clear when we look at Colbert's own policies, because while he did repeatedly inhibit the development with his regulations, we must not overlook the fact that he was hindering his *own* undertakings, that he issued all these regulations in order to move the development forward or to initiate it in the first place! He was the one pushing ahead and trying to secure France's participation in the international development that was sustained or set in motion by primitive accumulation, and if his methods ran counter to this attempt, in whole or in part, it was not because he fettered primitive accumulation, but because even the means of primitive accumulation did not provide the basis for liberating the capitalist mode of production.

When we compare the situation in France with that in England before the Revolution of 1649, we can abstract from the details and state that the slow development in France cannot be due to underdevelopment of manufacturing technology. Colbert not only imported whole branches of production into France, but also employed the most important domestic and foreign scientists (not least in the Académie des Sciences, which he founded) in activities such as the development of manufacturing, shipbuilding, and road construction. Such clear progress was made in all these areas that with the exception of agriculture, France reached among the highest standards on a world scale; at least the state of technological development in all areas was superior to that of the English means of production at the beginning of the seventeenth century. We must therefore ask what the French situation lacked in comparison to the English situation of that age. The obvious answer is the industrializing of agriculture, analyzed in detail by Marx; such industrializing not only provided raw materials for the production of the English manufactures, but also liberated the workers who were needed by the manufactures and who constituted the early stage of the modern proletariat.

These two crucial factors, *together* with commercial capitalism and the manufactures or their technology of production, revolutionized the relations of production in England. They did not exist in France; in view of the political and legal, feudal-agrarian constitution of the absolute monarchy, they could not exist there. A fundamental change, a revolutionary upheaval in the direction of modern capitalism could not take place within this system unless events occurred in the system that could have results similar to those of the two factors mentioned above. (To that extent, it was quite justified for the thinking of the leading economists of the time, from Boisguillebert to Quesnay, to center around agriculture,[5] even though they did not understand the interconnections, especially with the development of manufacturing production.) In a feudal-agrarian system of production, factors analogous in effect to the English "agricultural revolution" could only be a sudden surplus in production and a simultaneous demographic explosion; in fact, both of these events occurred between 1730 and 1770. We will not explore the manifold reasons for these two events, which are in part still unexplained today.[6] Nor will we investigate the differences between this situation and that of England before 1649. Of course, there were other contributing factors (political-ideological factors not least of all), but we can state that only this situation, which shared similar events with the English situation (though they were differently motivated), this coincidence of in part highly developed commercial capitalism, highly developed technology of production (although it was not fully applied), more or less underdeveloped manufactures, agrarian surplus production, and population explosion[7] created a condition that was objectively revolutionary, that is, ripe for revolution, so that a spark—the relative crisis after 1770—was enough to ignite political revolution.[8] Bourgeois scholarship has always cited the French Revolution, as a revolution in a feudal, agrarian country, to refute Marx's thesis about the origin of modern capitalism (and the fact that the revolution did not break out during one of the numerous crises but rather in an era of relative prosperity has always caused particular bafflement),[9] but this analysis bears out the Marxian thesis exactly.

It is in a certain sense misleading that scholars always talk about the failure of Colbert's policies. In fact, Colbert systematically and almost completely tested the efficiency of the whole economy, the developmental potential of commercial and manufacturing capitalism within a feudal-agrarian monarchy. To the extent he approved of the monarchy, Colbert may have felt as a personal tradegy the limitation of this developmental potential. But in truth the whole system turned out to be a brake on the realization of his plans for commercial and manufacturing capitalism, a fetter on the capitalist mode of production. Finances were exhausted by wars that were in the last analysis useless for the development of productive forces, wars started by Louis XIV to Colbert's despair and leading to the policy of excessive taxation. That is only one expression of the inefficiency inherent in the system, which also had repercussions on the political-intellectual front. Quite early on, therefore, ideological contradictions were kindled by this inefficiency in the system; the progressive alliance between monarchy and bourgeoisie soon lost the élan of the early 1760s and crumbled into groups more or less hostile to each other, until as a consequence of the development after 1770, of which we have given only a basic sketch, antagonism between the classes became ever more open. But up to that point, there was no real *practical* alternative to the way the whole society was constituted, and this lack also helps to explain the internal contradictions of the oppositional literature (for instance, the fundamental affirmation of the absolute monarchy by the ideologues of the Enlightenment, the philosophes).

Jacques de Caillière and the *Noblesse Commerçante*

The external sign for the decay of the alliance between monarchy and progressive bourgeoisie is the transfer of the court, and hence of the entire upper nobility, to Versailles in the seventies. Up until then, the movement toward consolidating the absolute monarchy and subjugating the oppositional feudal nobility had been sustained by the king and the absolutist nobility and bourgeoisie in common. In concrete terms, the absolutist nobility had still moved through the country with sword in hand, physically defeating the opposition. Now, after the oppositional feudal nobility had submitted itself to the monarchy, the nobility as a whole lacked a goal for further movement, further development. Colbert was pointing the bourgeoisie in the direction of developing its productive forces, but the nobility was left only the option of settling at court and becoming integrated into the courtly ritual. Settling in Versailles therefore signaled the moment when the upper nobility left the common movement and deserted the alliance. From that time on estrangement began; even Louis XIV and Colbert became estranged. When Colbert died, only the shared joy at his death united the alienated factions. In one of the numerous satiric poems issued on this occasion we read (in prose translation): "I have seen how the whim of profit-mad Colbert overturned the holiest laws of the state, how it attacked the nobility and oppressed the innocent [the common people—M. N.] and without scruple offended against right and law."[10]

Of course, it is the grudge-bearing feudal nobility speaking, from behind the mask of a friend of the people, for even in the ritualized inactivity at court, the most varied forces continued to mourn the lost past. By the way, not all the nobility took the path to inactivity, and not all who took it did so gladly (although the majority enthusiastically submitted for the price of a role in the courtly ritual). Many chose from the outset the path of resigned, conservative opposition (like La Rochefoucauld) or that of optimistic, scientific, artistic, or philosophical opposition (in approximation to the bourgeois intellectuals). Many others decided for political exile (like Saint-Evremond). There were even attempts—at least in the initial phases—to break through the ritualized fixity and to compete actively with the bourgeoisie. An especially interesting example is that of Jacques de Caillière (d. 1697), "maréchal de Bataille des Armées du Roi" (general of the Royal Armies), who published *La fortune des gens de qualité et des gentilshommes particuliers: enseignant l'art de viure à la cour, suiuant les maximes de la politique et de la morale* (Success of People of Talent and Superior Noblemen: A Handbook for Life at Court, Following Political and Moral Guidelines, 1658). Scholars have not dealt with this work in detail, perhaps because Maurice Magendie in his fundamental work on *Politesse mondaine et les théories de l'honnêteté* classifies it under the only aspect that interests him—and therefore wrongly—as one of the guides to *honnêteté*.[11] To be sure, Caillière (of course) applies the concept of *honnêteté*, but as his title makes clear, he is interested in something else. He pits his handbook (which, tellingly enough, is dedicated to one of the former leaders of the *Fronde*, the Duc de Longueville) against the bourgeois attitude toward life, based on *travail, utilité,* and *activité*. The aristocrat is to learn from Caillière's book how and with what activity he can resist the competition of the bourgeoisie.

Caillière's thoughts on Fortuna, who appears programmatically in the title, represent a variation on La Mothe le Vayer's thoughts:[12] in the dedication he writes that he is declaring war on Fortuna, and in the first chapter he states that there is no Fortuna as such, but rather only accidents that are basically explicable but are usually not understood by human beings. Caillière (again following La Mothe le Vayer) does not claim that these accidents are foreseeable and hence avoidable; rather he wants to show a human being (that is, a noble), who is "less weak than average"[13] and who can demonstrate with his experience how to defy coincidence and hence how to conquer Fortuna.

In fact much in this curious work sounds like an anticipation of the morality of the "master race" of later centuries (it is quite conceivable that Caillière was influenced by the *Oraculo manual* of Gracián, 1647). It is a question of success at any price:

> I am writing neither for the weak nor for the obdurate: it is the scatterbrain's own fault if he loses his way instead of following his leader. Our reason protects us from falls and abysses but it does not prevent them from existing, and it would be stupid not to cross a bridge because one could drown if one fell off.[14]

"Poverty is a monster that must be fought with every weapon," Caillière writes and recommends that the noble who needs money engage in financial speculation.[15] Success, fortune, is the highest maxim, and decisiveness, an entrepreneurial spirit, courage are needed to bend fortune to one's will. Caillière assumes (despite royal decrees to the contrary) that the noble who conducts trade will lose his privileges. For that reason many nobles refrain from conducting trade:

> Only with discomfort can I look at the situation of a second-born son [who is hence not the primary heir—M. N.] from a good house who is equipped by nature with a beautiful and generous soul but who is forced by necessity to seek his own fortune and social position. His social position [being a noble—M. N.], which seemingly should be to his credit, is only a burden, constitutes an impediment to his happiness and bars the ways for him that the laws open for non-nobles to gain wealth. Among others I find that law particularly harsh that forbids him to engage in trade. It seems to be based on principles that must be very weak, since it is so categorical. For in order to forbid something, this thing must either be bad in itself or must at least show bad effects. But can one censure trade as ruinous without insulting all the nations of the world? Is there anything more firmly established among human beings and more generally approved? The benefit is so great that it could not be eliminated without jolting all of civil society [*toute la société de la vie civile*]! It is trade that populates the large cities, it is trade that produces all the wealth and prosperity of the nations. . . . Are those effects that would be unworthy of the activity of a nobleman?[16]

It is already unusual for a nobleman to recommend the pursuit of trade to the nobility; the reasons Caillière gives to justify his praise of trade are still more unusual. They anticipate an argument that scholars date a century later; it is attributed to the treatise *La Noblesse commerçante* by the Abbé Coyer, 1765, although in view of the (in part almost verbatim) correspondences between Caillière and Coyer, one can assume that Coyer knew Caillière's treatise. This argument is of particular interest for the origin of the modern ideology of adventure in France. Caillière writes that people say trade is incompatible with the duties of the nobility, which is obligated to military service. But can all nobles perform military service? In reality, things look very different: the younger nobles, excluded from inheritance, are so poor—especially in the provinces—that they neither would be encouraged to perform military service nor would they see in it possibilities for rising in society:

> The conclusion to be drawn from the claim that chasing them out of their home is a means of sending them to war is not always correct: there are many living unhappily in the provinces who would serve as brave men in the army if they only had the appropriate equipment [*équipage*] and the means to finance it: poverty has such a depressing effect [*un ie ne sçay quoy de pesant*], that it robs some men of their courage and drives others to despair.[17]

These prejudices against trade are not shared by other nations. In Holland, for instance, nobles serve in the armies of merchants: "If this profession is so beneath the dignity of a noble that nobles cannot practice it, why do they serve in the armies of these merchants whom they acknowledge as their masters and whose pay they take?" The answer is very important for our purposes: trade and military service, *commerce* and *courage militaire*, are not only not incompatible, but inseparable.

> If one wants to allow nobles to pursue only military service, is there anything that can be combined so well with it as trade? The two things together have allowed the virtue of numerous great men to blossom, whose memory will never die. Do we know of anything more daring than the journeys of Paul Deruis, of Drake, and of Magellan? Do we read of more resolute undertakings than those of Pacheco, of Albuquerque, and of Soares in the New World? Would we not have to do without all the lovely things we enjoy in Europe if these famous merchants had not discovered them? Could they have planned such great projects if they were not great and noble spirits? And could they have realized them so successfully if their courage were not greater than the greatest dangers and their perseverance not equal to the greatest difficulties? Is there a better way to spread the glory and the name of our king to the other end of the world?[18]

Fortune-Hunters, Swindlers, Charlatans

Colbert did not find a propagandist in Caillière. On the contrary, the treatise arose out of an undirected feudal reaction against the bourgeoisie and hence also against Colbert. Despite the great difference in aesthetic quality, *La fortune des gens de qualité* belongs to the same ideological line as La Fontaine's praise of *aventure*. La Fontaine never forgave Colbert for bringing about the fall of his friend and patron, the finance minister Nicolas Foucquet, in 1661. The satiric poem La Fontaine wrote on the occasion of Colbert's death in 1683 is not the only expression of this rancor. His fables again and again mount polemics against Colbert's plea for overseas trade. In 1668, for instance, in the "Fable of the Shepherd and the Sea," La Fontaine says expressly that it is not casual advice but quite serious that one should avoid being seduced by sea trade and by delusions of grandeur, since for everyone who profits thereby there are ten thousand who bemoan it: "The sea makes shameless promises: / Watch out for the wind and the pirates!"[19]

La Fontaine's unfocused praise of risk in "Les deux aventuriers et le talisman" corresponds to his warning about overseas trade. Two "seigneurs aventuriers" (noble adventurers) are challenged to run an apparently senseless risk, and the survivor will receive an unknown prize. One of the two *aventuriers* declines the risk, the other takes it and wins—a kingdom. He wins (in contrast to Bassanio) blindly: "Blind Fortuna follows blind daring," writes La Fontaine and continues, "The wise man would sometimes do well to act first instead of leaving wisdom time to examine the matter."[20] Caillière writes in this same sense: "Great men have always loved danger."—"All great men have been adventurers." "The search for uncertain triumph"[21] is a mark of greatness, and "the world admires the conqueror."[22] If we think of Boileau and Fontenelle, these are very problematic utterances, to say the least. If despite everything they could be connected with some kind of heroic ideal (although such ideals could hardly appear attractive to nobles who were struggling to get to court), then the threshold to tasteless impossibility was crossed at the latest with Caillière's proposal for winning a fortune by gambling with dice: "I have always held that a tendency to gambling is a benefice of nature whose utility I have recognized."[23]

To be sure, there was gambling at the court,[24] but not as a form of livelihood; it was a diversion. But Caillière is not satisfied with even this out-of-place proposal; another of the many suggestions he makes to impoverished nobles is to don a cassock: "How many people of good background would don one if they recognized its advantages [i.e., that they could use it to make their fortune—M. N.]."[25] This is, of course, advice for creatures like Tartuffe (Molière's comedy appeared six years after Caillière's treatise) or for the Marquis who fleeces Monsieur Jourdain in *The Would-Be Gentleman*: advice for cheats and degraded, depraved nobles, with whom the upper nobility neither identified nor wanted to be grouped.

In fact, Caillière's treatise also expresses the malaise of the impoverished petty nobility that could not find a place at court or that preferred to avoid the court hierarchy for whatever reasons. But anyone who avoided this hierarchy lost his social connection to the courtly nobility, became an exotic element, a "court hustler" or *amuseur* in the best case, otherwise a fortune-hunter or swindler. One of the better sort of fortune-hunter, still possessed of the sympathetic youthful aureole of recklessness, was the famous Comte Philibert de Gramont (1621-1707), whose memoirs were published in 1713 by his brother-in-law Antoine Hamilton (1645-1720) and whose activities in Paris, London, and Italy amused or inflamed the courtly world. Gramont led a turbulent life between knightly soldiering and gambling (we will omit the details). What interests us is that the report on his deeds and those of his friend Matta once again buries the ideal of the *chevalier* (this time without the heroic stature we saw in Corneille). Hamilton, who did not hesitate to call Matta and Gramont *aventuriers*, distinguishes this new type of "knight" ironically from the ideal of the knight-errant of the Middle Ages:

> Fame in weaponry is only half of the glory that surrounds heroes.
> Love must complete the relief of their characters: in their struggles, in the boldness of their undertakings, and in the glory of their successes.

Fame in weaponry is only half of the glory that surrounds heroes. Love must complete the relief of their characters: in their struggles, in the boldness of their undertakings, and in the glory of their successes. We know of examples, not only in romances but also in the actual history of glorious warriors and of the most significant conquerors. The Chevalier Gramont and Matta, who hardly thought about these examples, did not omit to dream that it would be good to recover from the efforts of the seige of Trino [near Novara in Piemont— M. N.] by beginning a seige to the disadvantage of the beautiful women and husbands of Turin.... So they set off, a little like Amadis or Don Galaor after being knighted, to look for aventures, riding out for love, war, and magic. They were worthy of these two brothers, for even though they could not split any giants [with their swords—M. N.], smash armour, or carry lovely maids on their horses without speaking with them about something, they knew how to play cards, and the others did not.[26]

Thirty years after Gramont, Count Claude-Alexandre de Bonneval was born. He quickly became a legend, and his inauthentic memoirs, probably written by a group of Catholic freethinkers, appeared in London and The Hague in 1737: the *Mémoires du Comte de Bonneval*, a "roman pseudo-historique" about the life of the count whom Jean Sgard called "a feudal lord and a condottiere, a man of honor and an adventurer."[27] In this epoch, Sgard writes, there arose a new "type of adventurer philosopher":

These adventurers seem to go through the same course of experience: they are both libertine and sentimental, fortune-hunters and utopians.... They no longer rely on disorder, superstition, alchemy, arcane knowledge. Only a few of them from now on are without an economic plan, a financial system, a project for world peace or the draft of a system of belief that they want to present to the Sultan of Morocco or of Turkey.[28]

The answer to Sgard's question why no novelist has written about these "new heroes" is actually obvious. What Sgard considers new and correctly considers remarkable has lost its connection once and for all with the real powers of French society. Knight-errantry has long since ceased to exist, the upper nobility is resident at court, and the bourgeoisie can at first make relatively little of these existences, which are removed from the stage of the actual class confrontation in one way or another (whether the new heroes live the fringe existence of a criminal like the figures in Lesage's *Turcaret*, 1709, a meaningless gambler's existence like that of Chevalier Riccaut de la Marlinière in Lessing's *Minna von Barnhelm* [1760-63], or the existence of a magical mystifier of the type of Joseph Balsamo, called Count Alexandre de Cagliostro).

The Courtier Is Not an *Honnête Homme*

Although figures like Gramont or Bonneval were and remained basically alien to the bourgeoisie, they were still fascinating and enjoyable, especially since this type of adventurer without a position confronted the bourgeoisie with the decay of certain social relations and ideals of humanity that had become useless.[29] For of course neither the bourgeois public sphere nor the court moralists could overlook the fact that, after Colbert's death and after the secret marriage of Louis XIV and Madame de Maintenon, the courtly nobility underwent a serious crisis from which it would not recover.[30] This crisis was signaled by figures like the aristocratic "court hustlers" and gamblers as well as by the decay of aristocratic ideals including the knightly ideal. To be sure, as Robert Mandrou has demonstrated,[31] the knightly romance was still being consumed as mass entertainment literature, but we must also agree with Lew S. Gordon, who warns against giving this fact too much weight:[32] the knightly romances did not correspond to the objective needs of the bourgeoisie, to say nothing of the needs of the exploited masses, who also had access to political and philosophical treatises and pamphlets through chapbooks.[33] No one who wanted to confront the actual problems of the time could find anything of value in the knightly romances. Thus the commentary of the Jesuit *Dictionnaire de Trévoux*, reminiscent of *The Tatler* or *The Spectator*, is appropriately ironic: "There are people who suffer from the need to find adventures, and certain romantic spirits [*esprits Romanesques*] who set out on adventures. Don Quijote wanted to imitate the old paladins who went out in search of adventure."[34]

Even the upper nobility in Versailles—indeed, especially this nobility—could find nothing with which to oppose the decline of the heroic-noble ideal. On the contrary, the nobles themselves felt emptied, useless, without function—except for the one coveted, desired, despised function: being part of a decorative ritual. As Norbert Elias says, "Etiquette was borne unwillingly, but it could not be breached from within, not only because the king demanded its preservation, but because the social existence of the people enmeshed in it was bound to it."[35]

The crisis had been growing latently from the very beginning, as is clear in the writings of the most important theorist of the courtly aristocratic view of *honnêteté*, Antoine Gombaud, Chevalier de Méré (1607-84). His goal was to reconcile the ideal of *honnêteté* with the reality of the courtiers' existence at court, that is, with their fundamental inactivity and lack of social function. A great variety of difficulties had to be overcome in this attempt: for instance, how was the idealization of the inactive courtier existence to be made compatible with the ideal of a warrior hero to which the absolute monarch laid claim? In his posthumous *Discours de la vraie honnêteté* (1700), Méré, who with a certain (perhaps unconscious) distance had called the Crusaders "aventuriers" in his *Avantures de Renaud et d'Armide* (1678; inspired by Tasso's *Gerusalemme*) proposes a solution to the problem that occupied him all his life, as for instance his *Conversations* of 1668-69 demonstrate. He states that there is a fundamental difference between an *honnête homme* and an *honnête conquérant*, or "conqueror": the *honnête homme* must always remain *honnête*, but the conqueror must be *honnête* only during his time as conqueror. For that reason he places the *honnête homme* above every other human being, including the conqueror or the warrior hero, and his prototype of the *honnête homme* is the French courtier—a last attempt by the powerless great nobility to claim a little independence from or superiority to the absolute monarch through the ideal of *honnêteté*. War, as one of the discussants says in the *conversations* of 1668-69, "is the best profession in the world, we must all agree on that, but to be precise, the honnête homme has no profession."

The lack of profession or function that Méré postulates for the *honnête homme*, which is nothing other than the sublimation of the courtier's real lack of function, is elevated to a true ideal, the origin and precondition for realizing the ideal. The concept of *honnêteté*, Méré writes in the first *Discours de la vraie honnêteté*, is unique. It existed neither in the ancient world nor in Italy, Spain, England, or Germany, but only in France, and more precisely, at the French court. Everywhere else

> every individual devotes himself to a certain profession and those who are obligated to a profession hardly acknowledge any other goal than to succeed in it. But since the French court is the largest and most beautiful ever known, and since it is often so quiet that even the outstandingly active [*les meilleurs Ouvriers*] have nothing to do but rest [*se reposer*], there have always been certain idlers without a profession [*certains Fainéans sans métier*] who were certainly not without merit and whose only thought was to live well and to entertain themselves. It could be that we have them to thank for this important word [*honnêteté*—M. N.], and they are usually attractive minds and true hearts, proud and well raised, bold and modest people who are neither acquisitive nor ambitious, who place no value on reigning or occupying the first place at the side of the king.[36]

The accuracy of Méré's sociological classification of the origin of the courtly aristocratic version of *honnêteté* based on *repos, oisiveté*, even *fainéantise*, among the disempowered, unoccupied great nobility at the court is astonishing. Méré's description also clearly reveals the inherent contradictions and potential conflicts in this concept of *honnêteté*, especially since the action-oriented faction around Colbert was propagating a quite opposite ideal, one that could not be accepted by the courtiers. Both the ideal of *honnêteté* based on *activité* and that based on *oisiveté* were represented at court, as long as the fundamentally progressive alliance between monarchy and bourgeoisie lasted, and the two different views confronted each other as expression of antibourgeois, feudal-aristocratic class interests on the one hand and bourgeois class interests on the other, irreconcilable as a matter of principle. But while the concept of *honnêteté* based on *activité* implied change and movement into the future, the concept of the courtly nobles based on *oisiveté* implied preservation of the status quo, stagnation, the socially marginal—a defensive strategy.

At the latest when the progressive alliance between monarchy and bourgeoisie began to decay, the defensive ideological position of the courtly nobility, the courtiers, became obvious and was immediately registered by the moralists at court and by the representatives of the church. The clerics—Bourdaloue, Massillon, and others—took the offensive in defending the system and hence attacked the bourgeoisie (see the Church's polemic against the *commerçant/ négociant*, cited by Groethuysen in *Die Entstehung der bürgerlichen Welt- und Lebensanschauung in Frankreich* [Halle/Saale, 1927-30], a work rich in material). The courtly moralists, at least those who had not fallen victim to heroic pessimism like La Rochefoucauld, drafted new ideals in their criticism of the nobility. For the ideal of *honnêteté* as represented by Colbert or Boileau or Molière, based on *utilité* and *travail* or *activité*, is of course of no use to courtiers whose only function was to perform in the courtly ritual (about which Saint-Simon's memoirs give us the best information). Even Gracián's heroic ideal, which was propagated especially by the Jesuit reaction of 1685-1716,[37] found no response, not least because of its ascetic, intellectual components.

La Bruyère made an attempt to give criticism a new orientation, fundamentally affirming the nobility, although in his plea for the equality of magistrates and the nobility of the sword he admits that he does not understand the actual problems. In 1689, when the nobility in fact hardly fought any longer, he wrote:

> The noble risks his life for the good of the state and the glory of the prince, the magistrate [*noblesse de robe*] relieves the prince of part of his cares in judging the people: on both sides those are excellent functions of wonderful utility. Human beings are hardly capable of greater accomplishments, and I do not know why robe and sword think they have the right to hold each other in contempt.[38]

The upper nobility derived its right to hold the *noblesse de robe* in contempt from necessity. Since it could no longer orient itself by means of positive values, it tried to give itself value through negation. The noble who can afford to, La Bruyère states ironically in the same year, constantly praises his descent from a great house in conversation, "introduces his paternal and maternal ancestors into all his conversations, and even finds a little place for the *oriflamme* [the old French royal banner—M. N.] and the Crusades . . . ; he places value on having an old castle with towers, battlements, and balconies and at every opportunity says, my origins [*ma race*], my branch of the family, my name, and my weapons."[39] Another external means of distinguishing himself from the "merchant or peasant," mocks La Bruyère, is in the way the nobility names its members. Let the people name their children after saints and apostles and martyrs, Jean, Jacques, Pierre, or whatever, "we great ones" however should choose "profane [that is, not traditional Christian—M. N.] names" like "Hannibal, Caesar, Pompeius," but also "Renaud, Roger, Olivier and Tancrède: they were paladins, and there are no more wonderful heroes of novels than they."[40]

This kind of naming from the realm of old French *chevalerie* that La Bruyère mocks shows feudal-noble, antiabsolutist tendencies. It will come into its own later in the *Etat de la France* by Count Henri de Boulainvilliers (published in 1727-28).[41] This, and the waspishness of La Bruyère's remarks, demonstrate how lacking in orientation the nobility was, how it was looking for a foothold and—without this of course being a solution to the problem—was falling back on the stylish attitudes of the *précieux*. But La Bruyère is not only waspish toward the nobility. He also criticizes certain symptoms in the bourgeoisie. To be sure, he censures the courtier, reproaches him with hypocrisy, with *fausseté*, "falsity,"[42] censures his *fainéantise*,[43] but he also makes fun of "certain private persons" ("certains particuliers") who, "having become rich through the nobility of their fathers,"[44] now suddenly are imitating the nobility, the courtiers. Indeed, what disturbs La Bruyère about this type of bourgeois goes back once more to the courtier, about whom he has almost nothing positive to say. If his judgment does not fully annihilate the nobility, that is less out of sympathy for the courtier than from lack of political insight or lack of an alternative. He does not erect a positive new ideal of humanity (or of nobility), as even La Rochefoucauld tried to do, and La Bruyère's admission that he would rather be one of the "rude folk" than one of the "spoilt great ones," the result of pity and a sense of justice, is troubled by no thought of a revolution in social relations; he would have abhorred that, as his commentary on the Glorious Revolution proves.

What holds for La Bruyère tends to hold for Fénelon as well, but while La Bruyère finds only "certains courtisans" suspect and still distinguishes between the "gens aventuriers et hardis," the adventuring, bold people who appear at court as fortune-hunters, and the courtiers he evaluates positively,[45] for Fénelon, as early as 1712, the concept *courtisan* can no longer can be used in a positive sense:

> The métier of a competent courtier destroys everything in a state. Very often it is the stupidest and most corrupt minds that learn this unworthy métier the best. This métier spoils all the rest: the doctor neglects his medicine; the prelate forgets the duties of his calling; the general of the army thinks more about his career at court than about defending the state.... The art of excelling at court spoils the people of all professions and smothers true merit.[46]

Like Fénelon, Diderot considers the concepts *courtisan* and *honnête homme* to be irreconcilable. In the *Encyclopédie* article "Cour" (Court) he writes, with reference to Montesquieu, that beneath the varnish of fine courtly manners are hidden:

> ambition in laziness, baseness in arrogance, the desire to become rich without working, a disinclination toward the truth, flattery, betrayal, perfidy, the breach of every promise, contempt for the duties of a citizen...in a word, indecency and all its entourage [*la malhonnêteté avec tout son cortège*], in the guise of the most genuine honnêteté.[47]

D'Alembert follows suit with outrage, also in the *Encyclopédie*. In the article "Courtisan" he notes that this is a concept "that must not be confused with the 'homme de la cour,'" the (useful) "court official." It refers rather to that sort of person whom the bad luck of kings and nations has placed between kings and the truth. And after D'Alembert has given some advice, quite in the manner of Fénelon, on how the wise king should behave with respect to the courtier, he comes back to the difference between the courtier and the *homme de la cour*. It could happen, he says, that even an honorable man could be brought to court by his duties without becoming a courtier. But there he would have to become a misanthrope, although even that is only a means to success under some circumstances. In any case, it is impossible to be a philosophe at court, to say nothing of being both philosophe and courtier, and when D'Alembert closes ironically by saying that there are perhaps such philosophes, it is clear that the courtier is neither a philosophe nor an *honnête homme* but rather the scourge of the nation, its elitist, parasitical dregs. And thus the *chevalier*, via the *cortegiano* and the *honnête homme à la cour*, ends his career in history.

Mortal Risk; or, Senseless Resistance

If anything is obvious, it is that this social group and its moral and intellectual condition could not generate an ethical renewal, could not draft a new ideal of humanity, could not mobilize ideological or moral resistance to the rising bourgeoisie. Luc de Clapiers, Marquis de Vauvenargues (1715-47), who was radically opposed to the social changes, the rise of the bourgeoisie, faced a serious dilemma in his attempt to offer resistance to the age that seemed decadent in his eyes by drafting a new ideal of humanity. He wanted poor and rich to continue to exist: nature—later he will call on God's will here—will always see to it that the more intelligent, the more industrious, the cleverer person will rise above all those who are stupid, lazy, and reckless. "All means employed against this," he writes, "have been in vain: art cannot make people equal against the will of nature."[48] Vauvenargues is opposed to "les bas fonds," "the common people."[49] But he is also against the bourgeoisie, whom he despises and whose system of virtues, based on *intérêt*, desire for profits, he detests: "Trade is a school of deceit," he states laconically, and declares that many "bourgeois... lounge about idle in the cities and withhold their industry and their work from the kingdom."[50]

But Vauvenargues is not only opposed to *les bas fonds* and the bourgeoisie; he is also against the nobility as it currently exists: "Arrogance is the affair of the nobility just as rudeness is the affair of the people: the bourgeoisie borrows from both of them."[51] From this point we can determine Vauvenargues's position: he is on the side of the great aristocrats, the aristocratics of the intellect, the elite. Like Gracián, he is standing in an intellectual no-man's-land between the classes, on outpost duty in the irrational with his face turned toward the void, toward death: "Nobility," as Vauvenargues defines it, "is the preference for honor instead of profit (intérêt); baseness the preference for profit instead of honor."[52] That cannot be the point of view of the real nobility, the point of view of the still-dominant class.

But Vauvenargues is not talking about this real class as a whole. The *chevalier* and the courtier are not even worth his contempt; he ignores them. Thus he censures even La Rochefoucauld, whom he otherwise honors as a model, because of his affinity for the *précieux*.[53] And in fact Vauvenargues has not the least to do with the *précieux* or with preciosity: "Affected behavior is the outer appearance of tension and lies."[54] And what *précieux* like Scudéry considered the highest human happiness is odious to Vauvenargues: "It is doubtless a crude error to imagine that *oisiveté* can make human beings happier: health, strength of mind, satisfaction are the edifying fruits of labor."[55]

Labor as aristocratic virtue against the bourgeoisie? Yes, but against the *noblesse* as well. Vauvenargues is nearly obsessed with the affirmation of labor. His work, his thought represents an almost insane turning of noble ideals against the nobility, of bourgeois ideals against the bourgeoisie, and the two sets of ideals in conjunction against the whole society. One cannot imagine, understand, or explain the work of Vauvenargues without the social changes, the slow but irresistible rise of the active commercial, manufacturing, and financial bourgeoisie, the constant polemic of the ideologues of *activité, utilité,* and *honnêteté* against the representatives of the *honnêteté* based on *oisiveté*. Vauvenargues calls the apologists of *oisiveté* false prophets: "They do not know that enjoyment is the fruit and the reward of labor, that it is an activity [*une action*] itself, and that one can only enjoy as long as one is active."[56]

But for what purpose and to what end should one work? What profit does one gain from his ceaseless activity? The purpose cannot be grasped, is not material. On the contrary, anyone who acts with a material purpose in mind, undertakes voyages, runs risks, is wasting his time[57] because "very few activities have a useful purpose."[58] The goal of the activity Vauvenargues considers meaningful, of meaningful labor, is fame, *gloire*: "Intellect and labor [*activité*] carry the human being up to virtue and fame... fame stimulates us... to labor and virtue."[59] In activity, in labor the human being realizes himself, takes possession of the present in order to transform it into the past, and the hope of fame that grows out of the activity or that could grow out of it brings the future closer and makes labor (in hope of fame) easier: "The human being lives on, and fame, which cannot but follow on virtue, remains after it."[60]

Vauvenargues's praise is for a disinterested activity that has its meaning in itself, for great heroic deeds on the battlefield of war or—especially—on the battlefield of the intellect. For war dominates here as well as there; it dominates everywhere. Everyone wants success, wants to be the best: "Life is thus nothing but a long struggle in which human beings contend fiercely with each other for fame, pleasure, dominance, and wealth."[61] Anyone who wants to contend successfully must therefore be courageous—"Only courage directs life"[62]—but in contrast to the *courtisan* and the bourgeois (or the people), not for the sake of a sinecure or for profit (or for starvation wages), but for *gloire*: "Gloire fills the world with virtues, and like a beneficent sun it covers the whole world with flowers and fruits. Fame makes heroes beautiful. There is no perfect fame without the fame in warfare."[63] And finally, desperate and breathless: "The acme of courage is equanimity in the face of certain death."—"Le terme du courage est l'intrépidité à la vue d'une mort sûre."[64] This last design of a new aristocratic ideal, based on the bourgeois virtue of industry and the knightly virtue of courage, represents a new variant of the willingness to run risks, of the ideology of adventure: the adventurer dedicated to death, to the void, elitist and lonely, hostile to life, opposed to the common norm, that is, to everyone who does not share this ideal. Philosophers of the nineteenth and twentieth centuries use this variant as a source for their ideas of adventure and the adventurer. But the nobility as the dominant class in France could not even articulate itself heroically once more in the face of its actual fall; the machinery of representation at Versailles, the *perpetuum mobile*, was ready for the rubbish heap of history. Vauvenargues's criticism, however, could hardly have bothered the bourgeoisie, because if one read the maxims from the bourgeois point of view, the whole thing was quite useful. On the one hand, the nobility that Vauvenargues was talking about was not a matter of birth but of (intellectual) merit, with which the bourgeoisie could only agree; on the other, *activité*/labor was the most important element, the basis on which *gloire* and *fortune* were to be won, as Vauvenargues says,[65] and he must have plagiarized that (and much else as well) from the bourgeois himself.

Chapter 13
The Decay of the Alliance and the Formation of the Antiabsolutist Opposition

Bourgeois Opposition at the End of the Seventeenth Century

Scholars have repeatedly discussed whether there was a bourgeoisie at all in the seventeenth century, what it was like, how it was composed and articulated.[1] Let us disregard the fact that these discussions occasionally manifest a certain joy in verbal casuistry or that sometimes plainly anti-Marxist tendencies show through in them;[2] we must still admit that the definition of the term "bourgeois" in France at this time presents certain problems.[3] The most difficult problem in this context is probably defining the upper boundary of the concept, because the rise of members of the bourgeoisie into the nobility repeatedly involves class relations in a process of dissolving into each other (although this is primarily important only in a qualitative sense). The upper nobility (especially after several sporadic intensifications of the policy of ennobling the bourgeoisie after 1700) felt quite threatened by this process and firmly opposed it (as Saint-Simon did in his *Projets de rétablissement du royaume en France*, Proposal to Reestablish the Monarchy in France).[4] Nonetheless it is certain that the bourgeoisie existed, although it did not present a unified political picture; rather, it was divided into the commercial, manufacturing, and financial bourgeoisie, as well as the bourgeoisie of private means. Membership in one of these groups, however, did not exclude membership in another; for example, a member of the financial bourgeoisie might also conduct trade.[5]

What has obviously confused scholars from time to time and continues to do so is the fact that this splintered bourgeoisie did not have a unified class consciousness; there was a "lack of common interests," as Jean-Marie Goulemot writes about the time of interest to us, the time when the alliance between monarchy and bourgeoisie was disintegrating.[6] That is no doubt true, but we must not make the mistake of proceeding from this determination to assuming a coherent class consciousness of whatever description as a constituent of the bourgeoisie in the seventeenth century. Only if we assume the existence of such a coherent class consciousness do we find it surprising that this consciousness was in fact absent, especially if the bourgeois class consciousness is imagined only as an oppositional one to the monarch[7] (Goulemot and Rothkrug, against whom Goulemot polemicizes, both imagine it thus).[8] But if we start out from the objective class situation at the time of Colbert and in the years after his death, then a coherent oppositional literature as the expression of unified bourgeois self-consciousness would be nothing short of a miracle. The economic and political structures that had been created through the formation of the absolute monarchy and especially through Colbert's policies represent a framework for which the economic activities of the bourgeoisie as a whole were still too *insignificant*.[9] That is, the bourgeoisie did not yet completely fill this frame that had been constructed for it, and on the basis of the relations we have analyzed it could not yet fill the frame (as we have shown, the obstacle of mercantile overregulation was merely one more difficulty among many). Against what should or could the bourgeoisie as a class have been unified in opposition? We have shown that the monarch's hostile policy toward financial, commercial, or manufacturing capital was not the reason that the revolution in relations of production did not proceed more rapidly in the direction of the capitalist mode of production. With few exceptions, commercial and manufacturing capital were able to develop together only on such a small scale and often without a firm mutual involvement that the frame Colbert created for production became too narrow only after a relatively long time (and not equally in all sectors). That does not mean that there was no economic-political opposition in certain areas, but such opposition articulated itself sporadically (especially in the antifiscal revolts),[10] without unity, and with contradictions; it could not have done otherwise.

The state of affairs we have sketched out shows all too clearly how necessary it is not only to distinguish between subjective and objective interests but also to bear in mind their constant dialectical interrelation. Only in so doing can we recognize the following: the objective interests of the commercial and manufacturing bourgeoisie were what operatively could fill the potential for production— the structure of communications, transportation, and manufacturing—that Colbert created. The essential affirmation of the absolute monarchy is the political expression of these objective interests up to the moment when the potential within the framework of the absolute monarchy became a restraint on productive forces. In truth, however, this subjective affirmation of the monarchy masked objective antagonism. In other words, the bourgeoisie of that age expressed objective antagonism between the classes by affirming the possibilities for the development of commercial and manufacturing activities created by the absolute monarchy. As these productive forces developed, the ground became more unsafe for the absolute monarchy. Thus anyone who—like Jacques Savary in 1675— affirmed Colbert's platform for production in the framework of the absolute monarchy, and hence affirmed the monarchy itself, was acting in a revolutionary way. Goulemot, driven by an idea that runs counter to his efforts to reconstruct the consciousness of the epoch, the idea that objectively revolutionary behavior on the part of the bourgeoisie must also have an objectively revolutionary ideological expression, not only misunderstands Savary but twists him into his complete opposite: from the end of the century on, Goulemot writes, Savary complained "bitterly" "that one saw merchants and traders every day who earned remarkable fortunes and procured the best positions in the magistracy for their children."[11] But Savary does not utter a single syllable of complaint about this; instead he rejoices, since he sees this as proof of the importance of the *commerçant* and commerce.[12]

We call attention to this error in Goulemot's otherwise stimulating book because it clarifies the peculiar situation of the time between 1661 and about 1700 or 1720: the economic and political self-definition of the financial, commercial, and manufacturing bourgeoisie on principle *cannot* be explicitly oppositional in this epoch. This explains countless ideological manifestations that scholars consider more or less inexplicable, like the oppositional leadership role of the "reactionary" feudal nobility that Goulemot correctly notes. Goulemot's error explains why this oppositional feudal nobility sometimes represented the objective interests of the bourgeoisie while bourgeois (ideological) opposition appeared in aristocratic garb. For of course there was also a bourgeois (ideological) opposition, but it could not appear or could appear only in a sporadic and isolated way where Goulemot looks for it: in the sphere of production and circulation or among those who were active there as commercial or manufacturing capitalists. Instead, opposition appeared where it necessarily had to: among the intellectuals in *la cour et la ville*. The reasons for this are obvious. While the active commercial and manufacturing bourgeoisie did not yet fill the national framework of production delineated by Colbert and was active silently (which does not mean that it did not also participate passively in the ideological confrontations of the time), the "active conceptive ideologues" of the bourgeoisie (Marx) were orienting themselves toward the development of thinking on a world scale, and they were constantly bumping into boundaries set by church and government restrictions, prejudices, taboos, and censure at court and in the city.

The Difficulties of Thinking, Speaking, and Writing the Truth under the Absolute Monarchy in France

The internal contradictions in the intellectual movement of that age manifested themselves not least in Colbert's policy toward science and in his cultural strategy. Colbert tried to put all intellectual forces in the service of the throne, subsidized them in a way hitherto unknown, established the Academy of Sciences and placed its main accent on the research, presentation, and development of techniques of production, of technology. The Academy was charged with producing a *Description des arts et métiers* (Description of Techniques and Crafts), which, however, never appeared as a publication under that title. Not until 1704 did the academician Jaugeon present the first volume, entitled *Description et perfection des arts-et-métiers*, but this remained unpublished.[13] In the meantime Thomas Corneille had already produced an (insufficient) inventory of the technological vocabulary with his *Dictionnaire des arts et des sciences*, 1694, which Jacques Proust considers to be a precursor of Diderot and D'Alembert's *Encyclopédie*, along with various manuals on individual areas of technological development.[14]

Curiously, Proust and scholars of the *Encyclopédie* as a whole seem not to count among its precursors or to overlook altogether another work that I believe actually represents a first draft for an *Encyclopédie*: the plan for a reference library by La Mothe le Vayer, *Du moien de dresser une bibliothèque d'une centaine de livres seulement*, How to Assemble a Library with Only a Hundred Books, 1648.[15] This plan was conceived in an exclusively functional way, as a library with which one could do scholarly and scientific work. It extended from Latin, Greek, Hebrew, German, Spanish, and Italian dictionaries (among them only the best were named, like those of Santes Pagninus, Covarrubias, and Nebrija) to the poetic, geographical, mathematical, medicinal, and agricultural handbooks of all individual disciplines to manuals for special technologies: "In this way we see how the artisans alway have special tools that they handle better than all others."[16]

La Mothe le Vayer obviously considers it important that the latest state of research be represented, and works by Copernicus, Kepler, and Galileo are naturally among the authorities of his library. But the essential thing is that at the heart of this inventory of the individual disciplines and technologies (from which he pointedly bans alchemy and magic)[17] is the subjugation of the library to philosophy or the penetration of the sciences by philosophy. Of course, this does not take on so rigid a form as in the *Discours préliminaire*, the theoretical introduction by D'Alembert to the *Encyclopédie* of 1751, for here it is a library in which books and authors, while they are grouped together in the whole framework, still exist separately in individual volumes, and of course La Mothe le Vayer could not pass over religion and theology at that time (as even the *Encyclopédie* did not; but in the philosophical section, besides the ancient philosophers (such as Aristotle and Plato) there are moderns like Campanella, Giordano Bruno, Gassendi (whom La Mothe le Vayer counts among "nos amis intimes," "our closest friends"), and "Le grand Chancelier Anglois

Verulamius," Francis Bacon,[18] whose design of the sciences was the basis for Diderot and D'Alembert's in the *Encyclopédie*.

If we compare this technological panorama with the technological manuals or inventories from the time of the founding of the Académie des Sciences in 1666 to the beginning of the eighteenth century, one striking essential difference between the older and the newer works is that the older include works of philosophy or worldviews or embed the individual disciplines and technologies in philosophical reflection. The *Encyclopédie* of Diderot and D'Alembert in this respect takes up La Mothe le Vayer's design again, though with the eighteenth-century state of technology. In the epoch from 1666 to the end of Louis XIV's reign, on the other hand, technological research and development was government directed, in keeping with the government-directed manufacturing and commercial development, and basic research in the natural sciences or philosophy was largely banned, as Maurice Roelens has demonstrated in his excellent introduction to texts by Fontenelle.[19] This is quite clear in the instruction that Colbert's successor Michel le Tellier, Marquis de Louvois (1639-91) gave the Académie des Sciences "to dedicate itself above all to works that have a perceptible and quick application and hence contribute to increasing the glory of the king."[20]

Let us remember that this was a time of church and government reaction against any unorthodox thought, whether Jansenist or Protestant, against any freethinking movement whatsoever; starting in 1671 there was an official ban on spreading the teachings of Descartes; censorship hunted down everything that seemed to be dangerous in foreign intellectual imports.[21] Then the situation of the intellectuals in *la cour et la ville* becomes clear; despite all obstacles and bans, they naturally followed the international discussions in the area of natural sciences and philosophy and were in contact with the most important scholars (like Huyghens, Spinoza, Leibniz, and Newton). Thus until the 1720s, it was less the practical or administrative restrictions on commercial and manufacturing forces of production that drove the practical, active bourgeoisie into opposition than intellectual restrictions on basic scientific and philosophical research that of necessity drove the intellectuals into intellectual and political opposition, since they were fully informed about the international standard of research.

Two scientific-philosophical problems were clearly central: the infinity of space and matter and the laws of motion. As foreshortened as the following analogies might seem, they still appear in nearly all philosophical treatises of the time, applying the problem to all areas of life or drawing inferences from its conclusions. In view of the infinity of space and matter, the magnitude of the great king seems infinitesimal; in view of the constant motion in matter, the stagnation at the court is all the more unnatural, obstructive, hostile to life, and ridiculous. These and all other related questions necessarily led to a relativization of everything that existed, of all known hierarchies and orders of magnitude. When they were transposed into the intellectuals' own thinking in the particular situation of *la cour et la ville*, the result was the most varied strategies of thinking, speaking, and writing, for all of which the courtly tone was the basic precondition. The favored tactic was to present revolutionary thought in fictional dialogues with a conversation partner and to have the other partner, more or less outraged or amused, refute or "disprove" it, using all the current intellectual clichés. Another tactic was to impute revolutionary thought and action to people in distant, unknown, fictional or nonfictional lands. The various barriers of censorship and taboos on the one hand and the social and ideological disunity of the wholly or partly oppositional forces on the other led to extremely contradictory phenomena, but in view of the economic and political relations, we must look for and find the subjective oppositional articulation of objective class antagonisms in these contradictions.

The Alliance between the Feudal-Aristocratic and the Bourgeois Opposition

The most remarkable example of the internal contradictions of the ideological opposition is the famous *Querelle des Anciens et des Modernes*,[22] the battle between the advocates of antiquity and those of the modern period. All too often this has been considered only a battle about literature or the theory of art,[23] and not a political struggle in which class antagonisms become clear; this perspective provides the background against which the literary and aesthetic discussion reveals its true historical significance. We cannot see the political dimensions of the struggle merely by determining the social origins of those who took part in the *Querelle*:[24] social standing alone tells us nothing about this battle; this follows of necessity from the objective class situation of the bourgeoisie and the nobility with their factions that were either integrated into court life or not and especially with their ideologues. Not only do the interests of the different factions coincide in the common intellectual opposition across the boundaries of class, but they can be transformed, on the basis of the common opposition, from a starting position that is reactionary in principle, one that is for instance against the objective interests of the bourgeoisie, into a progressive thrust that corresponds to the objective interests of the bourgeoisie (and let us note here that in what follows the terms "reactionary" and "progressive" are used with certain reservations).

The work of Saint-Evremond (1614-1703) is particularly informative. As an advocate of enlightened despotism in the *Fronde* confrontations, he began by supporting the side of Cardinal Mazarin but then entered into a temporary alliance with Condé; in 1652 he entered the service of the king. For political reasons Saint-Evremond fell out of favor in 1659, on the occasion of the Peace of the Pyrenees; in 1661 he fled to England where, except for the period from 1665 to 1670, he stayed for the rest of his life, at first in voluntary and then in involuntary exile. Philosophically, Saint-Evremond is a passionate supporter of the sensualist materialism of Gassendi and Bacon and an avowed foe of Descartes.[25] In his *Jugement sur les sciences où peut s'appliquer un honnête homme* (Judgment about the Sciences to Which a Gentleman May Dedicate Himself, 1662), he writes that after he had studied scholastic philosophy, he recognized its casuistic arbitrariness: "I broke off all contact with it and began to be astonished that an educated person can waste his life with useless speculations."[26] But mathematics (Descartes) did not appeal much to him either: "Mathematics in fact grants a great degree of certainty, but when I think about the deep reflection it demands, how it alienates us from activity and pleasure, its price seems to me too high."[27]

He turns resolutely to ethics, polemics, and literature, from the point of view of social activity and utility. We must keep these determining criteria in mind if we want to come to an adequate evaluation of his thought, which is determined by the desire for a return to the old feudal constitution in the area of politics. This nostalgia for the past is relativized, however, by the criticism of absolutist despotism it contains: the old system with its *états généraux* and its parliaments, with its strong *noblesse* and its self-confident urban bourgeoisie, kept the king's power in check and thus guaranteed a play of forces that was favorable to ideological tolerance and social balance, as Saint-Evremond believed was the case in the reign of Caesar Augustus.[28] From this point of view, his experience especially with the Dutch republic, where he lived from 1665 to 1670, and with social relations in England later, even after the Glorious Revolution, results in his (progressive) affirmation of bourgeois-republican accomplishments: "After living rather a long time at courts," he writes in 1666 from The Hague, "I console myself with the fact that I will end my life in the freedom of a republic."[29]

Saint-Evremond's reflections on literary questions should also be considered under the aspect of the dialectical turn from backwards-oriented to future-oriented thinking. In his treatise *Du merveilleux qui se trouve dans les poèmes des anciens* (On the Miraculous in the Poems of Antiquity), written between 1675 and 1687, he praises the knightly romances in comparison with the epics of antiquity (with some irony, but, as a follower of Corneille, not without love)— but the conclusions he reaches are completely progressive. The knightly romances are preferable to the epics of antiquity because all the evil they portray is caused by magicians and devils, that is, by evil forces, whereas the evil in the works of antiquity results from the will of the gods[30] and is thus highly absurd and unbelievable for modern readers. Taking this thought as a point of departure, Saint-Evremond arrives not only at a relativization of aesthetic judgment that already contains the seeds of a historical approach, but also at a first understanding of literary texts from the point of view of the sociology of literature, which tries to uncover the interrelations of social conditions, the formation of consciousness, and literary articulation or production. In a comparison between Corneille and Racine (where Saint-Evremond once more starts out from his preference for *Frondiste* positions), he comes to a condemnation of Racine (and hence of the deliberately timeless art of representation under Louis XIV that aimed at validity for all eternity) because in Racine's heroic figures (in contrast to those of Corneille) historical local color is as little retained (or represented) as warriorlike heroic movement, which has been replaced by the stasis of the *précieux* casuistry of love.[31]

Movement had reached a crisis in Corneille's heroes in its irreconcilable contradiction to time and space but was preserved through tension even within the temporal and spatial restrictions. It is liberated again in Saint-Evremond and joins with the modern age's animated observation of nature (or with the modern observation of animated nature). As Saint-Evremond writes in *Sur les anciens* (On the Ancients), written between 1675 and 1687:

> Today, two heroes who wanted to fight would not stop to tell each other their genealogies. But one can easily see from the *Iliad*, the *Odyssey*, and the *Aeneid* that this was the practice earlier.... As to [poetic—M. N.] similes, we would today of course be more restrained.... The [poetic—M. N.] language was loaded with fictions, allegories, parables: nothing appears as it is [in reality—M. N.].... The spirit of our age is quite opposed to this drive for mystification. We love clear truths: rational insight outweighs fantastic illusions; nothing satisfies us today except solidity and reason. As there has been a change in taste, there has also been one in knowledge. We observe nature differently than the ancients observed it. The sky, this eternal domicile of so many divinities, is merely a huge, fluid space. It is, to be sure, still the same sun that shines on us, but we give it another course.... The earth, which earlier ideas held to be immobile, today turns in our ideas, and nothing approaches the speed of its movement.[32]

Saint-Evremond links the historical-sociological evaluation of the ancient hero and the polemic against the ahistorical immobility of Racine's heroes with the progressive thinking he reveals in his attitude toward the development of knowledge in the natural sciences. This linkage prepares the ground for a new image of humanity, which—in the union of the feudal-aristocratic and the bourgeois worldview—is sustained by the entirety of social change and the insight into it: "Everything has changed," he writes, "the gods, nature, politics, manners, taste, behavior. And should these many changes call forth no changes in our works?"[33]

The Imaginary Journey into the Real World

The new hero for whom Saint-Evremond boldly designs living space can in the last analysis be none other than the bourgeois and with him all the forces of the people that carry the process of change and the knowledge that has expanded through change. But Saint-Evremond's ideas thrive in (republican) exile. In France the strategic constraints on thinking, speaking, and writing the truth (but also the inner and outer lack of freedom) are different. Nonetheless, the thrust is not essentially different. When Charles Perrault (1604-1703) read his poem "Le siècle de Louis le Grand" (The Age of Louis the Great) in the Académie Française, it revealed forces, masked by the praise of the ruler, that were in growing opposition to the absolutist machinery of censorship. Boileau, who understood that this was the end of the the dream of the eternal alliance, that his time, which was also that of Colbert and Molière, was over, was angry at this, only too understandably, the more so since he knew elements among the moderns who—like Desmarest de Saint-Sorlin[34]—were wholly or partly in the reactionary camp.

It is not obvious where Perrault's thoughts originate. Perrault, the man of letters who made his start as a *précieux* writer, praises the literature of the *précieux* as the great literature of the age of Louis XIV and ranks as higher than the ancients these authors (especially Sarasin and Voiture);[35] among whom only Molière (described as naïve) is treated as a non-*précieux* exception. It is certain that this will not carry Perrault far, and so he combines his basically reactionary praise of second-rate *précieux* authors with that of progress in the natural sciences and of technology: "How much human knowledge about a number of objects of unimaginable magnitude has grown," he writes and continues (here in prose translation), "in the uncertain space of this great universe a thousand new worlds have been discovered, and new suns... are nearly as numerous as stars today."[36] Thus in Perrault too, we must distinguish cause and result while keeping the dialectic relations between the two in mind. In the attempt to raise the evaluation of (*précieux*) literature as part of the present, in the context of praising the entire present he refers especially to progress in the natural sciences and technology, a strategy that Hans-Robert Jauss has been quite right to examine.[37] In the area of natural science and technology, the superiority of the moderns is incontestable, and in this area—in England as well, with different premises—a new way of thinking about production is developing that is no longer borne by the repetition and imitation of ancient models but by the effort to develop further, by *inventio*, "invention," the creative production of the individual genius that does not result from application of the rules but from breaking them and going beyond them.[38] Here too the result is a breaking of the norms, a destruction and removal of hierarchies and constraints, an openness toward the new that is not restricted to the realm of the natural sciences and technologies but instead is transferred from that realm to all areas of thought and intellectual creation.

It was the new that the representatives of absolutist immobility hated, for the new, imaginary or real, or the previously unknown was the source of danger for the existing, the relativization of the traditional, dogmatically immobile. To the degree that a consciousness of history and progress developed, the stages of which Werner Krauss has described,[39] the new or the previously unknown moved from the realm of the exotic and became a political, ideological alternative or a possibility for the future. Literature about real or imaginary journeys of course had a special significance in this context. Travel literature is so extensive that we cannot treat it in detail here.[40] But we must describe some positions, especially since this literature, as Paul Hazard has correctly stated,[41] is an expression of the decay of a system of order oriented toward centralization and immutability and was experienced as a threat by the supporters of this order. In this connection, Hazard quotes La Bruyère, from the fifth edition of *Caractères* (1690):

> Some complete their demoralization by extensive travel, and lose whatever shreds of religion remained to them. Every day they see a new religion, new customs, new rites. They resemble those who go into a store and do not know which material they should buy. The great selection [of material—M. N.] makes them increasingly indifferent. All [materials—M. N.] have their advantages and good features. They [the buyers—M. N.] do not reach a decision [*ne se fixent point*] and leave again without having made a purchase.[42]

La Bruyère's criticism is very revealing: what he holds against the travelers is their mobility, their refusal to settle down, the fact that they do not decide on any worldview of style of life. It is noteworthy that this criticism is obviously already made from a defensive position, since it does concede the possibility of choice (of something other than the Catholic-absolutist regime). This development too was inevitable, although it ran counter to the desired centralization at the court. And here too it is once again Colbert who, in order to strengthen the absolute monarchy, introduced a development that necessarily led to its disintegration: he not only promoted travel to expand useful knowledge and to establish trade connections, but also promoted the production of travel reports wherever possible.[43]

Colbert had to overcome considerable prejudice in this attempt. Saint-Evremond, in his comedy of 1662, *Sir Politick would be*, had poked fun at the English and Germans as victims of travel fever,[44] and even those who affirmed travel in principle did so in a way that laid bare the contradictions of French absolutism. The work of François de la Mothe le Vayer is exemplary in this regard; he repeatedly treats the problem of travel. It is quite clear that his attitude toward travel is fundamentally positive. In one of his letters ("On being far from home") he writes:

> How can one indulge oneself more pleasantly and more usefully than in travel.... You will find in it utility joined with the greatest pleasure and it will teach you a certain indifference toward many things.... The intellectual elevation that you gain over so many different kinds of actions and thought, of which each nation considers its own the best, will place you on the fortunate and glorious level of the philosophers.[45]

La Mothe le Vayer here openly postulates things that would have made a La Bruyère anxious and angry: in the center of his thought is a tolerant relativism vis-à-vis everything out of the ordinary. In a collection of treatises that La Mothe le Vayer dedicated to Pierre Séguier, Gabriel Naudé, and Cardinal Mazarin, we find an essay, "Des Voiages" (On Travel), which begins with a polemic against recourse to antiquity, to Hercules and the Argonauts, when mounting arguments in favor of travel, because not until the discovery of the sea routes to the East and West Indies could one really talk about travel: "There is nothing more glorious in the history of the latest times than the names of Christopher Columbus, Amerigo Vespucci, Drake, [Jacques le—M. N.] Maire, and their ilk."[46] Therefore, he continues, the French would do well also to undertake voyages of exploration and to develop a colonial policy:[47] "Among the plans our great king has to make our kingdom famous and glorious in every respect, he should scorn neither the discovery of foreign lands nor good and verified information about certain areas whose names and geographical location we hardly know."[48]

"France is not incapable of supporting trading companies for overseas shipping, as some have claimed," La Mothe le Vayer states[49] and opens a vista on his real motives. For La Mothe le Vayer, the enthusiast of geography, the greatness of the monarchy, trade, and scientific research are all derived from travel (and vice versa). Merchants and explorers must, however, have certain qualities; they must know languages, geography, and astronomy, must be able to draw and must have "the drive that infuses us with the desire to travel."[50] With all his enthusiasm about travel, it is doubtful whether he himself felt this drive. La Mothe le Vayer's philosophical-skeptical position, in any case, is characterized by ambivalence. First, he unreservedly affirms the usefulness of travel in another treatise, "De l'utilité des voiages" (The Usefulness of Travel), in which he characteristically borrows a saying from Simonides to the effect that the disadvantage of being a king is the impossibility of travel. Then, he acts "according to the rules of skeptical philosophy"[51] and confronts this with another treatise, "De l'inutilité des voiages" (The Uselessness of Travel), in which he begins by stating that it is untrue that kings do not travel— witness Alexander the Great and other conquerors. He proceeds to state all the arguments against travel, which culminate in the claim that travel estranges the traveler from France: "What good is it to travel through the world like vagabonds in order to gain still more knowledge when the human soul is capable of going anywhere without one's having to move?"[52]

Fifty years later, Fontenelle strikes a similarly indecisive, now slightly world-weary, attitude (and fifty years after that, Diderot will advocate it scientifically and philosophically). In a posthumously published fragment, Fontenelle writes:

> I have discovered a kind of travel for myself which I intend to practice exclusively in the future. I am firmly convinced that human nature is everywhere the same but that it is susceptible of infinitely many external variations (especially as regards thinking and habits). I imagine all the differences as best I can: I use my imagination to shape customs and societies that despite everything do not contradict our principles, and I say: all this exists somewhere.[53]

The principle Fontenelle is paying homage to here is not new. From Thomas More on it has been the conception of utopian literature, which reached a remarkable high point in France in 1677, in the utopian-communist travel novel of Denis de Veiras (1635-85?).[54] Fontenelle will pay tribute to this literary genre with his *Histoire des Ajaoiens* (History of the Ajaoiens, published posthumously) and especially with his *Entretiens sur la pluralité des mondes* (Conversations on the Plurality of Worlds, 1686), and will thereby prove himself an advocate of travel without movement; this then becomes transfigured into such an ideal activity that even where real travels are undertaken, as by Louis-Armand La Hontan (1666-1715), the nonjourney is praised. In his *Dialogues avec un sauvage* (Dialogues with a Savage, 1704), he has a "noble savage" who embodies the principle of naturally correct thought and unspoiled feeling say:

> As to your sciences, they are useless to us. With respect to geography, we have no desire to burden our minds by reading travel books that all contradict each other, especially since we are not people who leave our land, whose smallest brook we know for four hundred miles around.[55]

La Hontan's polemic against travel is contradicted by his own travel activity. Fontenelle, on the other hand, stayed true to his maxim: he traveled in spirit, and far into space. Such imagined voyages were not new, either. Savignien Cyrano de Bergerac's (1619-55) report of voyages to the moon appeared posthumously between 1656 and 1662. What makes Fontenelle's travels unusual is their scientific-philosophical ambitions and the courtly strategic presentation of his enlightened thought that necessarily called into question the singularity of the absolute monarchy. The philosopher explains to his conversational partner, a marquise, that there are other worlds in the universe, and he proves it by the history of the discovery of the lands of earth. This ought at least to teach people to "reserve judgment" on the unknown.[56] In 1702 Fontenelle reiterates this idea in a rigorously scientific context, the *Préface sur l'utilité des mathématiques et de la physique* (Preface on the Usefulness of Mathematics and Physics), which was also a prelude to the *Encyclopédie* of Diderot and D'Alembert. The utility of mathematical research is obvious to only a few people, but this research is necessary in order to develop the natural sciences that can be applied. Contrary to Le Tellier's ordinance, one must therefore not neglect basic research:[57] "Even though it is true that not all the pure speculations of geometry and algebra can be applied to useful things, most of them that cannot be applied are connected with the applicable ones or lead to them."[58]

In technology, which Fontenelle complains receives too little attention, it is clear what can be applied.[59] Technology, he feels, is actually more important than many a "pleasant poem or a lovely speech."[60] In any case, research in mathematics and physics, together with technology, will open new horizons for humanity: "The human intellect's various modes of seeing are practically infinite, and nature is actually infinite. For that reason one can expect new discoveries every day, whether in mathematics or in physics, which represent a new sort of utility or singularity."[61] The knowledge that human beings have gained in the last hundred years can be judged, for instance, from the development of the telescope and the microscope, which are "a new organ of vision": "How amazed the ancients would have been if someone had prophesied to them that one day their successors, with the help of several instruments, would see an infinite number of objects that they themselves could not see: a heaven that was unknown to them and plants and animals whose existence they did not even suspect."[62]

Chapter 14
The Decay of the Alliance and the Rise of the *Commerçant*

Real Movement and *Aventure*

In "Du Bonheur" (On Happiness, 1691-99), Fontenelle sees the basis of happiness in a secure, peaceful existence, in immobility, in "duration without alteration";[1] still, we must not assume, as Robert Mauzi does, that Fontenelle expresses the general bourgeois worldview.[2] Fontenelle's essay doubtless presents an aspect of the bourgeois worldview, of the individual in his private sphere,[3] but we must overlook in Fontenelle neither the causes of such a desire for immobile happiness, inherent in the absolutist system, nor the fact that he did not belong to the active bourgeoisie but instead to its "active conceptive ideologues." In this function Fontenelle relativizes or annuls the wish for immobile happiness with a stream of contradictory and contrasting impulses: his scientific educational activity and his utopian travel reports or the vision of cosmic, distant, probable worlds. As Werner Krauss writes about Veiras's *Histoire des Sévarambes* (History of the Severambes), "The route of travel follows the known and the newly discovered world to its very limits, and where it goes beyond them the realm of probability begins, averse to any kind of miracles."[4] That means that the counterdesign to the feudal absolutist society of France is developing: "With its spatial fictions, the genre [of the utopian novel—M. N.] fully belongs to what we could call oppositional literature,"[5] Krauss continues, and Albert Soboul states: "From the end of the seventeenth century on, criticism of property and egalitarian tendencies begin to appear in the utopian framework and under the guise of literary fiction. The utopia that is close to communism is always set far away from the present in time and space."[6]

Imaginary journeys and the theme of the "noble savage" belong to the strategies of contrast that were also used when the criticism of social relations in France did not achieve the dimensions of utopian communism. But the real descriptions of travel in other countries were perhaps still more important. They did not need to be distant countries. Even England, about which an increasing number of reports were being written,[7] was an exciting, perhaps even the most exciting, country; its very existence and its national constitution (like that of all other countries) was so different from the French that it furnished incontrovertible proof of the possibility that one could also live in other social systems (and often even better). Versailles became smaller and smaller the farther away one traveled—all the way into the *Pluralité des mondes* (excursions into history served a similar purpose). And what is small is no longer so significant and fearful: fictional and real foreign travelers (as for instance in Montesquieu's *Lettres persanes*, Persian Letters, 1721) contributed to relativizing French conditions by their more or less sneering remarks about them. Through this flood of fictional and nonfictional travel literature in all its variants, movement was introduced into the thinking of an epoch in which little by little social relations also began to move.

In fact there was at this time something like an explosion in the area of the *histoire d'aventures*, of *aventure*, and of the *aventurier*. The body of literature that has the trademark *aventure* in the title is immense, which is due not least to the word's already having become an inflationary coin in the seventeenth century. In all of Molière's comedies, for instance, *aventure* could designate any process or event. But it is not enough simply to draw this conclusion, especially since contemporaries did not do so. At no other time have lexicographers had such a great interest in the concept *aventure*, or *aventurier*, and never again did lexicography achieve such subtle nuancing of the concept as at that time. "ADVENTURE, AVENTURE ou AVANTURE," we read in the *Dictionnaire de Trévoux*, "means simply an event, an action, a coincidence of several circumstances [*amas de plusieurs circonstances*], and the adjective with which one modifies *aventure* determines the meaning more exactly. One also says pleasurable aventure, irritating aventure...," then more precisely: "event, accident, something that intervenes unexpectedly. Eventus, casus, fortuna."[8]

The word *aventure* served to express approximately what we call *sensation* today. "ADVENTURE," the *Dictionnaire de Trévoux* continues, "is also what one calls surprising and extraordinary events [*accidens surprenans & extraordinaires*]" or "risky undertakings [*des entreprises hazardeuzes*]." The fictional *aventures* of knightly romance also belong to the extraordinary events that are designated as *aventures*, as we saw above, but the concept is by no means restricted to this realm any longer (or to that of the erotic *aventure*, which of course had moved from gallant courtly literature or language to general colloquial language and soon came to mean explicitly the sexual act).[9] From the *Avantures choisies* in the wake of the gallant courtly novels, which was published by Marteau in Cologne and Prault in Paris, to Marivaux's *La vie de Marianne ou les avantures de la Comtesse de* **** (The Life of Marianne or the Adventures of Countess ****), first two parts published in 1731; from the *Avantures de Télémaque* of 1691-99 to travel reports like the famous *Voyages et aventures de François Legnat, et de ses compagnons, en deux isles désertes des Indes Orientales* (Travels and Adventures of François Legnat and his Companions on Two Desert Isles of the East Indies, 1708); from the memoirs of the *aventurier* Gramont or those of the Count Bonneval to the adventures of the bourgeois social climber like Gil Blas de Santillane in Alain René Lesage's novel of the same name that appeared from 1715 to 1735, a type the *Dictionnaire de Trévoux* also treats under the category of *aventurier* ("as one calls especially those who are poorly favored by fortune and strive for social position"):[10] everything turns, moves, dances in a multifarious and nearly infinite *aventure*.

Gradually non-noble seekers after *aventure* replaced the noble *aventurier* or the traditional knight of *aventure* in the production of novels. At first these non-nobles (like Gil Blas) found their way into the aristocracy, but then more and more often the novels showed the bourgeois individual in his confrontation with a world in which the rise into the nobility no longer represented a serious solution to social and psychological problems, as for instance in Marivaux's *Paysan parvenu* (The Peasant Has Arrived, 1734-36) that however still describes the movement of rising. But by the *Histoire du Chevalier des Grieux et de Manon Lescaut* (Manon Lescaut, 1731), the Abbé Prévost no longer places the social rise or the integration of the individual into society at the center of his work; rather, it is the departure from society: "I must introduce a young blind man," Prévost writes, "who refuses to be happy in order to plunge of his own will into the worst unhappiness, and who—although equipped with all qualities which give rise to the most glowing merit—freely chooses an obscure vagabond existence over all advantages of property and nature."[11] We are no longer witnessing the construction of ideal figures (oriented perhaps toward the knightly or noble ideals); ideals are instead virtually destroyed in the turn to "problematic natures" (or to the "encanaillement du héros de roman," the "social degradation of the novel's hero"),[12] which Augustin-Simon Irailh, for example, bemoaned in 1661: "People turned away from great adventures, heroic projects, finely woven plots, the play of noble passions.... Heroes were no longer sought on thrones; one took them from anywhere, even from the dregs of the people."[13]

The Revolutionary Tightrope Act of the Bourgeoisie

Of course, the literature of travel or *aventure* expressed the actual movement in society, whose most mobile part was to be found in or was determined by the commercial bourgeoisie.[14] It is obvious that the travels of the *commerçants/*

négociants (who were often manufacturers as well) were often linked with the travels of scientists and scholars (like Montesquieu), but they were also linked with the travels of the journeying artisans, the *compagnons*.[15] How much the dominant class, the absolutist upper nobility and its ideologues, especially among the clerics, felt threatened by this activity is shown (besides by utterances like those of La Bruyère) by the polemics against the large-scale or overseas merchants in the sermons of the epoch that Bernhard Groethuysen has investigated.[16]

The polemic from the side of the reactionary forces corresponds to the glorification of the commercial capitalist on the side of the progressive forces. But in its historical development, this glorification is by no means unified; instead, it is subject to the most various deviations. Unless we take this into consideration we will necessarily arrive at a false evaluation of the public consciousness about commerce and the *commerçant* or about the process by which the *commerçant* became aware of himself, as Jean-Marie Goulemot, for instance, does:

> Bourgeois triumphing, the good conscience of commerce are rare [at the beginning of the eighteenth century—M. N.], and the proud declarations of the merchants find little echo. Moreover, they are disunified. Savary does not neglect to emphasize that according to the edicts of 1689 and 1701, nobles were allowed to conduct trade without losing their privileges, as if he were thereby trying to gild his shop sign.[17]

Almost nothing in this passage is correct. Jacques Savary, for instance, has been confused with his son Jacques Savary des Bruslons (for the Jacques Savary about whom Goulemot is writing in this passage, the author of the *Parfait négociant*, died in 1692 and could therefore not have known the edict of 1701). Jacques Savary did not want metaphorically to gild his shop; instead the monarch wanted to encourage the nobility to go into trade, thereby continuing an old tradition. Goulemot's error can be attributed to the fact that there are obvious difficulties in evaluating the class situation of the commercial and manufacturing bourgeoisie from 1666 to about 1720, so that Savary's book presents a puzzle to the scholar. It usually serves as a document for the development in the eighteenth century[18] (something similar is true for numerous arguments of the Abbé Coyer that can already be found in Caillière in 1661), although in view of the year in which the *Parfait négociant* appeared (1675), it would probably be well to assume that it represents approximately the time from 1650 on.

Nonetheless, Goulemot's incorrect evaluation is surprising because he quite rightly refers to the connection between English-French relations and the development of the ideal of the *commerçant*. However, in my opinion he dates this process much too late, at the beginning of the eighteenth century. In investigating the relationship of France to England, it is impermissible to ignore the policies and the writings of Colbert. Still, the laws of motion of historical thought in France that Goulemot uncovers in the material he analyzes, especially with respect to England and the English revolutions of 1649 and 1688, are quite apt to be useful to correct certain errors or even to undertake a better classification of Savary's thought. It is correct, and here we must agree with Goulemot completely, that the French Enlightenment may no longer be understood as an intellectual movement belonging exclusively to the eighteenth century. The fundamental philosophical points of departure were already defined in the first half of the seventeenth century, with Bacon, Descartes, Gassendi, and Hobbes. The political facts that are crucial for France are the triumph of the principle of the absolute monarchy under Henry IV, the English revolution of 1649, which coincides with the events of the *Fronde*, and the Glorious Revolution of 1688.[19] I believe that after 1649 the bourgeoisie performed a political-ideological tightrope act, at first within the alliance between monarchy and bourgeoisie, and outside it after 1688 and the decay of the alliance. But from the beginning the fact of the English revolution impeded French bourgeois action to change society, so that the burden of the successful revolution in England was added to all the previously described constraints.

No one at the French court failed to see that the English revolution of 1649 was a question of class conflict and that the bourgeoisie, under the leadership of their commercial-capitalist avant-garde, had done away with the absolute monarchy.[20] Thus from that time on, anyone who wanted to promote commercial and manufacturing capitalism or the commercial and manufacturing bourgeoisie in France, politically or ideologically, had to proceed very carefully: he had to present what in the last analysis had eliminated the absolute monarchy in England as a necessity in the interest of the absolute monarchy. The apology for trade, using as an example England where the nobility also conducted trade, had been completely unproblematic at the beginning of the seventeenth century; even in the forties, La Mothe le Vayer was able to use it without embarrassment. But now it could no longer function straightforwardly. In 1658 Caillière therefore referred only to Dutch trade (although with the same goal: in Holland nobles also conducted trade), and in 1675 Savary remains vague when he states that nobles engage in trade in many other "monarchies and states."

Of course we must be cautious in evaluating the concrete reasons for abandoning the English example. It is probable that in the course of depoliticizing or making taboo the revolution of 1649 at the French court, which Goulemot has analyzed capably,[21] praise of the English merchant also fell victim to the general silence about bourgeois England, so that an important argument for improving the reputation of trade could also no longer be used. But who were the apologists for commercial and manufacturing capitalism in this age of the alliance between monarchy and bourgeoisie? None other than Richelieu and Colbert themselves. When Goulemot refers to the wrong Savary, who allegedly called on certain edicts from the time around 1700 in order to improve the reputation of commerce, he overlooks that it was the royal representative Richelieu who "gilded" the first "shop sign" in 1627, then again in 1629 and 1634; that Mazarin continued this policy in 1645; and that Colbert again asserted the nobility of commerce in 1664 and 1669.

In fact—and typically—it was none other than Colbert who tried to perform the tightrope act as early as 1651, two years after the execution of Charles I, in the year of Cromwell's Navigation Bill; bourgeois ideologues would attempt the same act repeatedly after 1688. Colbert pleaded for recognition of the revolutionary English republic and for cooperation with it, giving exclusively reasons of commercial policy. Only when we have come to an understanding with England, he writes in a memorandum for Mazarin, will it be possible to reanimate French trade, "cet honneste excercice" (this honorable activity), which had come to a halt because of the events of the *Fronde*; then merchants will be encouraged to conduct commercial transactions.[22] A precondition for this understanding would be an alliance with England against Spain, as a result of which the English would stop their privateering war against the weak French commercial fleet: "What the English most want and what they are ready to make any concession for is the recognition of their republic." This recognition is particularly necessary since the Spanish have already anticipated the French: "It is the task of our ministers to find the form for this recognition and to determine how far we can go with it.... It seems that this affair, as delicate as it is, can be handled in such a way that this proud nation will be satisfied without doing the English king [in his French exile—M. N.] any harm or giving the poor example of devaluing the monarchy."[23]

When Mazarin—probably in part on the basis of Colbert's advice—came to an agreement with England in 1655, he became the target of conservative polemics.[24] But that did not change the fact that Colbert, as his balance sheet for world trade and the French economy for 1664 shows, still considered the economic development of England a commendable example. We can even say, as many documents prove, that he was fascinated by the economic and political power of England and was obsessed by the attempt to equal it. At times when the countries were cordially allied, Colbert was capable of gushing about the virtues of the English or of the English king,[25] but otherwise he did not hesitate to conduct privateering wars against the English merchant marine in his efforts to expand French trade. In 1666, in a letter to Colbert de Terron, he expressed his joy at the existence of enough shipbuilders ready "to engage in privateering and to disturb English trade"[26] (a joy that corresponds to the *Encyclopédie's* insight a scant century later, that France should conduct a privateering war against England). On 8 June 1672 when the English and French together were involved in confrontations with the Dutch, Colbert stated with satisfaction that the French privateering fleet was ready for battle, whatever the English might claim in their envy.[27]

The awareness that a revolution, the demolition of the absolute monarchy, and the establishment of a republic were all possible was repressed after the monarchy was restored in England in 1660 but continued to function as a latent determinant of political thought even in France. That is demonstrated by the reaction to the Glorious Revolution, which Goulemot has analyzed very competently: the bogeyman of Cromwell the Usurper was reanimated and used in the polemic against William of Orange. It is a moot point whether the reaction to the Glorious Revolution contributed to impeding or reducing the praise of all bourgeois forces and especially of the commercial bourgeoisie in France (still, Savary's *Parfait négociant* did not appear until 1675). It seems more plausible that praise of the *commerçant* had meanwhile become so much a matter of course that authors simply wrote it in passing, as we see in La Hontan's *Dialogues*. His "noble savage" says:

> Of all the occupations of the French, I like only trade, for I consider it the single occupation that is legitimate and necessary for us. Merchants provide us with pleasure; some of them sometimes bring us good wares, and there are many good and just people among them who are satisfied with small profits. They risk a great deal, they advance money, they lend, they wait; in short—I know enough merchants who are good and reasonable and to whom our people owe much.[28]

Apart from such casual praise that can be found in the writings of the time from Saint-Evremond to Montesquieu, we must not overlook the fact that, along with corresponding foreign treatises, Savary's *Parfait négociant* appeared in expanded new editions, and in 1723 his son Jacques Savary des Bruslons published his *Dictionnaire universel de commerce*, which Jacques Proust also counts among the precursors of the *Encyclopédie*.[29] Under the heading "Profession mercantille" we read:

> The occupation of merchant must be considered noble and independent. In France Louis the Great issued two edicts, one in August 1669 and the other in December 1701, allowing his nobility to conduct large-scale trade on water and on land without losing its privileges, and we have often seen that French and foreign merchants have been ennobled by our kings because they have established important manufacturing branches either in Paris or in the provinces.[30]

The qualities that the *commerçant/négociant/*manufacturer must have, according to Savary des Bruslons, do not differ essentially from those his father had enumerated half a century before: he must speak languages (Spanish, Italian, and even "Teutonic")[31] and have geographical, historical, and nautical knowledge (travel reports are cited for their usefulness here).[32] The only noteworthy thing is that Savary des Bruslons is already moving somewhat in the direction of separating the capitalist from his function as individual, from his own activity. In enumerating the skills the merchant (*commerçant*) should have, he writes: "Finally, and although it is not necessary that the merchant be very learned, it is not inappropriate for him to know a little history [*il est cependent à propos qu'il sçache un peu d'Histoire*]."[33]

Altogether, however, we must say (and this also explains Goulemot's oversight) that relatively little is known about the image of the commercial or manufacturing capitalist of that epoch, to say nothing of his self-awareness. No doubt the political dynamism and explosiveness inherent in the praise of commercial and manufacturing capitalists, especially in view of the English revolution of 1649 and the Glorious Revolution of 1688, must have shone through, particularly in the discussion about freedom of trade. As Goulemot correctly recognizes, Voltaire's *Lettres philosophiques* (Philosophical Letters) of 1733-34 give evidence of this political explosiveness. They make clear that the apologist position that Colbert had painstakingly integrated into the alliance between bourgeoisie and monarchy was now directed against the absolute monarchy in a more or less class-antagonistic way, although this is not explicitly developed.[34]

The *Lettres philosophiques* indicate the direction in which the bourgeoisie or its ideologues would now tend in relation to England or the new English social order after 1688 (or were already tending; the enthusiastic reception of *The Tatler* and *The Spectator* described by Hazard is on the same level as the reception of John Locke, with all due reservations that must be registered after Goulemot's investigation).[35] The bourgeoisie disapproves of the execution of Charles I in 1649 (while at the same time making every excuse and referring to French circumstances and events such as the murder of Henri IV by the forces of Catholic reaction) and praises the parliamentary monarchy after the Glorious Revolution as the ideal of a peaceful state that benefits the whole population, including the nobility, although in order to arrive at this state people had to wade through "seas of blood."

The *Lettres philosophiques*, which also contain apologias for Bacon, Locke, and Newton, were immediately condemned and burned in Paris; rightly so, from the point of view of the feudal-absolutist reaction: for if the English social constitution was to be an ideal model for France as well, then must France not also wade through those "seas of blood" that, according to Voltaire, were the price of freedom in England?[36] And if that is correct then who was the one to shed the "seas of blood" that the revolution brought forth? The *commerçant*, the merchant, the bourgeois. At least that is the result of Voltaire's arguments if one places them in a logical connection. The readers of the epoch, whether "rightist" or "leftist," were well schooled in establishing such logical connections, as we know from the writing strategy of smuggled political literature;[37] part of the strategy was that political works were written in a kind of code and were decoded by the readers. People had to wade through "seas of blood" in England in order to achieve the freedom that is now so desirable: "Commerce, which made the bourgeoisie in England rich, contributed to liberating them, and this freedom in turn expanded trade, and that resulted in the greatness of the state." The English merchant, Voltaire says, is right to be proud of his accomplishment, and his rank is equivalent to that of a noble. For that reason English nobles also have no qualms about engaging in trade themselves, while in France any [ragamuffin—M. N.] aristocrat thinks he has the right "majestically to despise the négociant."[38]

What Voltaire attempts in the *Lettres philosophiques* is what the philosophes of the Enlightenment up to the time of the *Encyclopédie* will pursue as a strategy: they who favor social change will use as a term of argument the bourgeois order in England, that England for which the name Locke is representative (that very Locke whom Voltaire made popular in his *Lettres philosophiques*). Put differently, they play the new bourgeois order (in England), which is the order of a new ruling class, off against the feudal-absolutist disorder in France, which is the (poor) order of the old exploiting class. They appear in the name of the (new) order and as supporters of order and thereby at the same time see to the destruction of the (old) feudal system. They must be Cromwell in the mask of Mr. Bickerstaff and Mr. Bickerstaff in the role of the *honnête homme*. They have to protest their virtue, their dutifulness, their usefulness to the state (something like a competition even begins between feudal-noble and bourgeois ideologues to prove the greater patriotism); they must improve circumstances in France or plead for their improvement while with every improvement they prepare the fall of feudalism; they must pretend to preserve what they are objectively destroying; and they must glorify the person who according to Voltaire's view played a leading role in preparing the revolution: the *négociant*, the *commerçant*. He forms a thoroughly militant unity with the philosophe, although we must not forget that fundamentally neither the one nor the other was working for the elimination of the monarchy (at least not consciously[39]—think of Montesquieu).[40] What they want is reform on the English model. What they do not see is that this reform is not possible; the demand to change conditions according to the English example *implicitly* means the overthrow of the feudal absolutist constitution, means revolution.

Honnêteté as Weapon; or, The Secularization of Knightly Virtues

In his *The European Mind: The Critical Years (1680-1715)*, Paul Hazard confirms the change in the courtier's thinking:[41] the ideal of the *honnête homme* is no longer applicable for him. The *honnête homme* "abdicated of his own accord...at the beginning of the eighteenth century, good manners and good morals were not necessarily concomitant any more. So now, the Gentleman [*l'honnête homme*] had fallen from his high estate, and we must look elsewhere for our pattern of the good life." "In his place, on struts the *Bourgeois*, the Business Man, beaming with smiles," Hazard continues and assumes that the bourgeois, "already highly pleased with himself," had no use for the ideal of *honnêteté*: "Steele and Addison were his sponsors."[42] In *The Spectator* and *The Tatler* they had sought to work out a new ideal of humanity—the result was the merchant who was, to be sure, not an *honnête homme*, but a gentleman: the equal of the (English) nobility, self-confident, rich, well reared. But, Hazard concludes this part of his considerations, the English model was not appropriate for the French temperament, for its fondness of *raison*. According to Hazard, toward the end of the seventeenth and the beginning of the eighteenth century the philosophe, oriented toward real life, became the new ideal of humanity in France.

So much for Hazard. Let us retain the following: for him, the ideal of the *honnête homme* disappeared at the beginning of the eighteenth century; the English ideal of the merchant did not prevail thanks to the Cartesian French turn of mind, but the philosophe did prevail as the ideal of humanity in eighteenth-century France. With respect to the ideal of the *honnête homme*, Robert Mauzi holds an opposed view. He believes that it continues to exist as an *ideal for the nobility* throughout the entire eighteenth century, much to the spiritual torment of the bourgeoisie:

> With regard to the nobility, the bourgeois of the eighteenth century suffers from an inferiority complex. The ideal of the "honnête homme" inherited from classicism is an aristocratic ideal that was in no sense designed according to the image of the bourgeois and in which no one will recognize him, as he knows.[43]

Without going into detail, we can state point-blank that both Hazard's and Mauzi's views are false, and the latter's are more ill-founded. We have already seen that the upper nobility was no longer in a position to make use of the ideal of *honnêteté*: the courtier was no longer an *honnête homme*. And if Colbert left the bourgeoisie of the eighteenth century any revolutionary ideological weapon, then it was the conception of *honnêteté* based on *utilité* and *travail*, which played a decisive role in the eighteenth century. For what Hazard overlooks and what the *Encyclopédie* bears witness to in almost every article on morality is that the philosophe and the *commerçant* are, in contrast to the parasitic nobility, *honnêtes hommes*. The ideology of *honnêteté* enabled the French bourgeoisie to develop their position as a social force that was objectively revolutionary but subjectively the sponsor of order. The dialectics of anarchic production and strict subordination within production, which were complemented and intensified in France by the political constitution of the absolute monarchy, as we attempted to analyze in the manifestations of interest to us, affect the formation of ideology in France as well. In other words, the carriers of the capitalist process of production tried to articulate the dialectics of their mode of production and existence ideologically and strategically in such a way that it served their interests. To be sure, this very articulation of interests of the bourgeois-active forces and tendencies of social change created difficulties in France because the absolute monarchy's entire official machinery of ideology was geared toward conserving the social constitution. The beginnings of a biologistic justification of the capitalist entrepreneur or adventurer were virtually absent, and typically enough, these beginnings were formulated as hints in the work of an oppositional emigrant in Dutch exile, in Pierre Bayle's *Continuation des Pensées diverses sur la comète* (Continuation of Various Thoughts on the Comet, 1704). But these beginnings had very little effect on the apologia for the entrepreneur in France during the time that interests us (whereas in England, for instance in Bernard de Mandeville's *Fable of the Bees*,[44] that biologistic justification was adopted and exploited). Even Hobbes has less effect in this regard than in his justification of absolutism, which met with considerable resistance from French Enlightenment thinkers.[45]

It is obvious that the French bourgeoisie thus had recourse to all the ideological, artistic, literary forms of social intercourse, ideologemes, and systems of ideology prepared by the nobility and the bourgeoisie in the past, in order to portray and to justify as socially necessary and irreproachable its activity in the interest of changing society. The concept of *honnêteté* based on *utilité* and *travail* provided operative possibilities in this attempt. While on the one hand, this concept did hinder the formation of an ideology of adventure comparable to the English one (as did the entire system), on the other hand, it provided the basis for designating and propagandizing the necessary change. The bourgeois strategy was the successive conquest and transforming appropriation ("refunctioning") of those ideals that had in earlier times at least guaranteed the mobility of the aristocracy or that expressed this mobility (and partial independence): the warriorlike virtues of the *honnête* military nobility or the former knightly virtues. The bourgeoisie appropriated them via the ideal of *honnêteté* based on *utilité* and *travail*. These ideals, made bourgeois, together with the trick we will analyze later of allowing other stand-ins to embody the destructive movement and activity that the capitalist or the capitalist mode of production exercised with respect to the old feudal order, represent the correlate to the presentation of the bourgeois as *père de famille*, "paterfamilias," "to the turn to the private, domestic sphere,"[46] to systematic order, which Robert Mauzi, basing himself on a (mutilated) quotation from Sombart,[47] absolutizes.

One piece of evidence for the extent to which the bourgeois, Colbertian ideal of *honnêteté* had already prevailed at the beginning of the eighteenth century is shown by the fact that even the Jesuit *Dictionnaire de Trévoux* (in one of its peculiar definitions) states as a matter of course: "Un honnête homme ne doit jamais être oisif" (An *honnête homme* must never be idle).[48] An *honnête homme*, as the Chevalier Louis de Jaucourt (1704-79) determines in the *Encyclopédie* in the 1750s, "is subject to his duties and he does honnête deeds that duty does not prescribe for him, out of pleasure in order and sentiment."[49] He notes about *oisiveté* that it is the source of all disorder (which is a clear jab at the courtiers)— an *honnête homme* must abhor it: "It would be desirable for us... to have laws against oisiveté, and for no one of whatever rank to be permitted to live without some kind of honnête physical or intellectual work."[50]

This is the basis on which Jaucourt is able to play the "great man" who serves "his native land in an excellent way" off against the "great lord" who has "ancestors, debts, and private means."[51] For according to the idea of the *encyclopédistes* (with the exception of Rousseau), the merchant is of course not only an *honnête homme* but also a patriot, and his patriotism (he provides wealth for the nation, work for the people, and the means to survive the battle against competing nations) is an essential ideological shield under the protection of which the bourgeois can tend to his business. Another component of this shield is the merchant's affirmation of the emancipatory virtues of the bourgeois *honnête homme*, including courage and the willingness to run risks. The *commerçant* represents all these qualities in the most brilliant way, and the *Encyclopédie* accordingly sings his praise under all possible headings from "Commerçant," "Merchant," "Négociant," all the way to (unsuspected) "Homme" (human being). Under "Homme" we read that the sovereign must take care to populate his land well, for the more human beings there are in a country, "the more traders, laborers, and soldiers" (in that order) he will have: "He will have industrious people at his disposal if they are free. The worst administration one can imagine is the one under which surplus sometimes becomes as terrible a scourge for a province as need, because the freedom of trade is not guaranteed."[52]

The number of articles in the *Encyclopédie* that praise the warriorlike virtues of the *commerçant*/bourgeois/*honnête homme* is as telling as the fact that they were edited almost entirely by the Chevalier de Jaucourt, one of the most acute ideologues in the battle especially against the nobility and its privileges, who by his own admission had no use for knightly romances and the knightly ideals glorified in them:

> The abolition of tournaments, the civil and foreign wars, the ban on dueling, the elimination of magic, witchcraft, and enchantments, the well-founded scorn for superstition, in a word: the new countenance that France and Europe donned under the rule of Louis XIV, transformed *bravoure*, bravery, and the *galanterie romanesque*, the romantic gallantry of novels, into a more spiritual and calm courtliness [*galanterie plus spirituelle & plus tranquille*]. People began no longer to hold the incomparable deeds of Amadís in high esteem.[53]

The articles in the *Encyclopédie* that glorify the militant virtues of the bourgeoisie are—how could it be otherwise?—pointedly worldly and opposed to knighthood. Even under the heading "Crainte," "fear," we do not find what we would have found previously: *la crainte de Dieu*, "fear of God," and the virtues contrasted to fear like *Courage* (courage), *Bravoure* (bravery), *Coeur* (manliness), and *Intrepidité* (fearlessness) are wholly or partly removed from the nobility and treated as universal human (that is, bourgeois) qualities. Under the heading "Hardiesse," "boldness," Jaucourt notes that there are five kinds of *hardiesse*, all similar to the single true *hardiesse* but not identical with it. True *hardiesse*, he concludes in accord with Montaigne, "manifests itself as gloriously in a domestic skirmish as in the clash of weapons, in an office as well as on the battle field, with lowered as with raised arms."[54] This single true *hardiesse* is not inborn noble virtue but rather "the fruit of reflection."[55]

Courage, Coeur, Hardiesse, Intrepidité, Fermeté (resoluteness) are the most important revolutionary virtues (besides industry and labor) that the bourgeois employs in the struggle for freedom. In this battle the bourgeoisie appropriates in a dialectical negation everything it can use as an ideological weapon to make its class interests prevail, and among these things are also the military virtues; a whole ideological system of the nobility's entitlement to rights had been erected on the assumption that such virtues were innate. The daring of the bourgeois *honnête homme*, the *commerçant*, the *négociant* in acquiring wealth, increasing his profit, thus receives a justification from many sides. According to the information of the bourgeois ideologues, that is necessary, for the risks that the bourgeois *commerçant* runs are great. That he runs them can be presented by bourgeois ideologues as an expression in turn of courage and of necessity because (as it says in the *Encyclopédie*) "the profit on a trade transaction is almost always proportional to the uncertainty of its success."[56] To be sure, that is why one should invest in risky undertakings only if one does not touch one's capital,[57] but an undertaking that allegedly only produces profit (i.e., that is foolproof) "is planned by someone who is either not very clever or not very honest."[58] Hence, the *Encyclopédie* continues, it would be "inconsistent to cancel an undertaking which one knew to be risky only because the risks have materialized."[59]

In the daring grasp of the *commerçant* who is willing to run risks, Fortuna undergoes a metamorphosis in France, and the sorcerer is none other than D'Alembert. Fortune, he believes, designates "either the sequence of events that make people happy or unhappy... or a condition of well-being, and in this sense one talks about 'faire fortune, avoir de la fortune'—making one's fortune, having [good] fortune."[60] Along these lines D'Alembert then sums up the quintessence of the confrontation between the nobility and the bourgeoisie:

> The honorable means of making one's *fortune* are those that are based on talent and industry. At the head of these means one must place

commerce. What a difference for the wise man between the *fortune* of a courtier, which is based on humiliations and intrigues, and that of a négociant, who owes his prosperity only to himself and who guarantees the well-being of the state with this prosperity. It shows a remarkable degeneration of our customs and at the same time a ridiculous contradiction that trade, that is, the noblest way of enriching oneself, is held in contempt by the nobility, and that it nonetheless serves to buy noble titles.[61]

Cliffs, Storms, and Pirates: The *Noblesse commerçante* of the Abbé Coyer

In 1756 the Abbé François-Gabriel Coyer, in his treatise *La noblesse commerçante*, again takes up arguments that Jacques de Caillière had circulated as early as 1661.[62] Coyer's motivation is, of course, completely different. For Caillière it was a question of giving the impoverished petty nobility a guideline for making their fortunes individually and in competition with the bourgeoisie; Coyer's concern is to integrate the nobility into the ranks of *commerçants* in order to help increase the prosperity of the nation. In his attempt Coyer (who in his other writings takes a plebian perspective, as a representative of the people) makes use of a stratagem (from class warfare); he argues in the name of patriotism (which, by the way, explains the title of the counterpolemic by the Chevalier d'Arc: *La noblesse militaire, ou le patriote françois* [The Military Nobility; or, The French Patriot]).

What Coyer actually has in mind is something else, basically something more rational: he is concerned about the condition of agriculture (although it had improved substantially since the 1730s). He sees that the feudal nobility, lured by Paris and Versailles, distracted by the desire for a courtier's career, is allowing their property to lie fallow or exploiting or managing it poorly, and he wants to find the lever that will move the nobility to a different attitude toward earning money in general and agriculture in particular. He believes this lever is the glorification of the "military" virtues of trade, the invitation to participate in trade. This invitation was not a product of his imagination, as Voltaire pretended to believe,[63] but rather was in the tradition of Richelieu's and Colbert's efforts, as we can see from the fact that Coyer cites Savary des Bruslons's *Dictionnaire universel de commerce* in the 1759 edition as an authority on this very question.[64] In an inversion of these efforts, the constant attempts of ideologues of the bourgeoisie (up to and including the *Encyclopédie*) to give commerce *titre de noblesse*, to ennoble trade, also allow us to deduce how topical Coyer's views were. Coyer's challenge to the nobility gives evidence of the dialectics inherent in the matter; this makes his treatise interesting to us, because the proof he tries to provide entails the proof of the nobility of trade and industry, which the *Encyclopédie* also strives for (for instance under the heading "Marchand," "merchant": "La profession de *marchand* est honorable," "the occupation of merchant is honorable").

A completely different question is how realistic it was to see the commercial, manufacturing, and in view of conditions in France, even the agricultural activity of the nobility as the solution to the economic crisis of the country. That will occupy us little here (history proves that it was not realistic and that Voltaire's mockery in this respect was not unjustified).[65] Coyer confirms that there are masses of nobles; only a fragment is needed for the army and the majority (also without a place at court) is living in financial dependence or even parasitism and in need. Instead of arranging for their fallow land to produce profitably, these nobles prefer financial dependence, even desperate need, to earning money on their own. Coyer invites these nobles to engage in trade, to become *commerçants*; he uses various arguments, among them the comparison with England, where the nobility is extensively active in trade and manufacturing. Interestingly, in his plea for nobles to engage in trade, Coyer refers to national history from Jacques Coeur to Colbert, but he also knows that his appeal will meet with great ideological resistance, as it was articulated especially by Montesquieu a few years before. "It is against the spirit of the monarchy," Montesquieu wrote in *De L'esprit des lois*, 1748, "for nobles to engage in trade. The custom that has allowed the English nobility to conduct trade is one of the factors that has contributed the most to weakening the monarchic government there."[66] Montesquieu thus pleads for retaining French conditions, with the division into *noblesse, noblesse de robe* ("who are between the great nobility and the people"),[67] and non-nobles, with a strict separation of their social functions. Montesquieu sees the social function of the great nobility in spending money (bringing it into circulation) instead of striving for profits; in conducting war and being moved only by the desire for military honors.

The fact that Montesquieu so pointedly takes a position against the idea of nobles engaging in trade (and even before Coyer's work) shows how much this idea was discussed. But for us, Coyer's counterargument is significant: people say that nobles must enter military service. That is correct. But France has many more nobles than it needs for military service.[68] These men apply themselves solely to idleness. People say that the spirit of trade makes men soft and corrupts their fighting spirit. Also true. But what is worse for the fighting spirit—trade or doing nothing?[69] To be sure, it is correct that war is more dangerous than trade,[70] but how often do we fight wars, and what are the nobles to do in the meantime?[71]

But if it is only a question of protecting the fighting spirit of the nobility, no one is asking them to become grocers:

> Why is this nobility of the sword, to which you sacrifice everything, so valuable to you? Obviously because it was gained with effort, with

dangers, and with blood. It is doubtless fine to suffer and die for one's country, but do you believe that trade does not have its troubles, its dangers, and its battles? If the trade carried on peacefully in the bosom of our cities does not appeal to your courage, throw yourselves into sea trade. That is the most interesting for the nation. There you will find cliffs, storms, pirates, and if there is open war, you will spill a more noble blood. There you will find food for your courage. The earth will never offer you so much.... A mariner, a négociant armateur, is the man for all seasons, all weathers, and all risks, and always contesting with hardships and death.[72]

Anyone who does not consider the shipping trade worthy of the nobility can chase "the Séguiers, the Davaux, and the Colberts" from the temple of fame. But Colbert did more for the kingdom "by establishing trade than he could have accomplished with victory in ten battles. That was glory [*gloire*], if I am not mistaken!"[73] Coyer exclaims.

Coyer will repeat this argument in his response to the rejoinder by the Chevalier d'Arc.[74] No wonder he also cites the *aventuriers* of the West Indies and even the *corsaires* of Dunkirk, especially Jean Bart.[75] For after all, everyone now agrees that the spirit of private enterprise can accomplish greater things than the will of an absolute monarch: "It is always the adventurers who do great deeds, and not the rulers of great nations," even Montesquieu must concede.[76] And the *Encyclopédie* yields nothing to the Abbé Coyer in admiration for the courage peculiar to the sea trader, the large-scale merchant, nor in its esteem for overseas trade: "Il élève des hommes à la mer," "it educates men to the sea," and "that is a great advantage for the nation."[77] At a time in which knights-errant had become courtiers, as Coyer states, a burden to princes (and as Coyer, the plebian ideologue, demonstrates in numerous other writings, especially a burden to the people),[78] the bourgeois ideologues are drafting new, attractive, adventurous ideals as a weapon in the battle to make their class interests prevail.

Apologia for Competition

The political targets of the bourgeoisie's efforts to make its goals, and hence the capitalist mode of production, win out were the liberation from mercantile regulation and hence the victory of the principle of free competition, which was considered the basis of (bourgeois) freedom altogether and for which all ideological strategies were set into motion, for which all those attractive new and often adventurous ideals were drafted. The word "competition," as Véron de Forbonnais writes in the *Encyclopédie*

> evokes the idea of several persons who are vying for a preeminent position. If for example various private persons are engaged in selling

one and the same commodity, each tries to offer the best commodity at the lowest price in order to be preferred by the buyer. One recognizes at first glance that competition is the soul and the impetus of industry and the most active principle of trade.[79]

Competition, which according to Véron de Forbonnais must be divided into internal and external and which must be based not on violence but on industry (from which one can assume that Véron saw violence at work everywhere), is

> the main foundation of freedom of trade; it alone contributes more than any other means to providing a nation with that external competition that makes it rich and powerful. The reason for this is quite simple. Each human being has a tendency by nature—I should perhaps not say, as would be tactless, a tendency to be active, but least to create prosperity for himself, and this prosperity, the reward for his labor, makes his occupation pleasant to him. Thus labor, unless an internal error of national government lays fetters on it, takes its free course.[80]

Véron's arguments can by this time be called classic. He considers the acquisition of property to be the realization of individual freedom; he thus describes what Marx and Engels called the "anarchy of production," whose laws they laid bare and which is active with undiminished force in capitalism up to the present as a factor creating peace, order, and freedom. Véron's plea for free competition is also a plea for the "anarchy of bourgeois society" as a *principle of order*, as Marx presented it with respect to the transition from feudalism to capitalism, the dissolution of the guild and corporation privileges of the feudal class society in free competition:

> The modern *"public system,"* the developed modern state, is not based, as Criticism thinks, on a society of privileges, but on a society in which *privileges are abolished and dissolved*; on developed *civil society* based on the vital elements which were still politically fettered in the privilege system and have been set free. Here *"no privileged exclusivity"* stands opposed either to any other exclusivity or to the public system. Free industry and free trade abolish privileged exclusivity and thereby the struggle between the privileged exclusivities. In its place they set man free from privilege—which isolates from the social whole but at the same time joins in a narrower exclusivity—man, no longer bound to other men even by the *semblance* of common ties. Thus they reproduce the universal struggle of man against man, individual against individual. In the same way *civil society* as a whole is this war among themselves of all those individuals no longer isolated from the others by anything else but their *individuality*, and the universal uncurbed movement of the elementary forces of life freed from the fetters of privilege.[81]

And somewhat later, Marx adds:

> *Anarchy* is the law of civil society emancipated from disjointing *privileges*, and the *anarchy* of *civil society* is the basis of the modern *public system*, just as the public system is in turn the guarantee of that anarchy. To the same extent as the two are opposed to each other they also determine each other.[82]

This was also clear to many of Montesquieu's contemporaries in the eighteenth century, as evidenced by his remark that while the "esprit de commerce," the "spirit of trade," might unite two nations that depended on each other for selling or buying goods, it did not unite the individuals.[83] For the eighteenth-century participants, the entire matter, however, is a question of the individual perspective on the manifestations of the capitalist mode of production, whose causes they do not comprehend. What made Montesquieu skeptical was interpreted in a positive sense by the Physiocrat and later minister Anne-Robert-Jacques Turgot (1727-81) in a letter to Du Pont de Nemours in 1764; here the motif of courage also bears fruit in the affirmation of large-scale, worldwide competition. Turgot writes that in speaking about the *commerçant*, Du Pont de Nemours must distinguish between the "little, stupid, greedy commerçants who concentrate only on the tiny sphere of their tiny profits... and fear foreign competition" and the "enlightened commerçants who desire nothing but freedom... and represent the unifying bond between nations and the mediators of worldwide peace."[84]

The Double Game of the Bourgeoisie

The opponents of the bourgeoisie did not fail to see the function of the bourgeoisie as destroyer of the existing feudal-absolutist society and founder of a future capitalist society based on the anarchy defined by Marx; they also saw the resultant ideological double game, although these opponents basically had no broad view and hence no alternative at their disposal, and their criticism remained mostly a simple negation. Jean-Jacques Rousseau (1712-78) is an exception, however. His relation to adventure is determined by both the rejection of the nobility and the upper bourgeoisie, including the rich *commerçants*, and fear of the preproletariat, the workers in manufactures and in the forges, the steelworks of the age. In opposition to these social forces, he develops something like an ideology of the modestly possible adventure, an ideology of the small travel adventure, meant on the one hand to secure independence and mobility vis-à-vis the preproletariat and on the other (especially in journeys on foot) to set itself off from the unadventurous travels of the nobility and the upper bourgeoisie. This aspect of Rousseau's ideology of the small travel adventure is of great importance for the further development of the ideology of adventure in the nineteenth and twentieth centuries; it originates in his plebian, petty-bourgeois worldview. It is of less interest in the context of our investigation, however, than his polemic against the softening effect of luxury and of the trade that produces this luxury. His apologia for a manly, toughening education and way of life (which he propagates, for instance, in *Emile ou l'éducation*, 1762) still has its roots in the traditional polemic of the nobility's ideologues against the bourgeoisie. But while these ideologues advocate an unreal reconstruction of the old society in which the nobility of the sword was the dominant class and performed a serious military function, Rousseau is pleading for an ideal of artisanlike self-sufficiency[85] and modest mobility[86] in the name of individual autonomy. He believes that this autonomy is guaranteed by disinterest, either pretended or actually believed, and Spartan frugality. At the same time, he has a negative view of the travels of merchants. They undertake their travels for the sake of profit, while he travels (and understands and recommends this as the true art of travel) in order to explore the world in closeness to nature, to absorb it into his soul, to deepen his sensibility to natural beauty.[87]

This is the positive aspect of his idea of the adventure of travel, that traveling becomes a spiritual enrichment of the human being and hence an indispensable component of his social being. But with this view he far exceeds (even in drafting new myths of the adventure of travel) the noble-reactionary forces in their destruction of the myth of bourgeois willingness to run risks, bourgeois daring, bourgeois love of travel and adventure, as Coyer developed it. In the same year in which Coyer's *Noblesse commerçant* appeared, 1756, Philippe-Auguste de Saint-Foix, Chevalier D'Arc (died 1779) published his anonymous treatise, *La noblesse militaire, ou le patriote français*, ironically enough with the printer's note, "A Paris. De l'imprimerie de la Noblesse Commerçante" (Paris, From the Press of the Commercial Nobility). D'Arc's arguments are given briefly here: he is outraged that one could even spread the suggestion of a *noblesse commerçant* in an "Etat belliqueux," a "militant nation," like France. The (patriotic) duty of the nobility is, as it has always been, military service. If he were writing in England, D'Arc continues, he would have something to say about the unhappy republican system there, which is fortunately kept in some kind of equilibrium by the English monarchy in a precarious balance of power, "but I am writing in France and for France, whose citizen [*citoyen*] I am."[88] In France, however, as in every self-respecting monarchy, there are and always have been "trois classes principales," "three main classes," "the clergy, the nobility, and the Third Estate,"[89] and each class has its own functions: "The functions of the nobility consist in general and particularly in France as in every militant nation in maintaining the gloire and the intérêts of the prince and of the nation and in spilling all its blood in the defense of those who contribute with their daily labor to their [the prince's and the nation's—M. N.] support and well-being."[90]

But when the nobility conducts trade instead of carrying a sword, who will then protect the traders, who will protect the nation? Perhaps the non-nobles? Would it not then be necessary, since the nobility was missing, to ennoble the non-nobles and to degrade the nobles to *roturiers*, to non-nobles? "Quelle absurde révolution!" D'Arc cries, appalled.[91] It has, after all, long since been proved that the desire for military honor cannot be united with commercial interests. Did anyone seriously believe "that a hand that was used to manipulating the tools of commerce could also learn to use weapons?" And then, alongside other more or less insignificant arguments, D'Arc continues:

> Nothing is as harsh, people cry to us, as the life of a commerçant: he works without respite, he constantly defies all the dangers of the sea; yes!—those whom he hires as subordinate employees, or apprentices [*apprentifs*] do so, but the commerçant, the successful commerçant, remains in his office, where he ceaselessly does accounts. He sends to the harbor or goes there himself and occupies himself only with loading, shipping, unloading, or with the return of his ships, while the captains of his ships have the task of selling in accordance with the instructions of their employer or of delivering the goods to trading partners, if they exist. If the commerçant boards a ship, then only to become acquainted with the country with which he wants to conduct trade. But as soon as he gets to know these countries, he returns home, where he stays in the warehouse that he has chosen as the center for his operations until his fortune has increased as much as he wishes.[92]

D'Arc adds that even if one admits that the life of a merchant is difficult, the "sufferings and dangers of war are of quite a different sort"—but that will not concern us here. We have mentioned what is important for us: the merchant, who or whose ideologue speaks about the courage the *commerçant* needs for his risky, daring commercial undertakings, is quite obviously playing with a marked deck. The *commerçant* does not run risks in person, does not meet dangers, does not venture into the storm, risking his life; instead, his employees do so, whether salesmen, captains, or apprentices.

It is just this aspect that Louis-Gabriel Buat-Nançay (1731-87) subjects to sharp criticism in his *Eléments de la politique, ou recherche des vrais principes de l'économie social* (Elements of Politics; or, Analysis of the True Principles of Social Economy), which appeared in London in 1773. About the entrepreneurs of his time, he writes:

> They have risked much to gain much? But they have risked men, and goods or money. As for the men, ... if they have exposed them to manifest peril for the sake of gain, they have done a very wicked act. As for the goods, if there is any merit in producing them, there should be no merit in risking them for the profit of one individual.[93]

Marx, who excerpted this quotation for his *Theories of Surplus-Value*, supplies the commentary: it "deals well with the prattle about the *risk* that the capitalist always runs."[94]

In fact, no one will question the courage of the philosophers of the Enlightenment, and no one will doubt the courage of the early commercial capitalists who still voyaged overseas themselves in order to export or import goods, just as no one will question that even in the eighteenth century there were still numerous capitalist undertakings demanding courage and willingness to run risks; but the capitalist as individual hero became obsolete at the latest when the physical and social risks were borne by employees and workers. The revolutionary deed of the bourgeois from that time on was only to promote the capitalist mode of production: he was no longer involved in the risks of its material execution, and even the risk of loss of capital, which Marx chiefly had in mind above, had become less and less with time. Even for the adventure trade the bourgeoisie (beginning, as we saw, as early as the Middle Ages) had developed a whole security system that removed risk from them and burdened others with it. Their risk is calculated against profit: "RISQUE," as the *Encyclopédie* states, "is the chance [*hazard*] to which one falls victim with loss or damage. . . . In order to avoid the risk to which goods and shipments on sea are subject, one usually insures them. See 'Insurance Policy.' "[95] Even where the word and the thing coincide, the safety net is open: "Aventure. . .commerce, to put money in a great aventure means to invest it in a ship; one runs the risk of losing it through shipwreck or to pirates unless one has insured it. See 'Insurance' and 'Insurer.' "[96]

The Robber as Hero of Liberation

The dual function and the ideological double strategy of the bourgeoisie we have presented explain why it can employ (or wear) quite different "character masks" for its interests. In an excellently documented investigation, Lew S. Gordon demonstrated what political, revolutionary function the glorification of the smuggler and bandit Louis Mandrin (1724-55) exercised in the so-called *littérature d'Epinal*, the popular literature of the epoch.[97] As a representative of the oppressed populace, Mandrin gives voice to their wishes and hopes, their dreamed-of rebellion against the system of constraints.

The philosophes of the Enlightenment, however, considered the figure of the bandit (except in Diderot's *Les deux amis de Bourbonne*) somewhat suspect. They could do little with his anarchic drive toward freedom. That does not mean that there was no attempt to employ the bandit for the purposes of the bourgeoisie; and this attempt already manifests the whole array of contradictions in interest on the part of the bourgeoisie in its relation to (political) anarchy. These contradictions result from the fact that the bourgeoisie, as the carrier of the capitalist mode of production, itself produces and affirms the anarchy of the social order. However, because bourgeois dominance absolutely requires subordination, either the bourgeoisie does not tolerate *political* anarchy, which is rebellious against its dominance, or the bourgeoisie plays political anarchy off against the organized working class. As early as the eighteenth century as well as for later times, we must sharply distinguish between the function that the social rebel has for the unorganized, exploited masses of the people (and how that function is reflected in the *littérature d'Epinal* investigated by Gordon) and the function that the ideologues of the bourgeoisie allot him.[98]

The use to which Laurent Angliviel de la Beaumelle (1726-73),[99] a Huguenot emigrant, puts the famous robber Louis Dominique Cartouche (executed 14 October 1721) in *Mes pensées* is still antiabsolutist and oriented toward freedom, but it contains several elements of the later bourgeois strategy of combating the working class by glorifying the social rebel or anarchist. La Beaumelle develops a remarkable theory of the origin of republics, speaking about antiquity but unmistakably referring to England: "The founders of monarchies were skilled usurpers, those of republics bold and fortunate bandits."[100]

In a society of criminals, La Beaumelle believes, the system of democracy must necessarily prevail, for no one would dare to try to rule despotically over such dangerous people: "The weakness of peoples elicited the power of kings."[101] A good thought if it were reversed: Strong peoples will drive out their kings. But that is less La Beaumelle's concern than the establishment of a myth:

> A society that consisted only of criminals of the first rank from all other societies would soon produce a people of philosophers, conquerors, and heroes. A republic founded by Cartouche would have had wiser laws than the republic of Solon and perhaps quicker successes than Romulus. The same qualities produce great heroes or great criminals, and the soul of great Condé resembled the soul of Cartouche.[102]

Cartouche, who in La Beaumelle's view was destined to become a great criminal or a great man on the basis of his talents, "would have started out as king by subjugating his subjects, would have divided his enemies with cunning and finally enslaved them with open force."[103]

It is not really surprising that La Beaumelle, who followed Vauvenargues's maxims in many things (especially in the contrast of *oisiveté-activité, gloire-intérêt*), admired Hobbes. One of La Beaumelle's maxims brilliantly exposes the dialectics of the absolutist despotically oriented *Leviathan*: "Hobbes was a great boon to England, for he ruined the kings who put him into practice."[104] His position on the courtier is clearly negative, determined by his condemnation of *oisiveté*; like a distant echo of Caillière, he quotes from the last pages of a courtier's will his exhortation to his son to follow "a strict plan for making your fortune."[105] Elsewhere La Beaumelle writes: "A courtier praising his prince almost always resembles a lover slandering his mistress. If there were princes who did not want to be praised, what would become of the courtiers? The only thing they can do is to flatter!"[106]

And yet, La Beaumelle's maxims give one pause. The censure of courtiers is linked with reactionary and anarchic ideologemes that show the direction that the glorification of the bandit by the bourgeoisie will take. His maxim "In oppression are born the great minds who conceive and give birth to freedom. Every people that wants to triumph will triumph"[107] must be seen in connection with the glorification of Cartouche. To be sure, all of this is openly directed against feudal oppression, but it is connected with contempt for the people, which is expressed throughout. In the last maxim something else announces its presence (as it does in the comments about Cartouche): the formation of the anarchic-fascist ideology of the adventure of the great leader, the *Führer*. La Beaumelle's utopian state on an island has no room for utopian-communist thoughts—one even has the impression that certain ideas were composed as a polemic against Jean Meslier's (1664-1729) *Testament*, which was circulating in manuscript form as early as 1734 before Voltaire published it in an "expurgated" form in 1762:[108]

> Goods would not be common property, for talents are different, and one must reward talent. There would be poor and rich, for could there be the arts and great virtues otherwise? All members of society who were weak, unhealthy, ugly, stupid, evil, would be extirpated.... Foreigners would not be tolerated on this island.... A hundred years would produce such pure and good blood that it would reestablish the nation. If I had my own kingdom, I would order that this policy be put into effect tomorrow...I do not doubt that in twenty or thirty years I would have a race of people in whose veins healthy common sense and virtue pulsed.[109]

The *Honnête* Philosophe as Propagandist of Piracy

To preclude misunderstandings: La Beaumelle was of course *not* a fascist. But during the bourgeoisie's transition from revolutionary rise to exploitative dominance, in the whole context of the ideological change or in connection with its formation, the ideological arguments within the revolutionary bourgeoisie, in all their conscious or unconscious variants (and not only in La Beaumelle), transformed much that was explosive, anarchic, that dismantled the feudal system into functions justifying the capitalist system, stabilizing it, supporting the exploitation and oppression of the proletariat (and these explosive factors themselves were in turn not always above moral reproach and challenge, even by the revolutionary bourgeoisie, the men of the Enlightenment). The glorification of the bold plebian, the great man whose quality as an extraordinary individual was not a question of social rank but of natural gifts, was a bold, revolutionary thought directed against the feudal class order which even Vauvenargues (the involuntary revolutionary) propagandized when he wrote: "If Cromwell had not been just as clever, steadfast, industrious, and generous as he was ambitious and revolutionary [*remuant*], then neither gloire nor fortune would have crowned his ventures."[110] But in the bourgeois class society, in the capitalist system, this glorification of the naturally exceptional person who decides the fate of peoples and nations necessarily became the apologia for the dominance of the bourgeoisie over the proletariat in general, of the capitalist or the politician who perceives the interests of capital in particular. There is no *direct* (intellectual-historical) path from the glorification of the naturally exceptional person by the revolutionary bourgeoisie under feudalism to the glorification of the fascist *caudillo, duce, Führer*, but there is the dialectical path of history.

The glorification of the criminal by bourgeois ideologues in the interest of the bourgeoisie, which can be explained only through the laws of motion of the capitalist mode of production analyzed by Marx, Engels, and Lenin, is associated with the glorification of the privateer or pirate; this glorification presents itself as a patriotic reflection but is in truth a component of the apologia for free trade and free competition, a component of primitive accumulation. Under the heading "Navigateur" in the *Encyclopédie*, the Chevalier de Jaucourt presents the line of ancestors of the great discoverers and conquistadors, especially the English pirate adventurers from John Cabot, Francis Drake, Martin Frobisher, and Walter Raleigh to George Anson (1697-1762), a contemporary of Jaucourt's whom he—for certain reasons—treats most extensively in his article. He is, of course, not ignorant of the function of these figures for English trade, for the English bourgeoisie. The political charge that this had in France is obvious from the fact that George Anson, who had conducted a privateering war against Spanish trade ships from 1718 on and especially after the outbreak of hostilities between England and Spain, had taken significant booty (in the amount of six hundred thousand pounds), and had also commissioned geographical surveys and descriptions, had conducted a marine war against France from the mid-1740s on, inflicting critical losses on the French fleet under Admiral Jonquière in 1747, and from 1758 on was in command of the fleet before Brest. Anson died shortly after being named commander-in-chief of the fleet, but was still living at the time Jaucourt wrote his article that states: "In this high function, the reward for his merits, he still leads the expeditions, the glory and the success of England's sea power."[111]

That Jaucourt touches on Anson's war against France only in an innocuous subordinate clause but spends over one and a half columns glorifying his privateering successes (Drake, for example, receives only one quarter of a column) is a first-rate political stratagem that is employed for a certain purpose. Jaucourt's description of the triumphal reception of Anson on his return from privateering voyages overseas in 1744 gives a key to this purpose:

> When he returned home, he had all the treasure he had conquered brought to London in triumph, with drumrolls and trumpets and the jubilation of the crowd. His various prizes in gold and silver amounted to ten million in French currency. This was given as a prize to the commander and his officers, the sailors and soldiers, without the *king demanding a share of the fruits of their efforts and their courage.* More: he named George Anson a Peer of the Realm.[112] (italics M. N.)

The reason Jaucourt speaks so extensively and with such great enthusiasm about the English pirates, privateers, and seamen, is the world trade that England, according to Jaucourt's view, owes to these brave men. For, as he explains at the beginning of his article, "There is no one who does not know that through shipping, the sea has become the link between the society of all peoples of this earth and that wealth and surplus are spreading."[113] Jaucourt places England in the center and refers to the high honors that the gentlemen adventurers received in England; he makes it clear that this success was possible only because the English monarch, as opposed to the French, did not intervene to no purpose in the overseas activities and in the resulting profits. This becomes all the more significant when we consider that France was currently at war with England. Jaucourt's skillful praise represents a decisive plea for a trade policy that would be more liberal in the domestic sphere and more aggressive and expansionist in the foreign sphere; the figure of the pirate serves the bourgeois or his ideologue well in this attempt. It is only against this background that we can understand all the implications of the definition of "Navigateur" placed at the beginning of his article: "this title is given only to those who undertake long ship voyages, and even among these it seems to be reserved especially for the enlightened, courageous, and bold men [*des hommes éclairés, courageux et hardis*] who have made important new discoveries of localities and countries."[114]

That Jaucourt's article is not an exception is proven by the article on the "Marine," the "navy," written by Jacques-Nicolas Bellin with the collaboration of André-François Boureau-Deslandes,[115] which had appeared three volumes earlier in the *Encyclopédie*. The authors, referring to the hostilities with England, especially in the year 1744, demanded an aggressive naval policy to protect French trade and openly advocated piracy. The ideologues of the bourgeoisie, the philosophes of the Enlightenment, remind the monarchy of its glorious past (which was also useful to the bourgeoisie): Colbert's marine policy is praised as exemplary, and the most famous *corsaires*, Duguai and Jean Bart, are called upon as witnesses. One section of this *Encyclopédie* article is entitled "On the Necessity of Practicing Privateering against English Trade." There we read: "We must declare war on English trade alone. There will be no lasting peace with these people without this policy. We must not aim to become powerful, but rather to become dangerous."[116] The candor of the following is unsurpassable: "The enemy's navy exists only thanks to their finances, and their finances rest on no other basis than trade. Therefore let us combat their trade and their trade alone... so you are pirates, people will say. Doubtless: that is the only role left for us."[117]

The Apotheosis of the *Aventurier*

It is natural that when one thinks of (especially) (English) privateers, pirates, conquistadors, and explorers under the common seal of utility for humanity, of commerce, one also thinks of the merchant adventurers. Even the *Dictionnaire de Trévoux* does not pass over them in silence,[118] and in Jacques Savary des Bruslons's *Dictionnaire universel de commerce*, sections of the adventure company's history are presented in detail.[119] Even in the *Encyclopédie*, under the heading "Aventurier," there is a section (largely copied from Savary des Bruslons's *Dictionnaire*)[120] in which special emphasis is placed on making clear the difference between *planteur* (settler) and *aventurier*/adventurer (shareholder in trade ventures)[121] (for the rest, the author obviously had little expertise).

But that was in England, that was the revolutionary music of bygone times. There the merchant could still call himself an adventurer, there he was not burdened with fighting the battle in the mask of an *honnête homme*. Now, in France, that was impossible: "Aventurier," the *Encyclopédie* reports, "in commerce: the title given a man without character and without a permanent domicile who involves himself boldly in business and whom one cannot completely trust."[122] That is—strategy. That is how the ideological confrontation was carried on in the class struggle of the eighteenth century. Of course there was also the *commerçant* who risked a great deal, went bankrupt, and plunged others into misfortune with his bankruptcy. But the *honnête homme* as *commerçant* had to take pains to distinguish himself from the bankrupt; to be sure, he did exactly the same things, but had had better luck. Anyone who lacked success in business could not have a good character, was a tramp, an *aventurier*.[123]

So far, so good: people would prefer to do business with a respectable *commerçant*—that is correct. But on the other hand, people love excitement, sensation, they admire the courageous man, the conqueror— how is this problem to be solved? Just as the problem with the bandit and the pirate was solved. Others were allowed to do the advertising. Not only were there adventurers in England, there were also French *aventuriers* who also called themselves *boucaniers* or *flibustiers*. Colbert and even Louis XIV had used them; why should the bourgeois of the eighteenth century not do the same, especially since he was not dirtying his own hands, did not even have to leave his desk? "Flibustiers," it says in the contribution by De Sacy for the *Supplément* to the *Encyclopédie* (1776-77), "is the name given in America to the bold and enterprising pirates who have formed an alliance against the Spaniards and who practice privateering, even against each other." "These aventuriers," whose contribution to French colonial policy in the West Indies Bellin had briefly praised in the "Marine" article, under the heading "corsaires d'Amérique,"[124]

> were originally boucaniers [hunters of wild bulls whose meat they prepared on a kind of grill, a *boucan*, from which they took their name—M. N.], who equipped *flibustes* [a kind of ship—M. N.] for fishing after they had killed off a great number of the wild bulls and wild boars in the Antilles. . . . They soon wearied of this arduous work, however, whose results provided the support necessary for them but did not quiet their lust for profit. They equipped their ships for battle and sought their fortune on the seas. This sort of knight-errant went to sea, but not as our old heroes did, who traveled on land in order to annihilate robbers; they themselves committed the most horrible robberies. The history of these pirates teaches us not to confuse true heroism with boldness. No military formation can boast of having furnished such extraordinary proofs of daring. They were wild and merciless, and when they captured a ship, they almost always massacred the crew. . . . This band of robbers, brought together by their greed for wealth, formed a state [*république*], obeyed laws that were seldom broken. These men, to whom justice meant nothing, were just to each other.[125]

After a series of further ostensible condemnations of the *aventuriers*, carried by unmistakable admiration, the *honnêteté* of an Enlightenment philosopher has received its due. He can raise his mask a bit:

> The aventuriers held their rendezvous in the Tortuga Islands near Santo Domingo. Around 1630 they settled there, drove out the Spaniards, were themselves driven out, came back and were able to maintain their hold. . . . Their leaders [*chefs*] had more authority than even the French governors. The court of Louis XIV, that is, Richelieu and Colbert, hardly dared to appoint governors without the agreement of this rabble of soldiers, which tended to do more harm than good. The greatest disadvantage of this institution, which was less authorized than tolerated, was that the flibustiers invited settlers in order to strengthen their ranks, and that these turned from robbers to idlers who would rather risk their lives to enrich themselves with the booty of their enemies than support themselves peacefully with the products of the earth that was to be cultivated.[126]

Let us bear in mind what could disappear in the verbal torrent of the author's moralizing: the institution of the *aventuriers* did "more harm than good," was more "tolerated" than "authorized"; thus it was both authorized and did some good, and that the monarch cooperated with the *aventuriers* or *boucaniers* or *flibustiers* is revealed not least by the fact that the monarch appointed governors to the islands with the agreement of the *aventuriers*. We have already seen how this was done from the Abbé Raynal's *Histoire philosophique et politique des établissements et du commerce des européens dans les deux Indes*, which appeared in three fundamentally different editions in 1772, 1774, and 1781, partly with the collaboration of Pechmeja and Diderot.[127] The chapter we are concerned with is probably by Raynal himself; in any case it is already present in the edition of 1772 and reports on the founding of French colonies in the West Indies by the *aventuriers/flibustiers/boucaniers*. Along with historical data, Raynal presents a portrait of the *aventuriers*: "They make up for what they lack in numbers and power by their activity, vigilance, and boldness. An immoderate inclination toward independence and freedom engendered and nourished in them this spiritual strength that is capable of undertaking and executing anything."[128] At this point the political polemic begins; it is united with a glorification of adventure, whose motivations are shifted into the general psyche of the human being (and pointedly out of the realm of economic motives) (it is no coincidence that Raynal assumes that Columbus felt "as if by instinct" "that there must be another part of the world, and that he was to discover it").[129] As Raynal writes:

> It is not easy to discover the basic drive that set these extraordinary and fantastic people in motion. We cannot say that it was need, for they had a country at their feet [France—M. N.] which offered them immeasurable wealth that people of much less talent than they were gathering before their eyes.[130]

Neither greed for profit nor love of fatherland nor desire for fame motivated the adventurers, according to Raynal:[131]

> What were the moral causes that gave the flibustiers such a strange direction? ... If we want to go back to the sources of this change, we will see that the flibustiers lived in the fetters of European government. The mainspring of freedom that had been compressed for centuries in their souls was released with incredible momentum and produced the most horrible moral phenomena that had yet been seen. Restless and enthusiastic spirits from all nations sided with the adventurers at the first news of their success. The attraction of novelty, the idea of and the desire for distant things, the need to change circumstances, the hope of better fortune, the drive of feeling that fires the imagination to great undertakings, the admiration that quickly entices to imitation, the necessity of surmounting difficulties...the encouragement of example; the equality of good and evil among free

comrades, in a word, that transitory ferment that had stimulated
heaven and earth and the seas, and nature and happiness among
human beings, who were now decked in gold and now in rags, now
sunk in blood, now in delights, made of the flibustiers a people
without equal in history, but also the people of a single day who shone
only for a moment.[132]

To be sure, the atrocities that Raynal says the *aventuriers* committed are inexcusable, but he does not name them. Instead, the author launches into an enthusiastic enumeration of their virtues: "How can one refrain from admiring, in the midst of these crimes, a throng of heroic deeds that would have done honor to the most virtuous peoples on earth?"[133] And the anecdote that is told at this point proves that one of the virtues of the *aventuriers* was not to break their word once it had been given. They gave their word to Spanish trade ships, to whom they had guaranteed safe conduct (in the *Encyclopédie* article "Marine," safe conduct is listed as one of the most important activities of the *corsaires*):

No, the history of past times and that of the future will not be able to
furnish an example of such a society that is as admirable as the
discovery of the New World itself. Only this significant event could
give rise to it because it drew all the spirits of our realm endowed with
spiritual strength and strong passions into these distant regions.[134]

"If that is not heroism, should one perhaps look for heroes in a century where everything great is made ridiculous under the name of enthusiasm?"[135]

A New Era of Humanity

It is obvious that this sort of ecstatic glorification of the *aventuriers*, which actually represents the first French systematization of the adventurer in the modern bourgeois sense, was not shared by all philosophes of the Enlightenment. Diderot, for instance, said he was no great admirer of the "esprit de voyage,"[136] the "spirit of travel," and he gives a mocking commentary on it and on the "voyageur" in the later editions of the *Histoire politique et philosophique*: "This traveler is the *aventurier colonial*," writes Yves Benot, "he is not the philosopher or the scientist."[137] Travels make sense for Diderot only if they serve to expand (scientific) knowledge. The traveler may not be too young, must have knowledge of mathematics, geometry, mechanics, hydraulics, experimental physics, natural history, chemistry, drawing, geography, "and even a little astronomy," and must know the languages of the country he is traveling to;[138] this catalog of qualities reads like a systematization of La Mothe le Vayer's thoughts. Diderot finally comes to understand the travels of a Bougainville, which are at first fully incomprehensible to him[139] (Bougainville was, after all, originally a mathematician with a "vie sédentaire," a "sedentary life," before he set out on his travels), through a projection of the immobility that characterizes his *Moi*, the philosopher in the *Neveu de Ramau* (*Rameau's Nephew*), into Bougainville's movement of travel. In the *Supplément au Voyage de Bougainville*, A expresses astonishment that Bougainville left his "vie sédentaire" in order to pursue the "métier actif, pénible, errant et dissipé de voyageur," the "active, arduous, unsettled, and disconnected *métier* of a traveler." B responds:

> By no means. If a ship is no more than a floating house, and if you observe a sailor who transverses huge spaces, locked in and immobile in a rather narrow space, then you will see that he travels around the world on a plank just as you and I travel through the universe on the floor of your room.[140]

Is this a last echo of the dream of imaginary journeys? Certainly; but it is also much more: the preference for immobility, the disinclination to travel, to expansive, restless movement, is much more progressive in this movement of interception, in the image of the internal rest of the ship and its external movement through space than the glorification of the anarchic rebellion against order, of adventuring in a foreign world. Raynal lacks perspective, which caused his apologia for directionless adventure to be propagated in the nineteenth and twentieth centuries: all the myths are already contained in his writing, including the bourgeois glorification and propagandizing of anarchy as an allegedly revolutionary attitude and praxis.

But Diderot is in pursuit of something completely different, which proves him, the materialist of the eighteenth century, to be a trailblazer for future historical and dialectical materialism. In the dialogue of the immobile *Moi*-philosopher and the constantly dancing nephew of Rameau, Diderot tries to express, as in the simile of the ship from the *Supplément au Voyage de Bougainville*, the fundamental dialectic determining the development of forces of production and—set in motion thereby—of the whole society, the same dialectic that we are tracking here, with a necessary emphasis on movement.

Diderot, who took his simile of the ship from mechanistic physics, the Newtonian laws of motion (see the article "Mouvement" in the *Encyclopédie*) is himself, with his work, the best witness for this dialectic. In the decades of work he put into the *Encyclopédie*, which made him largely immobile, chained him to Paris, in the gigantic inventory of the sciences of his age, in the systematization of the techniques of production, of technology, of the natural sciences and their applications, he produced the handbook of the forces with the help of which the world would be set in motion, kept in motion, even with which the old world would be blown to bits. Supported by experience in politics, science, philosophy, and aesthetics, he unites with his collaborators what had been laid out at the beginning of the seventeenth century but had been splintered, restricted, and fettered in France under the pressure of circumstances. The *Encyclopédie* is the tentative summation of the technologies of all branches of production and especially of manufacturing,[141] and to that extent it is not innovative, but its explosive force lies in the attempt to capture the movement through integrating progressive thought in all areas. The *Encyclopédie* is certainly a monumental work of ordering in production, in economics, in politics, in aesthetics, in moral philosophy, in all disciplines. But the order it introduces is the restlessness of the celestial clock, is the motor of world-historical movement, is the measure of the forces of production—and these forces are anarchic in social production: the glorification of piracy, the glorification of the *aventuriers* are no retrograde daydreams. The praise of the pirate *aventuriers* is one side of the coin; on the other side is engraved the most rigid order. The *Encyclopédie* is the monument of bourgeois order in anarchy or of anarchy out of order. It is the measure of the bourgeois revolution under the ideological guidance of the thinkers of the Enlightenment, in the guise of *honnête* philosophe, under whose protection and with the Church's blessing and many pious words genocide and the slave trade were conducted. The *Encyclopédie* is the geometrical order of the bourgeois upheaval in whose external harmony is hidden primitive accumulation: the great capitalist adventure.

None of this could be foreseen in 1759, when the great revolutionary novel of the French bourgeoisie appeared. It gives a brilliant artistic summary of what was analyzed circumstantially in the present work: the oppression of the people by the nobility, the futile direct revolt against the feudal caste system that ends with a kick in the rear, with exile, torture, and misery, until the enslaved human being begins to break out of this order, to set out for a new world, the New World, in which to be sure he gains gold and wealth but in which this wealth is won with renewed exploitation, with blood and misery. We will not treat in detail this novel, which is not merely a concentration of the most important philosophical problems, but also a historical compendium of the most important stations of primitive accumulation. It is Voltaire's *Candide*, whose subtitle, *Or, The Optimist*, is often misunderstood. Voltaire was not concerned with refuting Leibniz or Wolff; for that he would not have needed to take the trouble to create a (perfect) literary work. He was concerned with replacing speculative metaphysical optimism with a realistic optimism.[142] Voltaire sees the horror of primitive accumulation and abhors it as much as the crimes of feudal reactionary despotism. But despite this horror, he affirms—like Rabelais, like Shakespeare, like Defoe—primitive accumulation as a path in the human struggle for freedom. As Candide's companion, Pangloss, says at the end of their odyssey through the *only* world human beings have:

> There is a concatenation of all events in the best of all possible worlds; for, in short, had you not been kicked out of a fine castle for the love of Miss Cunegund; had you not been put into the Inquisition; had you

not travelled over America on foot; had you not run the baron through the body; and had you not lost all your sheep, which you brought from the good country of El Dorado, you would not have been here to eat preserved citrons and pistachio nuts.[143]

No shorter summary is possible of primitive accumulation and the history of the class struggles between nobility and bourgeoisie. But Voltaire also knows that that accomplishes nothing. He knows that primitive accumulation alone is worth nothing: anyone interested in economics and history (and who had these interests, if not Voltaire?) had known that from the time of Colbert at the latest. Spain's decline was a grim warning to everyone. In the twelfth volume of the *Encyclopédie*, which appeared several years before Voltaire's *Candide*, the article "Espagne" gives the reasons for this decline: a policy of depopulation (the expulsion of the Moriscos), the exploitation of the New World without simultaneous promotion of domestic production. The riches from the colonies "passed into other hands": "With little power on the foreign front, poor and weak domestically: even today no industry complements the gifts of nature in this happy climate."[144] And everyone who kept his eyes directed toward England, as the Anglophile Voltaire did, also knew how to gain lasting advantage from primitive accumulation: through labor, through production, through manufacturing. The better economists in France had also known this at the latest from Colbert's time; Colbert's secular attempt came up against one decisive barrier: the old feudal agricultural system. In 1759, however, the signs of the time are different—they foretell a storm. The *Encyclopédie* has summed up the scientific basis. Despite those seas of blood through which humanity had to wade, Voltaire's *Candide* delivers the literary-philosophical credo. Like the *Encyclopédie*, his novel characterizes the transition from commercial to industrial capitalism, from primitive accumulation, which after all makes possible the enjoyment of "preserved citrons and pistachio nuts," to modern capitalism: "Quite right," Candide conceded, "but we must cultivate our garden."

Notes

Notes

All translations are my own, unless otherwise indicated—R.C.

Chapter 9. Adventure in Bourgeois Order

1. Jürgen Kuczynski, *Studien zu einer Geschichte der Gesellschaftswissenschaften* (Berlin, 1975), 1:109-72.
2. Ibid., 1:155.
3. See Ernst Schulin, *Handelsstaat England: Das politische Interesse der Nation am Aussenhandel vom 16. bis ins frühe 18. Jahrhundert* (Wiesbaden, 1969), 92ff. (especially on Davenant, 269ff.); see also 155ff.
4. See ibid., 146ff.
5. See Karl Marx and Friedrich Engels, "Reviews from the *Neue Rheinische Zeitung*," "Guizot: *Pourquoi la révolution d'Angleterre a-t-elle réussi? Discours sur l'histoire de la révolution d'Angleterre*," in Marx and Engels, *Collected Works* (London, 1978), 10:251ff.
6. See on this period Jürgen Kuczynski, "Die Geschichte der Lage der Arbeiter in England von 1640-1760," in *Geschichte der Lage der Arbeiter unter dem Kapitalismus* (Berlin, 1961), vol. 22; William Cunningham, *The Growth of English Industry and Commerce* (Cambridge, 1907; reprint 1968); *The Cambridge Economic History of Europe* (1967), vol. 4.
7. Friedrich Engels to Conrad Schmidt, in Karl Marx and Friedrich Engels, *Werke* (Berlin, 1956-1971), 37:492.
8. Karl Marx and Friedrich Engels, *The Holy Family; or, Critique of Critical Critique* (Moscow, 1956), 169ff.; V. I. Lenin, "Materialism and Empirio-Criticism," in *Collected Works* (Moscow, 1962), 14:17-362, 126ff. See also Alfred Kosing and Dieter Wittich, "Erkenntnistheorie," in *Philosophisches Wörterbuch*, ed. Georg Klaus and Manfred Buhr, 10 ed. (Leipzig, 1974), 1:357ff.
9. See Winfried Schröder et al., eds., *Französische Aufklärung: Bürgerliche Emanzipation, Literatur, und Bewusstseinsbildung* (Leipzig, 1974), 154-59.
10. Karl Marx and Frederick Engels, *The German Ideology*, in *Collected Works* (London, 1976), 5:522.
11. Marx and Engels, *The Holy Family*, 169.

12. Karl Marx, *A Contribution to the Critique of Political Economy* (New York, 1970), 77.
13. And a distancing from Renouvier's positions. See *Ideology of Adventure*, chapter 8, 189-90.
14. Jean Chenesaux et al., "Das utopische Denken bis zur industriellen Revolution," in *Geschichte des Sozialismus*, ed. Jacques Droz et al. (Frankfurt / Main, West Berlin, and Vienna, 1974-1975), 1:133.
15. See in this context Engels to Conrad Schmidt, in Marx and Engels, *Werke*, 37:492.
16. See especially Walter Euchner, *Naturrecht und Politik bei John Locke* (Frankfurt / Main, 1969), 68ff.
17. John Locke, *The Second Treatise of Government*, ed. Thomas Peardon (New York, 1952), 4.
18. Cornelius Meyer-Tasch, "Nachwort," in John Locke, *Über die Regierung*, trans. Dorothee Tidow (Stuttgart, 1974), 201.
19. Locke, *The Second Treatise of Government*, 11.
20. Ibid., 12.
21. Meyer-Tasch, "Nachwort," 194.
22. Karl Marx, *Theories of Surplus-Value* (Moscow, 1963-1969), 1:365-67.
23. Ibid., 1:366-67.
24. Ibid., 1:367.
25. Ibid.
26. Locke, *The Second Treatise of Government*, 18.
27. Ibid., 18ff. See also Euchner, *Naturrecht und Politik bei John Locke*, 68.
28. Locke, *The Second Treatise of Government*, 24. See also Marx, *Theories of Surplus-Value*, 1:365.
29. Locke, *The Second Treatise of Government*, 27-28.
30. Ibid., 28.
31. Marx and Engels, *The German Ideology*, 5:409.
32. Ibid., 5:410.
33. Ibid., 5:411.
34. Ibid., 5:413-14.
35. In Karl Marx and Frederick Engels, *Collected Works* (London, 1975), 3:418-43, 442.
36. Ibid., 3:442.
37. Ibid., 3:423.
38. Ibid., 3:433.
39. Ibid., 3:434.
40. See among others Frederick Engels, "The Condition of England: The English Constitution," in Marx and Engels, *Collected Works*, 3:491-92.
41. *The Tatler* by Isaac Bickerstaff Esq., in *The Lucubrations of Isaac Bickerstaff Esq. Revised and Corrected by the Author* (London, 1712), 4:81.
42. Ibid., 4:278.
43. Ibid., 1:133-34.
44. Ibid., 3:163-64.
45. Ibid., 1:206ff.
46. Ibid., 3:201ff., 312ff.
47. See Jürgen Habermas, *Strukturwandel der Öffentlichkeit: Untersuchung zu einer Kategorie der bürgerlichen Gesellschaft* (Neuwied and West Berlin, 1968), 53ff.
48. *The Spectator* (London, 1747), 1:17.
49. See ibid., 3:33: "This is the economy of the merchant; and the conduct of the gentleman must be the same."
50. Ibid., 3:32.

51. Karl Marx, "The 18th Brumaire of Louis Napoleon," in Marx and Engels, *Collected Works* (London, 1978), 11:104.
52. Ibid.
53. Ibid., 11:104-5.
54. On Daniel Defoe's life, see Robert Weimann, *Daniel Defoe: Eine Einführung in das Romanwerk* (Halle, 1962), 7ff. See also the synoptic survey of Defoe's dates and contemporary social events in Daniel Defoe, *Romane*, ed. Norbert Miller, 2 ed. (Munich, 1974), 2:637-58.
55. See Ernst Gerhard Jacob, "Daniel Defoe: Essay on Projects (1697)," *Kölner Anglistische Arbeiten* 8 (1929): 61ff. On Defoe as an economic theorist, see Schulin, *Handelsstaat England*, 244ff.
56. See John Robert Moore, *A Checklist of the Writings of Daniel Defoe* (Bloomington, 1960), 7ff.
57. See in this context Weimann, *Daniel Defoe*, 30.
58. Norbert Miller, "Daniel Defoe oder Die Wirklichkeit des Puritaners," in Daniel Defoe, *Romane*, ed. Miller, 1:22.
59. Weimann, *Daniel Defoe*, 55. Robert Weimann also wrote an interpretation of Robinson Crusoe in *Phantasie und Nachahmung: Drei Studien zum Verhältnis von Dichtung, Utopie, und Mythos* (Halle / Saale, 1970), 13-67. In this study, Weimann develops the idea of what he had called in 1962 an "ethically advanced economic type": "Robinson masters nature by mastering himself. He draws his energy from the puritan postulate of self-control, from the worldly asceticism of English Protestantism, from the contemporary bourgeois image of man, and still he breaks through its ideological boundaries. He relies on the experience, the strength, and the confidence of a civilization which in its aspiring wholeness represents the fate of all of human culture. Crusoe's victory over unreason and the wild force of nature is in this sense the victory of all of humanity, which has not relinquished the belief in the powers slumbering in it."
Apart from the conclusion that Robinson is an allegory for "all of humanity," which seems to me to contradict what Weimann, together with Marx and Engels, correctly finds: that Robinson does not represent the abstract everyman, but the contemporary English merchant (17), the premises on which Weimann bases his conclusions seem somewhat problematic. Max Weber's key concept ("worldly asceticism") is so integrated into Weimann's interpretation that it is not even noted with quotation marks. We may assume that a course is thus set for an interpretation of Robinson Crusoe from the perspective of Weberian intellectual history, especially since immediately following the above passage, Weber's coordinates "adventure" and "asceticism" are offered as a key to understanding Robinson Crusoe: "The action is projected outward from the hero, and in the hero himself is staged the contest between adventure and asceticism, picaresque and spiritual drama, but also between utopia and reality." (36) But in his essay "Defoe: *Robinson Crusoe*," in *Der englische Roman: Vom Mittelalter zur Moderne*, ed. Franz K. Stanzel (Düsseldorf, 1969), 1:108-43, esp. 141-42, Weimann himself seems to indicate that he has gone beyond such positions.
60. Daniel Defoe, *The Life and Adventures of Robinson Crusoe*, in *The Novels and Miscellaneous Works of Daniel Defoe*, (Oxford, 1840; reprint New York, 1973), 1:15-16.
61. Ibid., 1:16.
62. Defoe, *The Complete English Tradesman* (New York, 1889; reprint 1970), 1:84. This remarkable quotation, twisted and misconstrued (applied, that is, to Robinson Crusoe or the merchant adventurer instead of to the small tradesman, although Defoe expressly emphasizes that he means the small tradesman), was used as a chapter motto by Jan Kott for interpretation of *Robinson Crusoe* in Kott, *Die Schule der Klassiker* (n.p., n.d. Berlin, 1954), 31.
63. Weimann, *Daniel Defoe*, 51.
64. See in this context Michael Nerlich, "Lazarillo und Felix sind keine Brüder," in *Kunst, Politik, und Schelmerei: Die Rückkehr des Künstlers und des Intellectuellen in die Gesellschaft*

des zwanzigsten Jahrhunderts, dargestellt an Werken von Charles de Coster, Romain Rolland, André Gide, Heinrich Mann, und Thomas Mann (Frankfurt / Main, 1969), 15ff.

65. See in this context Arthur Wellesley Secord, *Studies in the Narrative Method of Defoe* (New York, 1924; reprint 1963), 74ff.

66. See Michael Nerlich, "Plädoyer für Lázaro: Bemerkungen zu einer 'Gattung,'" *Romanische Forschungen* 80 (1968): 354-94. See also the polemical attack on my position in Alexander A. Parker, *Los pícaros en la literatura: La novela picaresca en España y en Europa (1599-1753)* (Madrid, 1971), 14ff.

67. See Secord, *Narrative Method of Defoe*, passim.

68. It is indicative that Defoe, in portraying the relationship between Robinson and Friday, quite obviously leans on Shakespeare's *Tempest* (Prospero and Ariel). See John Robert Moore, "Robinson Crusoe," in *Twentieth-Century Interpretations of Robinson Crusoe: A Collection of Critical Essays*, ed. Frank H. Ellis (Englewood Cliffs, N. J., 1969), 55-61, 58. Jürgen Kuczynski is therefore correct when he states that Defoe is celebrating the bourgeois revolution of the past with his "Hymn to the Mob" ("Defoe, Poe, und Swift," in *Gestalten und Werke* [Berlin and Weimar, 1971], 34).

69. See in this context Moore, "Robinson Crusoe," 57.

70. Karl Marx and Frederick Engels, *Collected Works* (New York, 1979), 12:149.

71. Moore, "Robinson Crusoe," 56.

72. Ibid., 55.

73. See Hermann Ullrich's work, which is still fundamental: *Robinson and Robinsonaden, Bibliographie, Geschichte, Kritik: Ein Beitrag zur vergleichenden Literaturgeschichte, im besonderen zur Geschichte des Romans und zur Geschichte der Jugendliteratur* (Weimar, 1898). Of course, the reasons for such a transformation must be kept distinct. Rousseau also pleads, from a "radical leftist" petty-bourgeois position, for the use of *Robinson Crusoe* as educational literature.

74. Marx, *Capital*, 1:169.

75. See Friedrich Engels, *Anti-Dühring: Herr Eugen Dühring's Revolution in Science*, 2 ed. (Moscow, 1959), 214ff.

76. Karl Marx, *Grundrisse: Foundations of the Critique of Political Economy*, trans. Martin Nicolaus (New York, 1973), 84-85.

77. See Engels's comments about Robinson's sword in *Anti-Dühring*, 229ff.

78. Marx, *Grundrisse*, 83.

79. Weimann, *Daniel Defoe*, 59.

80. Marx, *Capital*, 1:169.

81. That does not mean that Robinson / Singleton / Defoe would not have recognized how dubious was the inhumane treatment of the natives (or of the proletariat; in the figure of Friday one must see the native as well as the symbolic figure of the exploited proletariat of the age; see in this context Engels, *Anti-Dühring*, 220). Defoe describes it, discusses (literarily) the natural law positions in this description, but the bottom line is that despite the injustice, the right of the victor, the exploiter, the adventurer is greater (see Defoe's views on the slave trade in *A Plan of the English Commerce* [Oxford, 1927], 246ff.).

82. Defoe, *The Complete English Tradesman*, 2:126-27.

83. Ibid., 2:153. The reason for what appears as confusion may be the definition of trade that Defoe gives in the middle of the text as a *nota bene*, which runs counter to the declared intention of the book: "N.B. By trade we must be understood to include navigation and foreign discoveries; because they are, generally speaking, all promoted and carried on by trade." (1:243)

84. Ibid., 1:241-42.

85. Ibid., 1:242.

86. Ibid., 1:210.

87. See ibid., 1:36: "All rash adventurers are condemned by the prudent part of mankind;

but it is as hard to restrain youth in trade as it is in any other thing where the advantage stands in view, and the danger out of sight."

88. Ibid., 1:241.

89. Daniel Defoe, *Augusta Triumphans*, in *The Novels and Miscellaneous Works* (New York, 1973), 18:36.

90. See Daniel Defoe, *The Life and Actions of Jonathan Wild*, in *Romances and Narratives by Daniel Defoe* (London, 1895), 6:233-78.

91. See Daniel Defoe, *The History of the Remarkable Life of John Sheppard*, in *Romances and Narratives*, 6:169-210; *A Narrative of All the Robberies, Escapes, &c., of John Sheppard*, in *Romances and Narratives*, 6:211-32.

92. See Defoe, *Augusta Triumphans*, 18:34.

93. Ibid.

94. On the problem of criminality in Defoe's work, see Ian Watt, *The Rise of the Novel: Studies in Defoe, Richardson, and Fielding* (Berkeley and Los Angeles, 1957; reprint 1974), 93ff.

95. Defoe, *John Sheppard*, 6:175.

96. Ibid., 6:256.

97. Daniel Defoe, *The Fortunes and Misfortunes of the Famous Moll Flanders* (n.p., 1931), xviii.

98. Defoe, *Robinson Crusoe*, 1:16-17.

99. Ibid., 1:5.

100. Ibid., 2:1-2.

101. Ibid., 2:5.

102. Ibid.

103. Ibid., 2:9.

104. Ibid., 2:7.

105. Ibid., 2:9.

106. Defoe, quoted in Norbert Miller, "Daniel Defoe; oder, Die Wirklichkeit des Puritaners," in *Daniel Defoe: Romane*, 1:12. (This passage is translated from the German as I was unable to find it in English.—R. C.)

107. Defoe, *The Complete English Tradesman*, 1:59.

108. See Watt, *The Rise of the Novel*, 35-42.

109. Engels, *Anti-Dühring*, 222ff.

110. On the influence of *Don Quijote* and *Gil Blas* by Lesage on Smollet, see Paul-Gabriel Boucé, *Les romans de Smollett* (Paris, 1971), 127ff.

111. See Maximilian E. Novak, *Defoe and the Nature of Man* (Oxford, 1973).

112. Jonathan Swift, *Gulliver's Travels*, intro. Ricardo Quintana (New York, 1958), 55-56.

113. Ibid., 119-20.

114. See Swift's critique of feudal absolutist power politics, *Gulliver*, 199ff., and of the decadent nobility, 209.

115. Jürgen Kuczynski has correctly indicated that Swift criticizes English politics and social conditions from the perspective of the representative of an oppressed colonial people, which must be borne in mind in any discussion of his critique (Kuczynski, "Defoe, Poe, und Swift," 9-40; 37ff.).

116. See Swift, *Gulliver*, 205.

117. Swift, *Gulliver*, 212.

118. Ibid.

119. Ibid.

120. Ibid., 204.

121. Ibid.

122. Ibid., 198.

123. Ibid., 241.

124. Bernard Fabian, "Der Naturwissenschaftler als Originalgenie," in *Europäische Aufklärung: Herbert Dieckmann zum 60. Geburtstag*, ed. Hugo Friedrich and Fritz Schalk (Munich, 1967), 47-68, 51f.

125. Ibid., 63.

126. Ibid.

127. Ibid., 53.

128. See in this context Frank Wadleigh Chandler, *The Literature of Roguery* (1907; reprint New York, 1958).

129. See Manfred Naumann et al., eds., *Gesellschaft, Literatur, Lesen: Literaturrezeption in theoretischer Sicht* (Berlin and Weimar, 1973), 208ff. For the special situation in England see Watt, The *Rise of the Novel*, 35-59.

130. Arnold Hauser, *The Social History of Art* (New York, n.d.), 3:217.

131. Laurence Sterne, *The Life and Opinions of Tristram Shandy, Gentleman* (Oxford and New York, 1983), 48.

132. Compare the publication history of Diderot's *Encyclopédie*, as presented by Manfred Naumann in the foreword to *Artikeln aus der von Diderot und D'Alembert herausgegebenen Enzyklopädie*, ed. Naumann (Leipzig, 1972), 5ff.

133. Hauser, *The Social History of Art*, 3:54.

134. Published as a book edition, *The Adventurer* (London, 1753), from which all quotations are taken (pp. 1-6).

Chapter 10. The Metamorphosis of the *Chevalier*

1. Pierre Vilar, "La transition du féodalisme au capitalisme," in *Sur le féodalisme* (Paris, 1971), 35-55, 39.

2. See especially Jean Jacquart, "Immobilisme et catastrophes," in *Histoire de la France rurale*, ed. Georges Duby and Armand Wallon (Paris, 1975), 2:183-353. See also Robert Mandrou, *La France aux XVIIe et XVIIIe siècles*, 3 ed. (Paris, 1974), 75-84.

3. See especially Ernest Labrousse, *Esquisse du mouvement des prix et des revenus en France au XVIIIe siècle* (Paris, 1933); Labrousse, *La crise de l'économie française à la fin de l'Ancien Régime et au début de la Révolution* (Paris, 1944); as well as Labrousse's *Histoire économique et sociale de la France* (Paris, 1970).

4. See especially the study by Pierre Goubet, *Les Danse et les Motte de Beauvais, familles marchandes sous l'Ancien Régime* (Paris, 1959).

5. See Mandrou, *La France aux XVIIe et XVIIIe siècles*, 83-84.

6. Heinz Köller and Bernhard Töpfer, *Frankreich: Ein historischer Abriss* (Berlin, 1969), 1:217.

7. As for instance in ibid.

8. Norbert Elias, *The Court Society*, trans. Edmund Jephcott (London, 1983), 159.

9. See especially Roland Mousnier, *La vénalité des offices sous Henri IV et Louis XIII* (Rouen, 1946; new edition, Paris, 1971).

10. *Satyre Ménippée de la vertu du Catholicon d'Espagne et de la tenue des etats de Paris*, ed. Charles Labitte (Paris, 1841), 213.

11. Joachim Du Bellay, *La deffence et illustration de la langue françoyse*, ed. Emile Person, 2 ed. (Paris, 1892), 115.

12. Ibid., 121.

13. Ibid., 120.

14. René Bray, *La formation de la doctrine classique en France* (Paris, 1927; new edition Paris, 1961), 337.

15. See ibid, 191-214.

16. Elias, *The Court Society*, 158.
17. See among others Henri Sée, *Französische Wirtschaftsgeschichte* (Jena, 1930), 1:118.
18. Köller and Töpfer, *Frankreich*, 1:215.
19. Elias, *The Court Society*, 148.
20. Ibid., 160.
21. Ibid., 162.
22. De Bellay, *La langue françoyse*, 120-21.
23. Pierre Ronsard, *La Franciade*, in *Oeuvres complètes*, ed. Gustave Cohen, Bibliothèque de la Pléiade (Paris, 1950), 2:1011.
24. Ibid., 2:1009.
25. ibid., 2:1011.
26. Ibid., 2:1020.
27. Voltaire, "Essai sur les moeurs et l'esprit des nations," in *Oeuvres complètes de Voltaire*, ed. Condorcet (Paris, 1878), 12:145.
28. Elias, *The Court Society*, 148-49.
29. See among others Robert Mandrou, *Louis XIV en son temps (1661-1715)* (Paris, 1973), 244-68.
30. Nicolas Boileau-Despréaux, "Epitre I (1669): Au Roi [Contre les conquêtes]," in *Oeuvres complètes*, ed. Antoine Adam and Françoise Escal (Paris, 1966), 105.
31. Elias, *The Court Society*, 88.
32. Bernard Le Bouvier de Fontenelle, "La gloire des armes et des belles lettres sous Louis XIV," in *Oeuvres complètes*, ed. G.-B. Depping (Paris, 1818; reprint Geneva, 1968), 3:180-82, 180.
33. Nicolas Boileau-Despréaux, *L'art poétique*, in *Oeuvres complètes*, ed. Antoine Adam and Françoise Escal (Paris, 1966), 172-73. Emphasis is Nerlich's.
34. For the debate between Boileau and Desmarest de Saint-Sorlin concerning epic poetry, see Michael Nerlich, "La mythologie comme arme poétique dans la lutte pour la paix, propos hérétiques sur Boileau, le poème épique, et la doctrine classique," *Beiträge zur romanischen Philologie* 1 (1978): 65-80.
35. Werner Krauss, *Die Literatur der französische Frühaufklärung* (Frankfurt / Main, 1971), 43.: "The ancient framework deceived no one about the fact that this 'art' of ruling (*Les aventures de Télémaque*—M. N.) represented one long criticism of the absolutism dominating France. This criticism hid behind utterances like the following: 'Le gouvernement demande une certaine harmonie comme la musique, et de justes proportions comme l'architecture.'" [Government of a kingdom calls for a certain harmony like music, and correct proportions like architecture.]
36. For the contemporary response to *Les aventures de Télémaque*, see Hans Mattauch, *Die literarische Kritik der frühen französischen Zeitschriften (1665-1748)*, Münchener Romanistische Arbeiten 26 (Munich, 1968), 150-51.
37. On the "failure" of the French epic in the eighteenth century, see Eckart Richter, "Zum Problem des französischen Epos im 18. Jahrhundert," in *Beiträge zur französischen Aufklärung und spanischen Literatur: Festgabe für Werner Krauss zum 70. Geburtstag*, ed. Werner Bahner (Berlin, 1971), 315-36. It was not only the epic that was charged with glorifying the idea of the absolute monarchy or the figure of the absolute monarch; the whole of intellectual production was subordinated to this demand. That was especially true of historiography—it had to freeze movement in a snapshot of absolutist apotheosis: "For the epoch of absolutism it is characteristic to have a historiography in which the predominance of the absolute monarchy or of the nobility and the clergy is reflected: the history of dynasties, the narration of princely cabinet intrigues and military 'heroics.'" (Manfred Starke, "Das geschichtliche Weltbild der französische Aufklärung," in *Französische Aufklärung: Bürgerliche Emanzipation, Literatur, und Bewusstseinsbildung*, ed. Winfried Schröder et al., Reclams Universal-Bibliothek 562 [Leipzig, 1974], 250)

38. See in this context Maurice Magendie, *La politesse mondaine et les théories de l'honnêteté en France au XVIIe siècle, de 1600 à 1660* (Paris, [1925]), 1:2-3.

39. On the *précieux*, see among others René Bray, *La préciosité et les précieux de Thibaut de Champagne à Jean Giraudoux* (Paris, 1948), 202-28. On "heroic preciosity," see especially Paul Bénichou, *Morales du grand siècle* (Paris, 1948; reprinted in Collections Idées 143, Paris, 1967).

40. See in this context Magendie, *La politesse mondaine*, 1:150-409.

41. On *Astrée* see among others Elias, *The Court Society*, 246ff.

42. Ibid., 247-48.

43. In this context see Antoine Adam, *Histoire de la littérature française au XVIIe siècle* (Paris 1949-1956), 2:127-28.

44. See in this context ibid., 2:135ff.

45. Bénichou, *Morales du grand siècle*, 57-58.

46. On the problem of the three unities, see Jacques Schérer, *La dramaturgie classique en France* (Paris, 1968), 91ff.

47. Pierre Corneille, *Théâtre complet*, ed. Pierre Lièvre (Paris, 1950), 1:54.

48. Ibid., 1:79.

49. Jean Racine, *Oeuvres complètes*, ed. Raymond Picard (Paris, 1950-1960), 1:175-76.

50. Corneille, *Théâtre complet*, 1:79-80.

51. See in this context Erich Auerbach, "La cour et la ville," in *Vier Untersuchungen zur Geschichte der französische Bildung* (Bern, 1951), 12-50.

52. Pierre de Ronsard, *Oeuvres complètes*, ed. Gustave Cohen (Paris, 1950), 2:998.

53. Magendie, *La politesse mondaine*, 1:355-85.

54. Ibid.

55. Auerbach, "La cour et la ville," 38.

56. Ibid., 44.

Chapter 11. The Foundations of Modern Ideology of Adventure in France

1. See in this context Robert Mandrou, *Louis XIV en son temps (1661-1715)* (Paris, 1973), 159-90.

2. See in this context especially Alexandre Koyré, *Du monde clos à l'univers infini* (Paris, 1962), 89-123.

3. In René Descartes, *Philosophical Works*, trans. Elizabeth Haldane and G. R. T. Ross (Cambridge, Eng., 1969), 1:22.

4. See Herbert Pahl, *Die Kolonialpolitik Richelieus und ihre Beziehungen zu seiner Gesamtpolitik*, dissertation, Berlin (Heidelberg, 1932), 20-24.

5. See Guy Richard, *Noblesse d'affaires au XVIIIe siècle* (Paris, 1974), 31-33.

6. See among others Albert Soboul, *La civilisation et la Révolution française* (Paris, 1960), vol. 1, *La crise de l'Ancien Régime*, 228-29, 201, 279; Richard, *Noblesse d'affaires au XVIIIe siècle*, 121-30.

7. Jean Eon was one of the scholars working in this direction. On his book *Le commerce honorable ou considérations politiques*, see Ernst Schulin, *Handelsstaat England: Das politische Interesse der Nation am Aussenhandel vom 16. bis ins frühe 18. Jahrhundert* (Wiesbaden, 1969), 183ff.

8. François de la Mothe le Vayer, *Oeuvres*, new, expanded edition (Dresden, 1756-1759; reprint Geneva, 1970), 1:358.

9. See ibid.

10. See ibid.

11. Ibid., 1:466.

12. See in this context Daniel Dessert, "Finances et société au XVIIe siècle: à propos de la Chambre de Justice de 1661," *Annales* (1974): 847-82.

13. Alain Niderst, "Introduction," in Charles de Saint-Evremond, *Textes choisis*, ed. Niderst, Les classiques du peuple (Paris, 1970), 7-41, 12.

14. On Colbert see, in addition to C. W. Cole, *Colbert and a Century of French Mercantilism* (New York, 1939; new edition 1964), the still indispensable work by Alfred Neymarck, *Colbert et son temps* (Paris, 1877; reprint Geneva, 1970).

15. See Jean-Baptiste Colbert, *Lettres, instructions, et mémoires de Colbert, publiés d'après les ordres de l'Empereur*, ed. Pierre Clément (Paris, 1861-82), 2:cclxiii (the document is also printed in Neymarck, *Colbert et son temps*, 345-61).

16. Ibid.
17. Ibid., 2:cclxiv.
18. Ibid., 2:cclxv.
19. Ibid., 2:cclxvi.
20. Ibid., 2:cclxvii.
21. Ibid.
22. Ibid.
23. Ibid.
24. Ibid., 2:cclxviii.
25. Ibid.
26. Ibid., 2:cclxix.

27. See in this context François Hincker, *Les français devant l'impôt sous l'ancien régime* (Paris, 1971), 30-34.

28. Colbert, *Lettres, instructions, et mémoires*, 2:cclxix.

29. See ibid., 2:cclxxi.

30. Robert Mandrou, *Staatsräson und Vernunft, 1649-1775* (Frankfurt, West Berlin, and Vienna, 1976), 44.

31. See in this context Pierre Goubert, *Louis XIV et vingt millions de français* (Paris, 1966).

32. Colbert, *Lettres, instructions, et mémoires*, 3/1:329.

33. Mandrou, *Staatsräson*, 44.

34. Mandrou, *Louis XIV*, 113-21.

35. Colbert, *Lettres, instructions, et mémoires*, 2:760.

36. See in this context Ernest Labrousse et al., eds., *Histoire économique et sociale de la France* (Paris, 1970), vol. 2, *Des derniers temps de l'âge seigneurial aux préludes de l'âge industriel (1660-1789)*, 186-88.

37. On François Charpentier, see Schulin, *Handelsstaat England*, 88-89.

38. See for instance Franz Schalk, "Otium im Romanischen," in *Exempla romanischer Wortgeschichte* (Frankfurt/Main, 1966), 119-49.

39. Colbert, *Lettres, instructions, et mémoires*, 3/2:1. On Estienne Cleirac, parliamentary advocate in Bordeaux and author of *Us et coustumes de la mer* (Bordeaux, 1661), see Schulin, *Handelsstaat England*, 185.

40. Colbert, *Lettres, instructions, et mémoires*, 3/2:29.

41. Ibid., 3/2:30.

42. Ibid., 3/2:31.

43. See for instance the correspondence with Pierre Arnoul, naval superintendent in Toulon, to whom Colbert wrote on 3 February 1679: "You always only look for pretexts for doing nothing, and when you do not carry out the instructions I give you, then you prepare your lazy excuses." (*Lettres, instructions, et mémoires*, 3/1:144)

44. Colbert, *Lettres, instructions, et mémoires*, 2:656. See also 2:209, 356, 515, 289, 714-15.

Out of deepest conviction, Colbert also demands that children of the tenderest age be allowed to work (3 / 2:389-97).

45. On the organization of censorship or the police, see Mandrou, *Louis XIV*, 161-68.

46. Colbert, *Lettres, instructions, et mémoires*, 2:792-93.

47. Werner Krauss, "Molière und das Problem des Verstehens in der Welt des 17. Jahrhunderts," in *Gesammelte Aufsätze zur Literatur- und Sprachwissenschaft* (Frankfurt / Main, 1949), 339-68, 340.

48. It is characteristic of this policy that Louis XIV reintegrated even the *Frondeurs* into the absolutist system. On his policy toward the nobility see among others Mandrou, *Louis XIV*, 117-21.

49. The weakness of works like Charles Sorel's *Berger extravagant* of 1627 and especially Antoine Furetière's *Roman bourgeois* of 1666 is revealed in their exhibition of an intransigence with no point of view and hence with no meaning: Sorel against the *précieux*, Furetière, who opens up no perspective at all on the alliance of monarchy and bourgeoisie, against the bourgeoisie.

50. See in this context Michael Nerlich, "Notizen zum politischen Theater von Molière," *Lendemains* 2 / 6 (1977): 27-61.

51. See Antoine Adam, *Histoire de la littérature française au XVIIe siècle* (Paris, 1949-1956; reprint 1962), 3:289-90.

52. One of the most brilliant reactionary misinterpretations of Molière as an antibourgeois author is by Paul Bénichou in *Morales du grand siècle* (Paris, 1948; here quoted from the Collection idées 143, Paris, 1967). This analysis shows the kind of tricks one can use in this attempt. The figure of the bourgeois in Molière, says Bénichou, is incapable of loving; his examples are especially Sganarelle, Harpagon, and Arnolphe: "they cannot love." "The figure of Arnolphe," Bénichou elaborates, "is doubtless the most perfect that Molière gave of the bourgeois in love" (259). And with that, everything is proven, for it is a fact that Arnolphe is not capable of love. But what Bénichou (consciously) overlooks is that Arnolphe's opposite numbers, with their progressive ideas of love, are also bourgeois, and that the beloved woman Agnès belongs to the bourgeoisie and her lover Horace, who triumphs over Arnolphe, is also a bourgeois; here Bénichou's thesis collapses.

53. Werner Sombart, *The Quintessence of Capitalism: A Study of the History and Psychology of the Modern Business Man*, trans. and ed. M. Epstein (New York, 1915), 113-15.

54. Jacques Savary, *Le parfait négociant, ou instruction générale pour ce qui regarde le commerce des marchandises de France, & des pays étrangers...*, in Jacques Savary, *Oeuvres* (Paris, 1713), 1:1-2. On Savary's portrait of the merchant, see Henri Hauser, *Les débuts du capitalisme*, new edition (Paris, 1931), 275-80.

55. Savary, *Le parfait négociant*, 1:29.

56. Ibid.

57. Ibid.

58. Ibid., 1:30.

59. Ibid.

60. Ibid.

61. Ibid., 1:41-42.

62. Ibid., 1:426-30.

63. Ibid., 1:416.

64. Ibid.

65. Ibid., 1:201.

66. Ibid., 1:361-62.

67. Ibid., 1:521. See the whole chapter following 521.

68. See Jacques Dubois and R. Lagane, *Dictionnaire de la langue classique* (Paris, 1960), 37. See also Voltaire in the *Dictionnaire philosophique* (in *Oeuvres complètes*, ed. Louis Moland [Paris, 1877-1885], 17:502): "A proprement parler, *l'avarice* est le désir d'accumuler, soit en grains, soit

en meubles, ou en fonds, ou en curiosité." [Properly speaking, avarice is the desire to accumulate, whether it be grain, or furnishings, or funds, or rarities.]

69. In Franz Mehring, *Aufsätze zur ausländische Literatur: Vermischte Schriften* (Berlin, 1963), 15.

70. Molière, *The Miser*, in *Six Prose Comedies of Molière*, trans. George Graveley (London, 1968), 152, 1.3. Page numbers cited in the text refer to this edition.

71. Wolfgang Fietkau, in reporting on one of Peter Szondi's research projects, comes to an almost comic misunderstanding ("Molière in der Perspektive einer lecture sociologique: Versuche einer Rekonstruktion," in Peter Szondi, *Die Theorie des bürgerlichen Trauerspiels im 18. Jahrhundert: Der Kaufmann, der Hausvater, und der Hofmeister*, ed. Gert Mattenklott [Frankfurt / Main, 1973], 1:199-267). He writes: "Like the *Avare* (Harpagon's usury is the business of a rentier) and the *Malade imaginaire*, the *Bourgeois gentilhomme* takes place in the highest circles of the bourgeoisie that has become rich, which no longer ever speaks of commerce or trade" (219). This misinterpretation is augmented by the information on the same page that Colbert had "only contempt" (!) for merchants. How well Bertolt Brecht, on the other hand, understood the *Avare* can be seen from the "'Katzgraben'-Notaten": "Molière's public laughed at Harpagon, his miser. The usurer and hoarder had become ridiculous in a time that saw the great merchants arise, taking risks and assuming loans. Our public could laugh better about Harpagon's miserliness if it didn't see this as a quality, a peculiarity, something 'human, all-too-human,' but instead as a kind of class sickness, an attitude that only just became ridiculous, in short, as a social vice. We have to be able to present the human without treating it as the eternally human." (In Brecht, *Schriften zum Theater* [Berlin and Weimar, 1964], 7:191-92)

72. Karl Marx, *Capital* (New York, 1977), 1:735.

73. Colbert, *Lettres, instructions, et mémoires*, 2:ccxxxi.

74. Ibid., 7:180.

75. Ibid.

76. On November 24, 1680, Colbert forbade, as he claims, the further prosecution of a great usury affair in the interest of commerce (see ibid., 6:63-64).

77. See among others Lionel Rothkrug, "Critique de la politique commerciale et projets de réforme de fiscalité au temps de Colbert," *Revue d'histoire moderne et contemporaine* (April-June 1961): 81-102. See also, and especially, Klaus Malettke, "Colberts Werbung für die 'Compagnie des Indes Orientales': Mittel und Methoden merkantilistischer Wirtschaftsförderung," in *Aus Theorie und Praxis der Geschichtswissenschaft: Festschrift für Hans Herzfeld zum 80. Geburtstag*, ed. Dietrich Kurze (West Berlin and New York, 1973), 349-73. On the fact that Colbert himself later had these same difficulties with other commercial undertakings of this sort, see Pierre Boissonade and P. Charliat, *Colbert et la Compagnie de Commerce du Nord (1661-1689)* (Paris, 1930), 56-68.

78. See among others Jürgen Kuczynski, *Studien über Schöne Literatur und politische Ökonomie* (Berlin, 1954), 54. From the bourgeois side, this attempt was undertaken recently by Jürgen von Stackelberg, "Molière und die Gesellschaftsordnung seiner Zeit," *Germanisch-Romanische Monatsschrift* 56 / 3 (1975):257-75.

79. On the situation of the workers, see Emile Levasseur, *Histoire des classes ouvrières et de l'industrie en France avant 1789*, 2 ed. (Paris, 1901); for a short but very good survey see Maurice Bouvier-Ajam et al., "Préambule historique," in *Manuel d'histoire littéraire de la France*, ed. Pierre Abraham and Roland Desné (Paris, 1966), 2:23-34.

80. Nicolas Boileau-Despréaux, *Oeuvres complètes*, ed. Antoine Adam and Françoise Escal (Paris, 1966), 178.

81. Molière, *Scapin the Scamp*, in *Six Prose Comedies of Molière*, 324, 1.2. Page numbers cited in the text refer to this edition.

82. Nicolas Boileau-Despréaux, Satire VII, in *Oeuvres complètes*, 40.
83. See Satire V, in ibid., 30-33.
84. François de La Rochefoucauld, *Oeuvres complètes*, ed. Louis Martin-Chauffier and Jean Marchand, intro. Robert Kanters (Paris, 1964), 301.
85. On the Jansenist sources of La Rochefoucauld's criticism of the ideal of *honnêteté* see Bénichou, *Morales du grand siècle*; on La Rochefoucauld, see further Wolf Lepenies, "La Rochefoucauld: homme d'action und homme de pensée," in *Melancholie und Gesellschaft*, 2 ed. (Frankfurt / Main, 1972), 193-97.
86. La Rochefoucauld, *Oeuvres complètes*, 301.
87. Ibid., 444.
88. Ibid., 425.
89. Ibid.
90. Ibid., 432.
91. Moliere, *The Misanthrope*, in *Eight Plays by Molière*, trans. Morris Bishop (New York, 1957), 238.
92. Pierre Clément in Colbert, *Lettres, instructions, et mémoires*, 3 / 1:lvi.
93. Colbert, in ibid., 3 / 1:23.
94. Ibid., 3 / 1:114.
95. Ibid., 3 / 1:394.
96. See ibid., 3 / 1:lv.
97. This had an effect on literature as well. See Gilbert Chinard, *L'Amérique et le rêve exotique dans la littérature française au XVIIe et au XVIIIe siècles* (Paris, 1913), 246.
98. Colbert, *Lettres, instructions, et mémoires*, 3 / 2:476.
99. Ibid., 3 / 2:502, 551ff.
100. Ibid., 3 / 2:485.
101. Ibid., 3 / 2:670.
102. Boileau, Satire VIII, in *Oeuvres complètes*, ed. Adam and Escal, 42-43.
103. Ibid., 45.
104. See in this context Hans Kortum, *Charles Perrault und Nicolas Boileau: Antike-Streit der klassischen französischen Literatur* (Berlin, 1966), 99-107.
105. Ibid., 107-12.
106. Colbert, *Lettres, instructions, et mémoires*, 6:260-70, 266.
107. Ibid., 6:266.
108. Voltaire is right when he states that privateers were hanged like pirates, even in time of war and when they had letters of permission (*Essai sur les moeurs et l'esprit des nations*, in *Oeuvres complètes*, 12:477).
109. Leopold Ranke, *Französische Geschichte, vornehmlich im sechzehnten und siebzehnten Jahrhundert*, 2 ed. (Stuttgart and Augsburg, 1856-1861), 3:200.
110. See Armel de Wismes, *Jean Bart et la guerre de course* (Paris, 1965), 27-30.
111. Colbert, *Lettres, instructions, et mémoires*, 3 / 1:37-38.
112. Ibid., 6:287.
113. Ibid., 3 / 1:92-93.
114. Ibid., 6:287.
115. De Wismes, *Jean Bart*, 53.
116. Ibid., 55.
117. Christian Reuter, *Schelmuffsky*, ed. Ilse-Marie Barth (Stuttgart, 1964), 127.
118. *Nouveau dictionnaire historique-portatif. Par une société de Gens de Lettres* (Amsterdam, 1774), 1:242.
119. Cited in de Wismes, *Jean Bart*, 39.
120. The section "Buccaneers and Filibusters," pp. 361ff., in the chapter "Pictures, Strange

or Beautiful" in Paul Hazard, *The European Mind: The Critical Years (1680-1715)* (New Haven, 1953), is a paraphrase of the *Encyclopédie* article by Claude Louis Michel de Sacy (supplemented with quotations from Oexmelin). Hazard abstracts fully from the economic-political reality and shifts the cause of the *aventurier* existence completely into the *aventurier*'s mentality.

121. Despite its appropriateness here, for reasons of space I have omitted a discussion of *Histoire des aventuriers, flibustiers et boucaniers qui se sont signalés dans les Indes von Alexandre Olivier Oexmelin*, which Raynal doubtless consulted during the writing of his *Histoire philosophique et politique* (and which is now easily available in a reprint, 3 vols., Paris, 1967). On the literature of the corsairs and adventurers in the seventeenth century, see Adam, *Histoire de la littérature française au XVIIe siècle*, 5:317.

122. On the cooperation of Pechmeja and Diderot on the *Histoire philosophique et politique* by Raynal, see Yves Benot, "Diderot, Pechmeja, Raynal, et l'anticolonialisme," *Europe* (January-February 1963): 137-53; Yves Benot, *Diderot: De l'athéisme à l'anticolonialisme* (Paris, 1970), 162-259.

123. Guillaume Thomas Raynal, *Wilhelm Thomas Raynals philosophische und politische Geschichte der Besitzungen und Handlungen der Europäer in beyden Indien* (Kempten, 1783-1788), 6:141.

124. Ibid.

125. Ibid., 6:143. See also ibid., 5:226: "France, which up to then had disavowed robbers, whose fortune was of no duration, now recognized them as its subjects as soon as they became settled. It sent them in 1665 a virtuous and perceptive man to rule them."

126. Ibid., 6:143.

127. Ibid., 6:144.

Chapter 12. The Decay of the Alliance and the Departure of the Nobility

1. Guillaume Thomas Raynal, *Wilhelm Thomas Raynals philosophische und politische Geschichte der Besitzungen und Handlungen der Europäer in beyden Indien* (Kempten, 1783-1788), 6:144.

2. Ibid.

3. See Jacques Proust, *Diderot et l'Encyclopédie* (Paris, 1967), 167-77.

4. See in this context François Hincker, *Expériences bancaires sous l'Ancien Régime* (Paris, 1974), 11-13.

5. On Boisguillebert and Quesnay see among others A. W. Anikin, *Ökonomen aus drei Jahrhunderten* (Berlin, 1974), 93-108, 151-68.

6. In this context see among others Robert Mandrou, *La France aux XVIIe et XVIIIe siècles* (Paris, 1974), 138-44. See also Ernest Labrousse et al., eds., *Des derniers temps de l'âge seigneurial aux préludes de l'âge industriel (1660-1789)* (Paris, 1970), vol. 2 of *Histoire économique et sociale de la France*.

7. See especially Pierre Goubert, *Beauvais et le Beauvaisis de 1600 à 1730: Contribution à l'histoire sociale de la France du XVIIe siècle* (Paris, 1960).

8. See Ernest Labrousse, *La crise de l'économie française à la fin de l'Ancien Régime et au début de la Révolution* (Paris, 1944).

9. See among others Jean-Pierre Rioux, *La révolution industrielle 1780-1880* (Paris, 1971), 19-59.

10. Jean-Baptiste Colbert, *Lettres, instructions, et mémoires de Colbert, publiés d'après les ordres de l'Empereur*, ed. Pierre Clément (Paris, 1861-1882), 7:cxcvii.

11. Maurice Magendie, *La politesse mondaine et les théories de l'honnêteté en France, au XVIIe siècle, de 1600 à 1660* (Paris, [1925]), 2:722-29.

12. See François de La Mothe le Vayer, *Oeuvres*, new, expanded edition (Dresden, 1756-1759; reprint Geneva, 1970), 2:702-03.
13. Jacques de Callière, *La fortune des gens de qualité et des gentils-hommes particuliers* (Paris, 1661), 12.
14. Ibid., 332.
15. Ibid., 338.
16. Ibid., 175-76.
17. Ibid., 183.
18. Ibid., 177-78.
19. Jean La Fontaine, *Oeuvres complètes*, ed. Edmond Pilon et al. (Paris, 1954-1958), 1:91-92.
20. Ibid., 1:258-59.
21. Caillière, *La fortune des gens de qualité*, 353.
22. Ibid., 354.
23. Ibid., 324.
24. In addition to the memoirs of Saint-Simon, see Robert Mandrou, *Introduction à la France moderne (1500-1640)* (Paris, 1974), 226-27.
25. Caillière, *La fortune des gens de qualité*, 148.
26. *Mémoires de la vie du Comte de Gramont*, in *Romanciers du XVIIIe siècle*, introduction by Etiemble, Bibliothèque de la Pléiade (Paris, 1960), 1:11-247, 47.
27. Jean Sgard, "Aventure et politique: Le Mythe de Bonneval," in *Roman et lumières au 18e siècle* (Paris, 1970), 411-20, 416-17. That Bonneval ended up in Turkey as a pasha who converted to Islam must have impressed the ideologues of the Enlightenment as an expression of freethinking. See in this context among others *Nouveau dictionnaire historique-portatif. Par une société de Gens de Lettres* (Amsterdam, 1774), 1: Appendix, p. 14.
28. Ibid., 415-16.
29. See Paul Hazard, *La pensée européene au XVIIIe siècle de Montesquieu à Lessing* (Paris, n.d.), 1:338-44.
30. See in this context Robert Mandrou, *Louis XIV en son temps (1661-1715)* (Paris, 1973), 322-38.
31. Robert Mandrou, *De la culture populaire aux 17e et 18e siècles*, 2 ed. (Paris, 1975), 146-50.
32. Lew S. Gordon, "Le thème de Mandrin, le 'Brigand noble' dans l'histoire des idées en France avant la Révolution," in *Au Siècle des lumières* (Paris and Moscow, 1970), 189-207, 197-98.
33. See Ira O. Wade, *The Clandestine Organisation and Diffusion of the Philosophic Ideas in France from 1700 to 1750* (Princeton, 1938); Werner Krauss, "Über den Anteil der Buchgeschichte an der literarischen Entfaltung der Aufklärung," in *Studien zur deutschen und französischen Aufklärung* (Berlin, 1963), 73-155, 130-44.
34. *Dictionnaire universel françois et latin, vulgairement apellé Dictionnaire de Trévoux* (Nancy, 1734), 1:150.
35. Norbert Elias, *The Court Society*, trans. Edmund Jephcott (London, 1983), 87.
36. Antoine Gombard, Chevalier de Méré, *Oeuvres complètes du Chevalier de Méré*, ed. Charles-H. Boudhors (Paris, 1930), 1:11; 3:69-70. On the problem of the *conquérant-honnête homme*, see 3:90-91.
37. See Paul Hazard, *The European Mind: The Critical Years (1680-1715)* (New Haven, 1953), 321ff.
38. Jean de La Bruyère, *Oeuvres complètes*, ed. Julien Benda, Bibliothèque de la Pléiade (Paris, 1951), 260-61.
39. Ibid., 220-21.
40. Ibid., 254-55.
41. On Boulainvilliers, see among others Werner Krauss, *Die Literatur der französischen Frühaufklärung* (Frankfurt / Main, 1971), 48-50; Winfried Schröder et al., eds., *Französische*

Aufklärung: Bürgerliche Emanzipation, Literatur, und Bewusstseinsbildung, Reclams Universal-Bibliothek, 562 (Leipzig, 1974), 253-59.

42. La Bruyère, *Oeuvres complètes*, 215.
43. Ibid., 94.
44. Ibid., 207.
45. Ibid., 217-18.
46. François de Salignac de La Mothe-Fénelon, "Examen de conscience sur les devoirs de la Royauté," in *Oeuvres* (Paris, 1854), 6:8-32, 31-32.
47. *Encyclopédie; ou, Dictionnaire raisonné des sciences, des arts, et des métiers*, ed. D'Alembert and Diderot (edition used: Berne and Lausanne, 1778-1781), 9:795.
48. Luc de Clapiers, Marquis de Vauvenargues, *Oeuvres de Vauvenargues*, ed. Jean-Désiré-Louis Gilbert (Paris, 1857; reprint Geneva, 1970), 173.
49. Vauvenargues, *Oeuvres*, 349.
50. Luc de Clapiers, Marquis de Vauvenargues, *Oeuvres posthumes et oeuvres inédites*, ed. Jean-Désiré-Louis Gilbert (Paris, 1857; reprint Geneva, 1970), 68.
51. Vauvenargues, *Oeuvres*, 348.
52. Ibid., 60.
53. Vauvenargues, *Oeuvres posthumes*, 80.
54. Vauvenargues, *Oeuvres*, 60.
55. Ibid., 174.
56. Ibid., in the essay "Nulle jouissance sans activité," 67; see also "L'activité est dans l'ordre de la nature," 94-95.
57. Ibid., 200; see also "Essai sur quelques caractères: Titus, ou l'activité," 318-19.
58. Ibid., 99.
59. Ibid., 33.
60. Ibid., 129.
61. Ibid., 87.
62. Ibid., 441.
63. Ibid., 446.
64. Ibid., 484.
65. Ibid., 72.

Chapter 13. The Decay of the Alliance and the Foundation of the Antiabsolutist Opposition

1. See in this context among others Michel Vovelle, *La chute de la monarchie 1787-1792* (Paris, 1972), 62-73.
2. See among others Roland Mousnier, *Les hiérarchies sociales de 1450 à nos jours* (Paris, 1969); Roland Mousnier, *Les institutions de la France sous la monarchie absolue* (Paris, 1974), vol. 1.
3. See in this context Régine Robin, "Idéologie et bourgeoisie avant 1789," in *Aujourd'hui l'histoire*, ed. Nouvelle Critique (Paris, 1974), 301-31.
4. See in this context Jean-Marie Goulemot, *Discours, histoire, et révolutions: Représentations de l'histoire et discours sur les révolutions de l'Age Classique aux Lumières* (Paris, 1975), 313.
5. Ibid., 306.
6. Ibid.
7. Ibid., 302-10.
8. Lionel Rothkrug, *Opposition to Louis XIV: The Political and Social Origins of the French Enlightenment* (Princeton, 1965).

9. Scholarship—to a great extent in the wake of Sombart—has grown accustomed to seeing this only from perspectives that are negative for Colbert (Colbert as the rational dreamer who did not recognize the laws of "free enterprise," etc.): "le ministre a d'abord vu trop grand, trop haut" [the minister's vision was first too grand and too high], as André Rémond writes as a representative of many in "Economie dirigée et travaux publics sous Colbert," *Revue d'histoire économique et sociale* (1959): 295-327, esp. 295. That this view is undialectic and one-sided is made manifest by the question as to why there was no explicit bourgeois-capitalist opposition.

10. See among others François Hincker, *Les français devant l'impôt sous l'Ancien Régime* (Paris, 1971), 64-76.

11. Goulemot, *Discours, histoires, et révolutions*, 308.

12. Savary's actual wording is: "On ne peut douter de son utilité [du commerce—M. N.], premièrement à l'égard des particuliers qui vendent la marchandise, puisque la plus grande partie du royaume subsiste honnestement dans cette profession et que l'on voit tous les jours les marchands et les négociants faire des fortunes considérables et mettre leurs enfans dans les premieres charges de la Robe." [No one can doubt the utility (of commerce), primarily with respect to the individuals who sell merchandise, since the greatest part of the kingdom lives honestly from this profession and since one sees every day small and large merchants making considerable fortunes and putting their children in the best positions of the magistracy.] (*Le parfait négociant, ou instruction générale pour ce qui regarde le commerce des marchandises de France, & des pays étrangers...*, in Jacques Savary, *Oeuvres* [Paris, 1713], 1:2)

13. See in this context Jacques Proust, *Diderot et L'Encyclopédie* (Paris, 1967), 182-85.

14. Ibid., 177-81.

15. François de la Mothe le Vayer, *Oeuvres*, new, expanded edition (Dresden, 1756-1759; reprint Geneva, 1970), 2:372-75.

16. Ibid., 2:373.

17. Ibid., 2:374.

18. Ibid.

19. Maurice Roelens, "Introduction," in Bernard Le Bouvier de Fontenelle, *Textes choisis*, Les classiques du peuple (Paris, 1966), 7-33.

20. Quoted in ibid., 19.

21. See among others Robert Mandrou, *Louis XIV en son temps (1661-1715)* (Paris, 1973), 159-90.

22. On the *Querelle des Anciens et des Modernes* see especially Werner Krauss and Hans Kortum, "Der Streit der Altertumsfreunde mit den Anhängern der Moderne und die Entstehung des geschichtlichen Weltbildes," in *Antike und Moderne in der Literaturdiskussion des 18. Jahrhunderts*, ed. Werner Krauss and Hans Kortum (Berlin, 1966), ix-lx.

23. On the aspect of this battle bearing on literary or art theory, see especially Hans Robert Jauss, "Ästhetische Normen und geschichtliche Reflexion in der 'Querelle des Anciens et des Modernes,'" in *Charles Perrault: Parallèle des Anciens et des Modernes en ce qui regarde les arts et les sciences*, ed. Hans Robert Jauss and Max Imdahl (Munich, 1964), 8-64; and in the same work, Max Imdahl, "Kunstgeschichtliche Exkurse zu Perraults Parallèle des Anciens et des Modernes," 65-79.

24. See in this context among others Antoine Adam, *Histoire de la littérature française au XVIIe siècle* (Paris, 1949-1956), 5:80-81.

25. This by no means excludes respect for Descartes, as the sentence quoted by Jauss proves: "Descartes & Gassendi ont découvert des vérités qu'Aristote ne connaissait pas." [Descartes and Gassendi discovered truths which Aristotle did not know.] (Jauss, "Ästhetische Normen," 35)

26. Charles de Saint-Evremond, *Textes choisis*, ed. Alain Niderst, Les classiques du peuple (Paris, 1970), 76-77.

27. Ibid., 76-77. For the criticism of "immovable mathematics" and the related discussion,

see Werner Krauss, introduction to *Cartaud de la Villate: Ein Beitrag zur Entstehung des geschichtlichen Weltbildes in der französischen Frühaufklärung* (Berlin, 1960), 1:49-58.

28. See Saint-Evremond, *Textes choisis*, 139-215.
29. Ibid., 84.
30. Ibid., 305.
31. See ibid., 107-24.
32. Ibid., 316-18.
33. Ibid., 318.
34. See Krauss, introduction to *Cartaud de la Villate*, 1:36.
35. See Charles Perrault, "Le siècle de Louis le Grand," in *Perrault: Parallèle des Anciens et des Modernes*, 165-71, esp. 167 (Vincent Voiture, 1597-1648; Jean-François Sarasin, 1614-54: *précieux* poets).
36. Ibid., 165-71.
37. Jauss, "Ästhetische Normen," 44-45.
38. Ibid., 53-54. On this problem see also Martin Fontius, "Ästhetik contra Technologie—eine Voraussetzung bürgerlicher Literaturauffassung," in *Funktion der Literatur: Aspekte, Probleme, Aufgaben*, ed. Dieter Schlenstedt et al., Reihe Literatur und Gesellschaft (Berlin, 1975), 123-32.
39. See for instance Werner Krauss, "Das historische Weltbild und die Geschichtsschreibung in der ersten Hälfte des XVIII. Jahrhunderts," *Lendemains* 1 / 4 (1976): 21-30.
40. See the bibliography in Michèle Duchet, *Anthropologie et Histoire au siècle des lumières: Buffon, Voltaire, Rousseau, Helvétius, Diderot* (Paris, 1971), 483-546.
41. See Paul Hazard, *The European Mind: The Critical Years (1680-1715)* (New Haven, 1953), 3-28.
42. La Bruyère, *Oeuvres complètes*, ed. Julien Benda, Bibliothèque de la Pléiade (Paris, 1951), 450.
43. See among others Hazard, *The European Mind*, 8-9.
44. See in this context, ibid., 6.
45. La Mothe le Vayer, *Oeuvres* 2:537.
46. Ibid., 1:336.
47. Ibid., 1:338.
48. Ibid., 1:336.
49. Ibid., 1:338.
50. Ibid., 1:339.
51. Ibid., 2:358.
52. Ibid., 2:359. Elsewhere he says, in another antithetical discussion: "The useful journeys are those of the mind." (281)
53. Quoted by Maurice Roelens, Introduction, in Fontenelle, *Textes choisis*, 67.
54. On this subject see Werner Krauss, "Überblick über die französischen Utopien von Cyrano de Bergerac bis zu Etienne Cabet," in *Reisen nach Utopia: Französische Utopien aus drei Jahrhunderten* (Berlin, 1964), 5-59; see also Albert Soboul, "Aufklärung, Gesellschaftskritik und Utopie im Frankreich des 18. Jahrhunderts," in *Geschichte des Sozialismus: Von den Anfängen bis 1875*, ed. Jacques Droz et al. (Hamburg, 1972-1974), 1:130-340. See also especially Irmgard Harting and Paul Soboul, *Pour une histoire de l'utopie en France, au XVIIIe siècle* (Paris, 1977). See Harting and Souboul, *Pour une histoire*, 14, on Veiras: "De la Régence à la Révolution...le roman utopique...ne manifests plus l'audace d'un Vairasse ou d'un Gueudeville." [From the Regency to the Revolution, the utopian novel no longer shows the daring of a Vairasse or a Gueudeville.]
55. Louis-Armand La Hontan, *Dialogues avec un sauvage*, ed. Maurice Roelens, Les classiques du peuple (Paris, 1973), 140.

56. Fontenelle, *Textes choisis*, 97-98.
57. Ibid., 267-70. On the preface see Alain Niderst, *Fontenelle à la recherche de lui-même (1657-1702)* (Paris, 1972), 559-73.
58. Fontenelle, *Textes choisis*, 271.
59. Ibid., 269.
60. Ibid.
61. Ibid., 276.
62. Ibid.

Chapter 14. The Decay of the Alliance and the Rise of the *Commerçant*

1. In Bernard Le Bouvier de Fontenelle, *Oeuvres complètes*, ed. G.-B. Depping (Paris, 1818; reprint Geneva, 1968), 2:378.
2. See Robert Mandrou, *L'idée du bonheur dans la littérature et la pensée française au XVIIIe siècle* (Paris, 1960).
3. See in this context Martin Fontius, "Zur Menschenbildproblematik des bürgerlichen Dramas," in *Französische Aufklärung: Bürgerliche Emanzipation, Literatur, und Bewusstseinsbildung*, ed. Winfried Schröder et al., Reclams Universal-Bibliothek 562 (Leipzig, 1974), 428-37.
4. Werner Krauss, "Überblick über die französischen Utopien von Cyrano de Bergerac bis zu Etienne Cabet," in *Reise nach Utopia: Französische Utopien aus drei Jahrhunderten* (Berlin, 1964), 22.
5. Ibid., 23.
6. Albert Soboul, *Geschichte des Sozialismus: Von den Anfängen bis 1875*, ed. Jacques Droz et al. (Hamburg 1972-1974), 1:137.
7. See in this context especially Georges Ascoli, *La Grande-Bretagne devant l'opinion française au XVIIe siècle* (Paris, 1930), 1:255-73. Among newer works about the relationship between England and France, see Werner Krauss, "Das Verhältnis der Franzosen zu England im 18. Jahrhundert," *Lendemains* 2/6 (1977): 73-87; Michael Nerlich, "Anmerkungen zu Werner Krauss, 'Das Verhältnis der Franzosen zu England im 18. Jahrhundert,'" *Lendemains* 2/6 (1977): 87-90; Janos Riesz, "Zum Verhältnis der Franzosen zu England im 18. Jahrhundert: Weitere Anmerkungen zum Aufsatz von Werner Krauss," *Lendemains* 2/7-8 (1977): 197-204.
8. *Dictionnaire universel françois et latin, vulgairement apellé Dictionnaire de Trévoux* (Nancy, 1734), 1:150.
9. To give a striking example from the *Dictionnaire*: "The Portuguese are so superstitious that they drape all pictures in their room before they complete an *aventure amoureuse*." *Aventure* here means the completion of sexual intercourse. The definition of *one* meaning of *aventurier* corresponds to this; the concept was used, according to the *Dictionnaire*, to designate a man "who loves no one woman but seeks the favor of all" (151). The complementary term *aventurière* is not mentioned in the *Dictionnaire de Trévoux*, although it was already current and often referred to a more or less elegant coquette or prostitute, though that was not necessarily the case: *aventurière* was not yet as clearly defined as the term *courtisane*. But the path the term was to follow is already sketched out in the *Dictionnaire*: "That is a woman who is out for *aventures* (*C'est une femme à avantures...*), when she causes talk by her *galanteries*" (150).
10. Ibid., 151.
11. Abbé Prévost, *Histoire du Chevalier des Grieux et de Manon Lescaut*, ed. Frédéric Deloffre and Raymond Picard (Paris, 1965), 4-5.
12. See in this context Georges May, *Le dilemme du roman au XVIIIe siècle: Etude sur les rapports du roman et de la critique (1715-1761)* (Paris, 1963), 182-203.
13. As quoted in Geissler, *Französische Aufklärung*, 502.

14. For a great deal of material on Germany, see the study by Fritz Redlich, "Frühindustrielle Unternehmer und ihre Probleme im Lichte ihrer Selbstzeugnisse," in *Wirtschafts- und sozialgeschichtliche Probleme*, ed. Wolfram Fischer (West Berlin, 1968), 339-412, 343-50.
15. On France see especially Emile Coornaert, *Les compagnonnages en France du Moyen Age à nos jours* (Paris, 1966).
16. Bernhard Groethuysen, *Die Entstehung der Bürgerlichen Welt- und Lebensanschauung in Frankreich* (Halle / Saale, 1927-1930).
17. Jean-Marie Goulemot, *Discours, histoire, et révolutions: Représentations de l'histoire et discours sur les révolutions de l'Age Classique aux Lumières* (Paris, 1975), 308.
18. See among others Pierre Léon, "La vie du marchand," in *Des derniers temps de l'âge seigneurial aux préludes de l'âge industriel (1660-1789)*, vol. 2 of *Histoire économique et sociale de la France*, ed. Ernest Labrousse et al. (Paris, 1970), 612-17. Henri Hauser already censured the fact that scholars constantly confused Jacques Savary with his son, Jacques Savary des Bruslons (see in this context *Les débuts du capitalisme* [Paris, 1931], 275ff.). On the origin of the merchant's self-awareness, see also Jean Ehrard, *L'idée du nature en France à l'aube des lumières* (Paris, 1970), 226-35.
19. See Michael Nerlich, "Zum Widerspruch zwischen 'Aufklärung' und Geschichte," *Lendemains* 1 / 4 (1976): 9-12.
20. See Goulemot, *Discours, histoire, et révolutions*, 34-78.
21. Ibid.
22. Jean-Baptiste Colbert, *Lettres, instructions, et mémoires de Colbert, publiés d'après les ordres de l'Empereur*, ed. Pierre Clément (Paris, 1861-1882), 2:405.
23. Ibid., 2:409.
24. See in this context Ascoli, *Le Grand-Bretagne devant l'opinion française*, 1:112-20.
25. See for instance Colbert, *Lettres, instructions, et mémoires*, 1:432.
26. Ibid., 3 / 1:38.
27. Ibid., 1:446.
28. Louis-Armand La Hontan, *Dialogues avec un sauvage*, ed. Maurice Roelens, Les classiques du peuple (Paris, 1973), 140-41.
29. Proust, *Diderot et l'Encyclopédie* (Paris, 1967), 179-80.
30. Jacques Savary des Bruslons, *Dictionnaire universel de commerce* (Paris, 1723, supplement volume, Paris, 1730), 2: cols. 1222-23.
31. Ibid., 2: col. 649.
32. Ibid.
33. Ibid.
34. On the *Lettres philosophiques* in this context, see Goulemot, *Discours, histoire, et révolutions*, 374-402.
35. On the reading and reinterpretation of Locke under James II, see ibid., 222-75. On the reception of *The Tatler* and *The Spectator* as well as of Locke, see among others Paul Hazard, *The European Mind: The Critical Years (1680-1715)* (New Haven, 1953), 239-51, 325-32.
36. Voltaire, *Lettres philosophiques*, ed. Raymond Naves (Paris, 1951), 35.
37. See Werner Krauss, "Über den Anteil der Buchgeschichte an der literarischen Entfaltung der Aufklärung," in *Studien zur deutschen und französischen Aufklärung* (Berlin, 1963), 73-154, esp. 96-124.
38. Voltaire, *Lettres philosophiques*, 45, 46-47.
39. See Manfred Naumann, foreword to *Artikel aus der von Diderot und D'Alembert herausgegebenen Enzyklopädie*, ed. Manfred Naumann, Reclams Universal-Bibliothek 90 (Leipzig, 1972), 11-12.
40. See Louis Althusser, *Montesquieu, la politique et l'histoire* (Paris, 1959).

41. Hazard, *The European Mind*, 325. To be sure, Hazard concentrates on externalities, and his chief witness before the court of history is Count Gramont, who sees the essence of *honnêteté* in correct behavior alone. For Hazard, the views of this marginal figure constitute the collapse of the world of the *honnête homme*.

42. Ibid., 320-21.

43. Mauzi, *L'idée du bonheur*, 271.

44. See Pierre Rétat, *Le Dictionnaire de Bayle et la lutte philosophique au XVIIIe siècle* (Paris, 1971), 223-25.

45. See Ascoli, *Le Grand-Bretagne devant l'opinion française*, 2:105-10; Ian M. Wilson, *The Influence of Hobbes and Locke in the Shaping of the Concept of Sovereignty in Eighteenth Century France*, Studies on Voltaire and the Eighteenth Century 101 (Oxford, 1973), 48-51.

46. Martin Fontius, "Zur Menschenbildproblematik," 429.

47. Robert Mauzi's philosophical foundation is actually a partially accepted Sombart, whose conception of the burgher as the opposite pole to the bourgeois and other ideas Mauzi adopts and to which he also, unfortunately, subordinates all the valuable eighteenth-century material he reviewed. Thus Mauzi writes, in *L'idée du bonheur*, 268: "If one is to believe the wonderful book by Sombart [*The Quintessence of Capitalism*], then the bourgeois must be defined as 'homo oeconomicus.' There are two types of human being: one that heaps things up, the other that squanders them; the closed and the open human being... one that converts his energy into the money he accumulates, the other that changes it into love which streams forth from him. The 'economic' temperament of the bourgeois is directly opposed to the 'erotic' temperament, which is its contrary."

48. *Dictionnaire de Trévoux*, 3:266.

49. D'Alembert and Diderot, ed., *Encyclopédie; ou, Dictionnaire raisonné des sciences, des arts, et des métiers* (edition used here, Berne and Lausanne, 1778-1781), 17:697.

50. Ibid., 23:585.

51. *Artikel aus der... Enzyklopädie*, ed. Naumann, 928.

52. D'Alembert and Diderot, ed., *Encyclopédie*, 17:682.

53. Ibid., 19:345.

54. Ibid., 17:54.

55. Ibid.

56. Ibid., 8:716-17, under "Compagnie de Commerce."

57. Ibid., 8:716.

58. Ibid.

59. Ibid.

60. Ibid., 15:98.

61. Ibid., 8:99.

62. On Coyer's treatise, see especially Guy Richard, *Nobless d'affaires au XVIIIe siècle* (Paris, 1974), 53-62.

63. See Lew S. Gordon, *Studien zur plebejisch-demokratischen Tradition in der französischen Aufklärung* (Berlin, 1972), 280.

64. Jacques Savary des Bruslons, *Dictionnaire universel de commerce* (Copenhagen, 1759-1765), 2:120.

65. See Guy Richard, *Noblesse d'affaires*, 265: "La 'noblesse commerçante' en tant qu'essai d'adaptation dans le cadre de l'Ancien Régime d'une caste féodale à une économie capitaliste, fut incontestablement un échec." [The 'commercial nobility' as an attempt of a feudal caste to adapt to a capitalist economy within the framework of the Ancien Régime was an incontestable failure.]

66. Montesquieu, *Oeuvres complètes*, ed. Roger Caillois, Bibliothèque de la Pléiade (Paris, 1949-1951), 2:598.

67. Ibid., 2:99.

68. François-Gabriel Coyer, "La Noblesse commerçante," in *Oeuvres de M. l'Abbé Coyer*, new edition (London, 1765), 2:33-35.
69. Ibid., 2:22-25; 46-50.
70. Ibid., 2:22.
71. Ibid., 2:36-38.
72. Ibid., 2:161-62.
73. Ibid., 2:162-63.
74. Coyer, "Développement et défense du système de la noblesse commerçante," in *Oeuvres*, 2:152-55.
75. Ibid., 2:106.
76. Montesquieu, *Oeuvres complètes*, 1:1426.
77. D'Albert and Diderot, ed., *Encyclopédie*, 8:540.
78. See "Les Bagatelles morales" and "Plusieurs dissertations sur différents sujets," in Coyer, *Oeuvres*, vol. 1.
79. As quoted in *Artikel aus der... Enzyklopädie*, ed. Naumann, 252-53.
80. Ibid., 254.
81. Karl Marx and Friedrich Engels, *The Holy Family, or Critique of Critical Critique* (Moscow, 1956), 156-57. See in this context Martin Fontius, "Zur Menschenbildproblematik," 355-57.
82. Marx, in Marx and Engels, *The Holy Family*, 158.
83. Montesquieu, *Oeuvres complètes*, 2:586.
84. Anne-Robert-Jacques Turgot, *Oeuvres de Turgot et documents le concernant*, ed. Gustave Schelle (Paris, 1912-1923), 2:508.
85. See Jean-Jacques Rousseau, *Emile ou l'éducation*, ed. François and Pierre Richard (Paris, 1964), 226.
86. Ibid., 522.
87. See in this context *La nouvelle Héloïse*, in Jean-Jacques Rousseau, *Oeuvres complètes*, ed. Bernhard Guyon et al., Bibliothèque de la Pléiade (Paris, 1964), 2:79-80.
88. Philippe-Auguste de Saint-Foix, Chevalier D'Arc, *La noblesse militaire, ou le patriote françois* (Paris, 1755), 19.
89. Ibid., 22.
90. Ibid., 25.
91. Ibid., 63.
92. Ibid., 63-64.
93. As quoted in Karl Marx, *Theories of Surplus-Value* (Moscow, 1963), 1:381.
94. Ibid.
95. D'Alembert and Diderot, ed., *Encyclopédie*, 29:240.
96. Savary des Bruslons, *Dictionnaire universel de commerce* (Copenhagen, 1759-1765), 1: col. 263.
97. See Lew S. Gordon, "Le thème de Mandrin," in *Au Siècle des Lumières* (Paris and Moscow, 1970), 189-90.
98. On this change on function of the bandit or the bandit theme, see Annechristel Recknagel, "Der Brigant in der italienischen Literatur des 19. Jahrhunderts. Ein Beitrag zur Sozial- und Ideologie-geschichte des italienischen Bürgertums," dissertation (Bremen, 1973).
99. On La Beaumelle see Werner Krauss, *Die Literatur der französischen Frühaufklärung* (Frankfurt/Main, 1971), 54-58.
100. Laurent Angliviel de la Beaumelle, *Mes pensées*, 6 ed. (London, 1752), 79-80.
101. Ibid., 79.
102. Ibid.

103. Ibid., 80.
104. Ibid., 263.
105. Ibid., 54.
106. Ibid., 264.
107. Ibid., 39.
108. See in this context *Französische Aufklärung*, ed. Schröder et al., 329.
109. La Beaumelle, *Mes pensées*, 88-91.
110. Luc le Clapiers, Marquis de Vauvenargues, *Oeuvres*, ed. Jean-Désiré-Louis Gilbert (Paris, 1857; reprint Geneva, 1970), 128.
111. D'Alembert and Diderot, ed., *Encyclopédie*, 24:261.
112. Ibid.
113. Ibid., 24:257.
114. Ibid.
115. See Rolf Geissler, *Boureau-Deslandes: Ein Materialist der Frühaufklärung* (Berlin, 1967), 53-54.
116. D'Alembert and Diderot, ed., *Encyclopédie*, 21:103-11, esp. 107.
117. Ibid.
118. *Dictionnaire de Trévoux*, 1:151.
119. Savary des Bruslons, *Dictionnaire universel de commerce* (Copenhagen, 1759-1765), 1: cols. 1624-28.
120. Ibid., 1: cols. 263-64.
121. D'Alembert and Diderot, ed., *Encyclopédie*, 4:30.
122. Ibid.
123. Much the same is true for piracy. While the great war of piracy was called for and received every possible justification, the small pirate was hung from the yardarm, as the *Encyclopédie*, in accordance with the *Dictionnaire de Commerce*, writes: "INTERLOPER... is a man who does not respect the privileges of a trading company and without permission conducts the same trade in the same place. These men are also called *aventuriers*." Relations have been completely reversed from the time of the merchant adventurers.
124. D'Alembert and Diderot, ed., *Encyclopédie*, 21:109.
125. D'Alembert and Diderot, ed., *Encyclopédie*, 4:30, in the first edition in a supplementary volume under "Aventuriers."
126. Ibid.
127. On the passage we are discussing here, which is probably only by Raynal, Benot remarks (and would seem not to go far enough with this comment) that it should have captured the attention "des historiens du cinéma, en raison de l'importance de cette source de films d'aventures" [of film historians, because of its importance as a source of adventure films] (Yves Benot, *Diderot: De l'athéisme à l'anticolonialisme* [Paris, 1970], 206). To be sure, the text is important for the aspect Benot mentions; but it is still more important as a document of the times.
128. Guillaume Thomas Raynal, *Wilhelm Thomas Raynals philosophische und politische Geschichte der Besitzungen und Handlung der Europäer in beyden Indien* (Kempten, 1783-1788), 5:264.
129. Ibid., 3:274. Turgot represents the opposite opinion in his *Oeuvres*, 1:141-42: "Je n'admire pas Colomb pour avoir dit: 'La terre est ronde, donc en s'élançant toujours à l'Occident je rencontrerai la terre,' quoique les choses les plus simples soient souvent les plus difficiles à trouver; mais ce qui caractérise une âme fort, c'est la confiance avec laquelle il s'abandonne à une mer inconnue sur un raisonnement. Si le courage est la connaissance de ses forces, quel doit être le génie de celui à qui la vérité connue en donne tant." [I do not admire Columbus for having said, "The earth is round, so if I proceed constantly eastward I will discover the earth," although the simplest things are often the hardest to find; but the mark of a strong spirit is the confidence with which

it abandons itself to an unknown sea on the strength of reason. If courage is the knowledge of one's strength, what must be the genius of someone to whom known truth gives so much courage.]

130. Raynal, *Philosophische Geschichte*, 5:264-65.
131. Ibid.
132. Ibid., 5:265-67.
133. Ibid.
134. Ibid., 5:268.
135. Ibid.
136. Denis Diderot, "Voyages autour du monde par la frégate du roi La Boudeuse et la flûte L'Etoile," in *Oeuvres complètes de Diderot*, ed. Jules Assezat and Maurice Tourneux (Paris, 1875-1877; reprint 1966), 2:199-206, esp. 206.
137. Diderot, *Oeuvres complètes*, 2:205.
138. Diderot, "Des moyens de voyager utilement," in *Oeuvres complètes*, 17:365-68.
139. Ibid., 2:199.
140. Ibid., 2:208.
141. See in this context Proust, *Diderot et L'Encyclopédie*, 163-88.
142. I agree completely with the interpretation by Herbert Dieckmann in "Philosophie und literarische Form in Frankreich im 18. Jahrhundert," in *Diderot und die Aufklärung* (Stuttgart, 1972), 59-79, esp. 74-79.
143. Voltaire, *Candide*, in *The Works of Voltaire, A Contemporary Version* (Paris, London, New York, and Chicago, 1901), 1:208.
144. D'Alembert and Diderot, ed., *Encyclopédie*, 12:992.

Index

Index

Addison, Joseph, 259, 381
Ad-venture, 3, 36, 52, 81
Adventurer: 51, 76, 195, 224n, 243n; antitype to, 113; associations of the, 59, 78, 120-28; knightly, 133; merchant, 88; in Rabelais, 105. *See also Aventure*
The Adventurer, 281-83
"Adventurers of the Mercery," 58
The Adventures of Roderick Random, 275
Aeneid, 289
Aesthetics: 288-89, 301, 302, 352, 382; knightly-courtly, 291, 292-94; neo-Aristotelian, 297, 300, 303-5. *See also* Ideology; Monarchy; *Précieux*
Aithiopika of Heliodorus, 5, 214n
Alanus ab Insulis, 172
Alberti, Leon Battista, 66-67, 118, 150, 324
Aleman, Mateo, 39
Alembert, Jean Le Rond d', 310, 356, 362, 384-85. *See also Encyclopédie*
Alexandre le Grand, 304-5
Alfonso the Wise, 22, 23
Amadís de Gaula: 12, 29-35 *passim*, 164, 185, 190; translation of, 290-92, 301
Anarchy: xx, xxii, 9, 50, 96, 98; capitalist, 89, 112-15, 195, 198, 392-93; in Italy, 46, 65; in *Pantagruel*, 101-2; social, 109, 196,

388-89, 394. *See also* Engels, Friedrich; Marx, Karl
Anti-Semitism, 180-82
Anson, George, 395-96
Apuleius, 4
Aquinas, Thomas, 56
Arcadia, 130, 301
Ariosto, Lodovico, 45, 289, 291, 293
Art, Politics, and the Picaresque, xviii
The Art of Cutting with a Knife, 24
L'art poétique, 296, 298-99, 300, 331
Artois, Robert d', 63
Astrée, 302
Auden, W. H., 139, 140, 141
Auerbach, Erich, 13, 105, 306
Augusta Triumphans, or The Way to Make London the Most Flourishing City in the Universe, 271
Aulularia, 327
Avantures de Renaud et d'Armide, 352
L'avare, 181, 327, 329, 330
Aventure: 3-6, 54, 59-63, 80; in *Amadís*, 29; dialect variants of, 57-58; etymology of, 51-52; and Fortuna, 56, 349-50; ideological origins of, 12-17; and piracy, 340-42; social origins, 7-9, 10; in Spain, 20-23; transformation of, 291, 298, 373-74, 397
Les aventures de Télémaque, 300, 374

Bacon, Francis: 118, 154, 194, 198, 199, 208; and bourgeois ideology, 188-201, 249, 309, 363; and free trade, 192-93; and Shakespeare, 168, 169; on usury, 94-95. Mentioned, 261, 273, 279, 284, 310, 376, 379. *See also Essays, Novum Organum, New Atlantis*
Baïf, Jean-Antoine de, 288
Bakhtin, Mikhail, 4, 63, 233n
Balzac, Honoré, 26
Balzac, Jean Louis Guez de, 301
Bart, Jean, 339, 387, 396
Bastiat, Frédéric, 266
Bataillon, Marcel, 37, 38
Bayle, Pierre, 19, 208, 382
Beaumelle, Laurent Angliviel de la, 393
Beaumont, Francis, 135, 163, 184, 186
Beggar's Opera, 271
Bellay, Joachim de, 288, 289, 290, 300, 301
Bellin, Jacques-Nicolas, 396
Bénichou, Paul, 302-3
Benjamin, Walter, xviii
Benot, Yves, 400
Berkeley, George, 250, 251
Bible du soldat, 301
Boccaccio, Giovanni, 45
Bodin, Jean, 287, 294, 312
Böhme, Jacob, 189
Boiardo, Matteo Maria, 45, 291
Boileau-Despréaux, Nicolas: 302, 324, 340, 350, 367; and Colbert, 336-37; and Louis XIV, 295-97. *See also L'art poétique*
Boisguilbert, Pierre de, 345
The Boke named The Governor, 132
Bonneval, Count Claude-Alexandre de, 351, 374
Book of the Knightly Order, 23, 25
Borgia, Cesare, 48
Borinski, Karl, 40
Borjois, xx, 6, 53-54. *See also* Bourgeoisie
Borkenau, Franz, xix, 194-200 *passim*
Borst, Arno, 9
Boscán Almogaver, Juan, 35
Bougainville, Louis-Antoine de, 400
Boulainvilliers, Count Henri de, 355
Boureau-Deslandes, André-François, 396
Bourgeois gentilhomme, 54, 320, 327, 350
Bourgeoisie: 11, 12, 50, 55, 169; avant-garde, 63, 107; English, 61-62, 250; Italian, 46; and monarchy, 286, 288, 302, 352, 355;

modern, 260; in *The Prince*, 49; Spanish, 34-44 *passim*; world view of, 372, 392. *See also Aventure*; Class Struggle; *Honnêteté*; Ideology; Monarchy; *Noblesse de robe*
Brakel, Simon von, 78-79, 121, 126
Bray, René, 289
Brecht, Bertold, xviii, 155, 164, 238n, 417n
Brevisme relacion de la destruccion de las Indias, 36, 133
Bruno, Giordano, 171, 176, 362
Buat-Nançay, Louis-Gabriel, 391
Budé, Guillaume, 98
Bueil, Jean de, 18
Burckhardt, Jacob, 48, 106, 195, 204

C'est les marchands, 64
Cabot, John, 127, 262, 264
Cabot, Sebastian, 127, 128, 129
Caellanus, Andreas, 14
Caillière, Jacques de, 347-49, 350, 376, 385
Calvin, John, 93, 154
Campanella, Tommaso, 362
Candide, 278, 402-3
Cantar de geste, 21-25 *passim*
Canterbury Tales, 55-56
Canto de Mio Cid, 21, 304
Capellanus, Andreas, 62
Capital, 76, 89, 141, 148, 202, 268. *See also* Marx, Karl; Use-value
Capitalism: xix, 34, 79, 121, 233n, 237n; commercial, 65, 83-89, 96, 109-15 *passim*, 132, 345, 360, 379; French, 286, 310-11; in Shakespeare, 146, 159, 172. *See also* Bourgeoisie; Colbert, Jean Baptiste; Monarchy; *Noblesse de robe*
Captain Singleton, 265
Les Caractères, 368
Carey, Henry Charles, 266
Carlos famoso, 36
Cartier, Jacques, 104
Cartouche, Louis Dominique, 393, 394
Cassandre, 302
Carus-Wilson, E. M., 59
Castiglione, Baldassare, 14, 35, 132, 290, 306
Cavendish, Sir Thomas, 130, 131
Cervantes, Miguel de, 25, 30, 39, 40
Champlain, Samuel de, 310
Chanson de geste, 21, 53
Charles *II*, 205
Charles *V*, 34-42 *passim*, 128, 227n

Charles *VII* of France, 18, 20, 49
Charles *IX*, 292
Charpentier, François, 318
Chaucer, Geoffrey, 55-56, 179
Child, Josiah, 96
Chrestien de Troyes, 5-12 *passim*, 53
City Book, of London, 58
Class struggle: 133, 188, 226n, 236n; in *Della Famiglia*, 66; early modern, 81, 286, 306, 359, 364, 376; feudal, 32-33, 87; in Machiavelli, 48; in Shakespeare, 172. See also *Borjois*; Engels, Friedrich; Ideology; Marx, Karl; Monarchy; *Noblesse de robe*
Clélie, 302
Cléopâtre, 302
Clitandre, 304
Colbert, Jean-Baptiste: 349, 352, 367, 396, 403; and the bourgeoisie, 323, 330, 346, 353, 376, 379; cultural policies of, 360, 362; economic policies of, 316, 329, 334, 338, 343, 345; and Louis XIV, 299-300, 317, 320, 328; and world trade, 313-14
Columbus, Christopher, 85, 229n
Commerçant, 323-26, 354, 379, 391, 398. See also *La noblesse commerçante*
The Complete English Tradesman, 263, 269, 274
Conjectures on Original Composition, 279
Continuation des Pensées diverses sur la comète, 208, 382
Les Conversations, 352, 353
Coornaert, E., 55
Copernicus, Nicolas, 309, 362
Corneille, Pierre, 303-4, 324, 365, 366
Corneille, Thomas, 362
Il Cortegiano, 35, 132, 290, 302, 306
Cortrugli, Benedetto, 118
Cotgrave, Randle, 19
Couvin, Watriquet de, 56
Coyer, Abbé François-Gabriel, 348, 375, 385, 386, 390
El Criticón, 40-44
Crohn-Wolfgang, Herman Felix, 133
Cromwell, Oliver, 205, 260, 378, 380, 395
Crusade: 15, 52, 54; Fourth, 16, 22, 26; Seventh, 63
Curtius, Ernst Robert, 53
Cyrano de Bergerac, Savignien, 370

Dante, Alighieri, 65

De Amore, 14
De cive, 201
De Dignitate et Augmentis Scientiarum, 191
De L'esprit des lois, 386
De gli eroici furori, 171, 176
De Jure Belli et Pacis, 253
De Jure Naturalis et Gentium, 253
De merveilleus qui se trouve dans les poèmes des anciens, 365
De Officio Hominis et Civis, 253
Declaration of the Demeanor and Carriage of Sir Walter Raleigh, Knight, 186
Declaration of Rights (1689), 207
Deffence et illustration de la langue françoyse, 288
Defoe, Daniel, 256, 260-69 *passim*, 402
Della Famiglia, 66-67, 118, 150, 151, 324
Deloney, Thomas, 183
Descartes, René, 194, 198, 309, 310, 363, 376
Description et perfection des arts et métiers, 362
Desmarets de Saint-Sorlin, Jean, 300, 367
La desordenada codicia de los bienes ajenos, 39
Deutsche Zeitschrift für Philosophie, xix
Les deux amis de Bourbonne, 392
Dialectical materialism, xviii, xxiii, 65, 197, 246n
Dialogo di Fortuna, 172
Dialogues avec un sauvage, 370
Diana, 301
Diaz de Bivar, Rodrigo, 21
Dictionnaire de l'ancienne langue française, 51
Dictionnaire des arts et des sciences, 362
Dictionnaire de Trévoux, 352, 374, 397
Dictionnaire Universel de Commerce, 323, 378, 385, 397
A Dictionary of the French and English Tongues, 19
Diderot, Dennis: 341, 355-56, 362, 370, 392, 400-401. Mentioned, 323, 340, 344, 399
Discours préliminaire, 362
Discours de la vraie honnêteté, 352
A Discourse of Trade, 96
A Discourse upon Usury, 93-94, 126, 240n, 328
Dit d'aventures, 63
Dit des marchands, 64
Don Quijote, 29, 39, 40, 221n
Doren, Alfred, 67

Drake, Francis, 129-33 *passim*, 264, 265, 275
Du Fail, Noël, 19
Du moien de dresser une bibliothèque d'une centaine de livres seulement, 362
Du Pont de Nemours, Pierre Samuel, 389
Duby, Georges, 8, 135
Duchat, Jacob le, 19
Dühring, Eugene Karl, 82, 275
Dürer, Albrecht, 109

East India Company, 95, 96, 133, 207, 208
Ebenwein, Elena, 5, 51
L'école des femmes, 321, 323, 326-27
Edward *IV*, 60
"The 18th Brumaire of Louis Napoleon," 260
Eléments de la politique, 391
Elias, Norbert, 286-87, 290, 296, 302, 352
Elizabeth *I*, 60, 121, 124, 130, 131, 183
Elyot, Thomas, 132
Emblemata of Alciati, 176
Emile ou l'éducation, 390
Encyclopédie: 323, 344, 377, 378, 381, 401; and the bourgeoisie, 383-88 *passim*, 392, 395. Mentioned, 310, 340, 356, 362, 371, 396
Engels, Friedrich: xix, 17, 19, 46, 75, 207; on the *homo novus*, 108-13, 118, 250, 256; on the medieval merchant, 76-79; on private property, 82; on social anarchy, 115, 195, 196, 198, 388; on trade, 87, 88; on usury, 90. Mentioned, 84, 85, 120, 122, 141, 152, 275, 285, 286, 287, 388, 395, 409n. *See also* Guilds; "The Peasant War in Germany"
England's Treasure by Forraign Trade, 95-96
Enlightenment: 346, 376, 392, 396; French, 250, 255-56, 274, 277, 382, 400-402
Enrique IV, 24
Entretiens sur la pluralité des mondes, 370
Entstehung der bürgerlichen Welt- und Lebensanschauung in Frankreich, 354
Epic, 36, 45, 291-98 *passim*, 413n
Erasmus, 38
Essai sur les moeurs et l'esprit des nations, 294
Essais, 306
An Essay Concerning Human Understanding, 250
An Essay upon Projects, 261

Essays, 94-95, 168, 191, 208. *See also* Bacon, Francis; *New Atlantis*; *Novum Organum*
Estienne, Henri, 19
Etat de la France, 355
The European Mind: The Critical Years, 310
Exchange-value, 83, 86, 87, 111, 117. *See also* Use-value

Fabian, Bernhard, 279
Fable of the Bees: or Private Vices, Publick Benefits, 208, 382
The Faery Queen, 131, 132
Famous Tragedy of the Rich Jew of Malta, 183
Faret, Nicolas, 306
Felipe *IV*, 41, 42
Fénelon, François de Salignac de La Mothe, 300, 355
Fernando of Aragon, 24
Fielding, Henry, 259
Flor, Roger de, 25, 26, 27
Fontenelle, Bernhard le Bovier de, 296-97, 350, 370, 371, 372
Fontius, Martin, xix
Forbonnais, Véron de, 387-88
La formation de la doctrine classique en France, 289
Fortuna, 56, 67-68, 170-79 *passim*, 347, 350, 358
Fortunatus: 66-75 *passim*, 110, 117, 118, 273; and *Pantagruel*, 103-5
La fortune des gens de qualité et des gentilshommes particuliers, 347, 349
Foucquet, Nicolas, 349
The Four Prentices of London, 183
La Franciade, 292, 294
François *I*, 106, 286-96 *passim*
Freud, Sigmund, 170
Fritz, Kurt von, 37
Frobisher, Martín, 129, 130, 134, 264, 265
Fronde, 295, 302, 313, 315, 320, 377
Fugger, Jacob, 90, 96, 227n

Gail, Jörg, 117
Galba, Martí Joan de, 20, 27
Galileo, Galilei, 309, 362
García, Carlos, 39
Gargantua, 19
Gassendi, Pierre, 362, 365, 376
Gazette de France, 339

Georges Dandin, 327
The German Ideology, 249, 255
Gerusalemme liberata, 45
Gesta Dei per Francos, 15
Gesta Romanorum, 175
Giacometti, Félix Henri, xviii
Gilbert, Humphrey, 131
Giovanni, Ser, 141
Godefroy, Frédéric, 51-52
Goffredo, 45
The Golden Ass, 4
Gonçalvo de Córdoba, 27
Gordon, Lew S., 352, 392
Goulemot, Jean-Marie, 359-61, 375-79
Gracián, Baltasar, 40-44, 347, 357
Gramont, Comte Philibert de, 350, 374
Gramsci, Antonio, 66
Grand Cyrus, 302
Gresham, Sir Thomas, 124, 129, 141, 264
Grotius, Hugo, 253
Grouthuysen, Bernhard, xix, 354, 375
Grundrisse, 117
Guevara y de Noroña, Antonio de, 27, 28
Guilds: 54-58 *passim*, 115, 116, 244n; Engels on, 77-78; and Hanseatic League, 100, 121-22; and usury, 119
Gulliver's Travels, 266, 275

Hakluyt, Richard, 264
Hamilton, Antoine, 350
Hanseatic League, 57, 100, 121-22
Harvey, William, 201
Hauser, Arnold, 219n, 280-81
Hawkins, John, 130, 132, 264, 265
Hazard, Paul, 310, 324, 368, 379, 381
Die Heilige Johanna der Schlachthöfe, 155-56
Heine, Heinrich, 180
Heliodorus, 5
Henri *IV*, 294-95, 301, 311, 376
Henri Quatre, 310
Henry *VIII*, 60, 128
Heraclitus, 203
Hercules, 4
Herder, Johann Gottfried, xvii
Hermes, 107
El Héroe, 44
Heywood, Thomas, 183
Histoire des Ajaoiens, 370
Histoire des aventuiers, flibustiers et boucaniers, 341
Histoire du Chevalier des Grieux et de Manon Lescaut, 374
Histoire philosophique et politique des établissements et du commerce des européens dans les deux Indes, 399, 400
Histoire des Séverambles, 372
Historia de la vida del Buscón, 39
An Historical Account of the Voyages and Adventures of Sir Walter Raleigh, 264
The History and Remarkable Life of the Truly Honourable Col. Jacque, 272
History of the Royal Society, 279
Hobbes, Thomas: 251, 252, 255, 382; and Bacon, 191, 194; and emergent capitalism, 200-205, 207, 249. Mentioned, 161, 198, 275, 376, 393
The Holy Family, 194, 250
Homer, 36, 204, 214n
Honnêteté: 313, 347, 356, 380-85, 397-98; and Descartes, 309; ideology of, 318-19, 322, 332-37; and Méré, 353-54; and Montaigne, 306-7. *See also* Utility
L'honnête homme ou l'art de plaire à la cour, 306
Hörz, Herbert, xxii, xxiii
Humanism, 34, 35, 43, 45
Hume, David, 250, 251
Hundred Year's War, 18, 55
Hythlodeus, Raphael, 99, 118

Ibrahim ou l'illustre Bassa, 302
Ideology of Adventure: Studies in Modern Consciousness, 1100-1750, xix, xx, xxiii
Ideology of adventure: xx, xxi, 192, 209, 214n, 228n; bourgeois, 60-62, 81, 183-86, 259-60; courtly, 5, 14, 57, 131, 135, 164, 188; in England, 55, 61-63, 236n; and fascism, 394-95; in *Gulliver's Travel's*, 276-79; and Hobbes, 202; and *honnêteté*, 382; knightly, 10-11, 32, 39, 40, 258, 300-302, 350; modern, 45-46, 80, 92, 113-114, 280-85, 317-18, 348; in *Robinson Crusoe*, 262-65, 272-74; and Rousseau, 389-90; in Shakespeare, 164, 179-86 *passim*; Spanish, 20, 33-34, 35. *See also* Aventure; Christian de Troyes; *Honnêteté*; *The Merchant of Venice*
The Iliad, 290
Individual: v, 76, 109-17 *passim*; in Shakespeare, 145, 172

Ingenioso Hildago Don Quijote de la Mancha. See *Don Quijote*
Instaurio Magna, 189
Irailh, Augustin-Simon, 374
L'Italia liberata dai Goti, 176

James: *I,* 134, 149, 183, 184, 206; *II,* 205, 206
Jankélévitch, Vladimir, xviii
Jauncourt, Chevalier Louis de, 383, 384, 395-96
Jauss, Hans-Robert, xix, 367
Jawkesworth, John, 281
Jodelle, Étienne, 288
Joseph Andrews, 275
Le Jouvencel, 18
Juan *II,* 24
Judde, Andrew, 129, 141
Jugement sur les sciences où peut s'appliquer un honnête homme, 365

Kartschoke, Dieter, 71-72
Kepler, Johannes, 309, 362
King Henry IV, 135-38, 139
Kipling, Rudyard, 270
The Knight of the Burning Pestle, 135, 163, 184, 186
Knights Templar, 25
Köhler, Erich, 7
Kott, Jan, 269
Krauss, Werner, xviii, 33-43 *passim,* 213n, 320, 368, 372
"Die Kritik des Siglo de oro am Ritter- und Schäferroman," 33
Kuczynski, Jürgen, 141, 184, 249, 250
Kunst, Politik, und Schmelerei, xviii
Kuske, Bruno, 58

La Baumelle, Laurent de, 393-94
La Bruyère, Jean de, 354-55, 368-69, 375
La Calprenède, Gautier de Costes de, 302
La Fontaine, Jean, 324, 349-50
La Hontan, Louis-Armand, 370
La Mothe le Vayer, François de, 312, 347, 362, 368-69, 376, 400
La Rochefoucauld, François de, 332, 333, 346, 354, 355, 357
Lais of Maire de France, 51
Landauer, Gustav, 177
Langland, William, 56

Las Casas, Fray Bartolomé de, 36, 133, 159
Law, John, 264, 344
Lazarillo, Guzmán de Alfarache, 39
Le Goff, Jacques, 54
Le Tellier, Michel, 300, 371
Leibniz, Gottfried Wilhelm, 402
Lenin, V. I., 79, 195, 198, 238n, 250, 395
Lesage, Alain René, 351, 374
Lessing, Gotthold Ephraim, 351
Lettres persanes, 373
Lettres philosophiques, 380
Leviathan, 201, 205, 393
Ley, Hermann, xix, xx
Libel of English policie, 127
Libro áureo del Emperador Marco Aurel, 27
Libro de caballería, 20
Libro del Caballero y del Escudero, 23
Libro del Orde de Cavallería, 23, 25
Literatur und Gesellschaft, xviii
Llull, Ramón, 23, 25
Locke, John, 250-56 *passim,* 260, 264, 275, 276
The London Merchant, 184
Louis *XIV,* 295-97, 304-5, 319-20, 328, 366, 314-15. Mentioned, 290, 294, 345, 346. See also Colbert, Jean Baptiste; Monarchy
Louvois, Michel le Tellier, Marquis de, 363
Lukács, Georg, xviii, xix
Luther, Martin: 109; on merchants, 118, 119, 120; on usury, 91, 92, 96-98

Mably, Gabriel Bonnot, 256
Machiavelli, Niccolò, 47-50, 65, 109, 120, 132
MacOrlan, Pierre, xviii
Magendie, Maurice, 347
Malthus, Thomas Robert, 256
Mandeville, Bernard de, 208, 332, 382
Mandrin, Louis, 392
Mandrou, Robert, 316, 352
Manley, Thomas, 96
Mann, Heinrich, 310
Manuel, Don Juan, 23
Marivaux, Chaimblain, 374
Marlowe, Christopher, 183
Martorell, Joannot, 20, 25-27, 54
Marvell, Andrew, 205, 206
Marx, Karl: xix, xxi, 250, 256, 260, 409n; and anarchy, 112-13, 388-89; on Bacon, 188-89; and Borkenau, 193-98; on modern trade, 84-86, 89, 208, 249, 265, 392; on

INDEX □ 439

Hobbes, 200, 202, 203; on the individual, 117-18, 266; on Locke, 253; on primitive accumulation, 285-86, 328; on usury, 91-93, 96, 141, 152, 159. Mentioned, 48, 79, 94, 109, 122, 196, 199, 344, 345, 395. *See also* Class struggle; Engels, Friedrich; Exchange-value; Sombart, Werner
Maschke, Erich, 57
"Materialism and Empirio-Criticism," 250
Matire de Bretagne, 12-13, 21-29 *passim*
Mauzi, Robert, 372, 382
Mazarin, Jules, 295, 313, 338, 364, 369
Medici, Lorenzo di, 49
Médicis, Catherine de, 292
Mehring, Franz, 327
Melancholy, 28, 39, 159, 239n
Mémoires du Comte de Bonneval, 351
Menosprecio de Corte y Alabanza de Aldea, 28
The Merchant of Venice, 138-82, 183, 184, 323, 326. *See also* Class struggle; Ideology of adventure; Individual; Monarchy
Méré, Antoine Gombauld, Chevalier de, 307, 352-53
Mes pensées, 393
Meslier, Jean, 256, 394
Meun, Jean de, 62, 63
Meyer-Tasch, Cornelius, 251-52
Miller, Norbert, 261
Milton, John, 129, 205
Minna von Barnhelm, 351
Li miroir as Dames, 56
Misanthrope, 320, 331-32, 333
Molière (Jean Baptiste Poquelin): 54, 181, 326-27, 329, 350, 416n; and *aventure*, 373; and the bourgeois-absolutist alliance, 302, 320-21, 323, 330-33. Mentioned, 304, 324, 367
Moll Flanders, 265, 268, 272
Monarchy, absolute: 60, 343, 370, 423n; alliance with bourgeoisie, 89, 115, 129-32 *passim*, 286, 302; and Bacon, 193, 194; establishment of, 308-9; ideology of, 102, 290, 372, 382; and knighthood, 35, 49-50, 87; reactionary, 184-88 *passim*; in Shakespeare, 135, 164. *See also* Colbert, Jean Baptiste; Epic; Goulemot, Jean-Marie; Louis *XIV*; Molière; *Noblesse de robe*
Le Moniage Guillaume, 53, 56

Monluc, Blaise de, 301
Montaigne, Michel de, 191, 200, 306, 384
Montalvo, García Ordoñes de, 29
Montchrestien, Antoine de, 310
Montemayor, Jorge de, 301
Montesquieu, Baron de la Brède et de, 4, 166, 380, 386, 389. Mentioned, 356, 373, 375, 378
Moore, J. R., 265
More, Thomas, 98-106 *passim*, 139, 199, 370
Morgante, 291
Muisit, Gilles de, 64
Mun, Thomas, 95-96, 192, 249, 261, 273
Muntaner, Ramón, 25
Müntzer, Thomas, 120
Mussolini, Benito, 50

Naudé, Gabriel, 369
Naumann, Manfred, xviii, xix
Navarre, Marguerite, 106
Neuschäfer, Hans-Jörg, 29, 45
New Atlantis, 198
Newton, Isaac, 379
Niderst, Alain, 313
Nietzsche, Friedrich, xxiii, 80, 195, 204
La noblesse commerçante, 348, 385
La noblesse militaire, ou le patriote françois, 385, 390
Noblesse de robe, 285-88, 306-16 *passim*, 354
Norris, John, 131
Novum Organum, 118, 169

Odysseus, 3
Oexmelin, Alexândre, 341
"On Trading and Usury," 96-98
Oraculo manual, 347
Orlando Furioso, 45, 289
Orlando innamorato, 45
Othello, 139

Palmerin of England, 185
Parfait négociant, 323, 375, 378
Pasquier, Etienne, 19
Patch, Howard R., 172
Paysan parvenu, 374
"The Peasant War in Germany," 31-33
Peckham, George, 131
Il Pecorone, 141
Pegolotti, Giovanni, 118
Peirce, Charles Sanders, xxiii

Perrault, Charles, 300, 367
Petronius, 4
Petrus von Amiens, 16
Petty, William, 249
Philippe *II* of France, 17
A Philosophical History of Adventure: Prolegomena to Another Aesthetics, xx
Picaresque, xvii, xviii, 40, 104
Piracy, 80, 83, 130-31, 229n
Plato, 292, 301
Politesse mondaine et les théories de l'honnêteté, 347
Polo, Marco, 117
Practica della mercatura, 118
Précieuses ridicules, 302, 320
Précieux, 302, 322-23, 333, 355, 357, 366
Préface sur l'utilité des mathématiques et de la physique, 371
Prévost, Abbé Antoine-François, 374
Prigogine, Ilya, xxiii, xxiv
Le Prince, 301
Principal Navigations, 264
Il Principe, 47-50
Projets de rétablissement du royaume en France, 359
Proletariat, 37, 38, 113
Proudhon, Pierre-Joseph, 266
Proust, Jacques, 362, 388
Pufendorf, Samuel, 253
Pulci, Luigi, 291

Querelle des Anciens et des Modernes, 300, 364
Quesnay, François, 345
Quevedo y Villegas, Francisco Gómez de, 29, 39
Quiller-Couch, Arthur, 180
The Quintessence of Capitalism, 79-80

Rabelais, François, 19, 101-7, 161, 402
Rachfahl, Felix, 195, 196
Racine, Jean, 304-5, 324, 366
Raissbüchlin, 117
Raleigh, Walter, 129, 133, 149, 206, 264, 275
Raynal, Guillaume Thomas, 341, 343, 399, 401
Reali di Francia, 45, 291
Recherches de la France, 19
Reconquista, 20, 23, 24

Réflexions ou sentences et maximes morales, 332
Reformation, 33, 39
Regulae ad directionem ingenii, 309
Reinke de Vos, 63
Renaissance, 5, 65, 66, 102, 106, 150
Renouard, Yves, 46
Renouvier, Charles Bernard, 200
Reuter, Christian, 339
The Review, 261, 274
Revolution: English, of *1649*, 376, 379; French, of *1789*, 260, 285; Glorious, 250, 355, 376, 378, 379
Ricardo, David, 266
Richelieu, Armand-Jean du Plessis, Cardinal de: 295, 301, 311, 340; and bougeoisie, 376; and Champlain, 310, 343; economic policy under, 377, 385
Robinson Crusoe, 263, 266, 267, 275-78
Roelens, Maurice, 363
Roman de Renart, 63
Roman de la Rose, 62
Ronsard, Pierre de, 288, 292-93, 294, 305
Rothkrug, Lionel, 360
Rousseau, Jean-Jacques, 256, 265, 267, 383, 389
Roxana, 265

Sacy, Claude-Louis de, 399, 419n
Sade, Marquis de, 256
Saint-Evremond, Charles de, 364-68 *passim*, 378
Saint-Foix, Philippe-August de, Chevalier d'Arc, 387, 390
Saint-Simon, Claude-Henri de Rouvroy, 359
Sannazzaro, Iacopo, 301
Sapori, Armando, 63
Satiricon, 4
Savary, Jacques, 323, 361, 375, 376, 377
Savary de Bruslons, Jacques, 323, 388
Scapin, Fouberies de, 331-32, 335
Schopenhauer, Arthur, 204
Schröder, Winfried, 201
Scudéry, Madeleine, 302
Séguier, Pierre, 369
Sforza, Francesco, 47, 48
Sgard, Jean, 351
Shakespeare, William: 135-82 *passim*, 240n, 245n, 324, 327, 402. See also The Mer-

chant of Venice; Monarchy, absolute; *The Two Gentlemen of Verona*; Usury
Sheppard, John, 271
The Shortest Way with Dissenters, 261
Siciliano, Italo, 54
Sidney, Henry, 129, 130
Sidney, Philip, 130, 131, 171, 176
Siete Partidas, 22, 23
Siglo de Oro, xviii
Simmel, Georg, xviii
Six Books of the Republic, 287
Smith, Adam, 256, 266
Smollett, Tobias George, 275
Soboul, Albert, 251, 372
The Social History of Art, 219n
Sombart, Werner, 96, 228n, 323-24, 382, 422n; and "the spirit of enterprise," 79-80, 82; and Weber, 195, 204
Some Thoughts Concerning Education, 253
Song of Roland, 21, 291
Spaccio della bestia tronfante, 176
The Spectator, 259, 261, 270, 284, 379, 381
Sprat, Thomas, 279
Spengler, Oswald, 111
Spenser, Edmund, 131, 132
Steele, Richard, 257-59, 381
Stengers, Isabelle, xxiii, xxiv
Sterne, Lawrence, 280
Stirner, Max, 256
Stucken, Eduard, 170
Studien zu einer Geschichte der Gesellschaftswissenschaften, 249
Sur les anciens, 366
"Sur l'homme," 336-37
Swift, Jonathan: 256, 265, 266, 275; on capitalism, 276-79, 411n
Szondi, Peter, 417n

Tartuffe, 326
Tasso, Torquato, 45, 301
The Tatler, 257-61 *passim*, 270, 282, 284, 379, 381
Tawney, R. H., 94
Terron, Colbert de, 377
Theories of Surplus-Value, 392
Thorne, Robert, 127, 130
Tiers Livre des Faucts et Dicts Héroiques du Bon Pantagruel, 101-7
Timon of Athens, 148

Tirant lo Blanc, 18-29 *passim*
Tom Jones, 275
Traité de l'économie, 310
Trissino, Giovanni Giorgio, 176
Tristram Shandy, 280-81
Troilus and Cressida, 172
The True-born Englishman, 261
Turcaret, 351
Turgot, Anne-Robert-Jacques, 389
The Two Gentlemen of Verona, 187
Two Treatises of Government, 250, 251
Tyard, Pontus de, 288

Ulenspiegel, 63
"Umrisse zu einer Kritik der Nationalökonomie," 256
Urfé, Honoré d', 302
Use-value, 83, 84, 111, 117, 197. See also Exchange-value
Usury: 119, 121, 224n, 231n, 240n; in Shakespeare, 144, 152-61, 171. See also Bacon, Francis; Engels, Friedrich; Luther, Martin
Utility: 255, 258, 365, 381; of free trade, 265, 311, 324, 357; and *honnêteté*, 382
Utopia, 98-101, 105, 199
Uzzano, Giovanni da, 118

Valin, René-Joseph, 340
Vauvenargues, Luc de Clapiers, Marquis de, 356-58, 393, 395
Veiras, Denis de, 370, 372
Venette, Jean de, 18
Vespucci, Amerigo, 99
La vida de Lazarillo de Tormes y de sus fortunas y adversidades, 36-40
La vie de Marianne ou les avantures de la Comtessa de ****, 374
Vilar, Pierre, 20, 285
Villehardouin, Geoffroy de, 16, 22, 26, 52, 54
Vinci, Leonardo da, 108
Virgil, 36, 288, 289, 293
Voltaire, François-Marie Arouet de, 294, 379-80, 394, 402-3. Mentioned, 385, 386
Von Nogent, Guibert, 15
Voyages et aventures de François Legnat, 374
Voyages et découvertes faites en la Nouvelle France depuis 1615-1618, 310

Walter Ohne Habe, 16
Weber, Max, xix, 133, 195-204 *passim*, 409n
Weimann, Robert, 135, 140, 262, 263, 267, 409n
Weinrich, Otto, 214n
Welzig, Werner, 58
Wilde, Jonathan, 271
William of Aquitaine, 53

William of Orange, 207, 261, 378
Wilson, Thomas, 93-94, 126, 328
Wolff, Christian, 402

Young, Edward, 279, 281

Zapata, Luis, 36
Zufall—Eine philosophische Untersuchung, xxii

Theory and History of Literature

Volume 18.	Thomas G. Pavel *The Poetics of Plot: The Case of English Renaissance Drama*
Volume 17.	Michel de Certeau *Heterologies*
Volume 16.	Jacques Attali *Noise*
Volume 15.	Peter Szondi *On Textual Understanding and Other Essays*
Volume 14.	Georges Bataille *Visions of Excess: Selected Writings, 1927–1939*
Volume 13.	Tzvetan Todorov *Mikhail Bakhtin: The Dialogical Principle*
Volume 12.	Ross Chambers *Story and Situation: Narrative Seduction and the Power of Fiction*
Volume 11.	Edited by John Fekete *The Structural Allegory: Reconstructive Encounters with the New French Thought*
Volume 10.	Jean-François Lyotard *The Postmodern Condition: A Report on Knowledge*
Volume 9.	Erich Auerbach *Scenes from the Drama of European Literature*
Volume 8.	Mikhail Bakhtin *Problems of Dostoevsky's Poetics*
Volume 7.	Paul de Man *Blindness and Insight: Essays in the Rhetoric of Contemporary Criticism* 2nd ed., rev.
Volume 6.	Edited by Jonathan Arac, Wlad Godzich, and Wallace Martin *The Yale Critics: Deconstruction in America*
Volume 5.	Vladimir Propp *Theory and History of Folklore*
Volume 4.	Peter Bürger *Theory of the Avant-Garde*
Volume 3.	Hans Robert Jauss *Aesthetic Experience and Literary Hermeneutics*
Volume 2.	Hans Robert Jauss *Toward an Aesthetic of Reception*
Volume 1.	Tzvetan Todorov *Introduction to Poetics*

Michael Nerlich is professor of literary criticism and romance philology at the Technical University of West Berlin and chief editor of the scientific quarterly *Lendemains, Etudes comparées sur la France*. He has written books on epic theory in Spain, Hebraic thought in Fray Luis de León, and political engagement in the German and French artistic "picaresque" novel of the twentieth century.

Currently self-employed, **Ruth Crowley** has been an assistant professor of German at the University of California, Irvine, and assistant professor of comparative literature at Queens College, CUNY. She was assistant editor of *German Quarterly*, in 1980-81. Crowley received her Ph.D. in German Studies from Stanford University in 1975.

Wlad Godzich is professor of comparative literature and French studies at the Université de Montréal as well as professor of comparative literature and director of the Center for Humanistic Studies at the University of Minnesota. He serves, with Jochen Schulte-Sasse, as editor of the series Theory and History of Literature.